HOLISM

HOLISM

A shopper's guide

Jerry Fodor and
Ernest Lepore

BLACKWELL
Oxford UK & Cambridge USA

Jerry Fodor and Ernest Lepore are hereby identified as authors of this work in accordance with Section 77 of the Copyright, Designs and Patents Act 1988.

First published 1992
Reprinted with corrections 1992

Blackwell Publishers
Three Cambridge Center
Cambridge, Massachusetts 02142, USA

108 Cowley Road, Oxford, OX4 1JF, UK

Library of Congress Cataloging in Publication Data
Fodor, Jerry A.
Holism: a shopper's guide / Jerry Fodor & Ernest Lepore.
p. cm.
Includes bibliographical references and indexes.
1. Holism.   2. Meaning (Philosophy)   I. Lepore, Ernest, 1950–
II. Title.
B818.F66   1992   91–29538
149—dc20
ISBN 0–631–18192–X (alk. paper)
ISBN 0–631–18193–8 (pbk. alk. paper)

British Library Cataloguing in Publication Data
A CIP catalogue record for this book is available from the British Library.

Typeset in 11 on 13½pt Sabon
by Hope Services (Abingdon) Ltd
Printed in Great Britain by
T. J. Press Ltd, Padstow, Cornwall

for Janet and Francesca

I am sent with broom before
To sweep the dust behind the door.
A Midsummer Night's Dream, Act V

CONTENTS

CONTENTS

PREFACE

It seems that it all depends on the context. "The bark," for example, means one thing in the context ". . . of the tree," but something quite different in the context ". . . of the dog." "Flying planes" means *aircraft* in the context ". . . are dangerous," but it means *piloting* in the context ". . . is dangerous." "The" out of context means nothing at all (so, anyhow, Bertrand Russell assures us), but "the F is G" is adequately well defined. [Empedikli:s li:pt] means that someone leaped in English, but it means that someone loves in German. "Je vais" means nothing in English, but it means *I go* in French.

Meaning is, therefore, something that words have *in sentences*; and it's something that sentences have *in a language*. Just as nothing is a heart except as it is part of a whole *system* of organs, and nothing is a Ministry of Finance except as it is part of a whole *system* of institutions, so nothing is a symbol except as it is part of *a whole system of signifiers*. "Only in the context of a sentence does a word have a meaning" says Frege ("On sense and reference"), and "to understand a sentence is to understand a language," says Wittgenstein (*Philosophical Investigations*, para. 199). And Davidson puts the two together: "Only in the context of the language does a sentence (and therefore a word) have meaning" ("Truth and meaning," p. 22). It looks as though some of the arguments for these conclusions require only *truisms* for their premises. No wonder the conclusions themselves are so widely taken for granted.

This is a book about holism about meaning; roughly, it's about the doctrine that only whole languages or whole theories or whole belief systems *really* have meanings, so that the meanings of smaller units – words, sentences, hypotheses, predictions, discourses, dialogues, texts, thoughts, and the like – are merely derivative. Meaning (or semantic) holism must be distinguished from a number of related ideas with which it's easily confused: from holism about confirmation, for example, or about interpretation or about the individuation of functional properties. These other kinds of holism might be true even if meaning holism isn't. Or at least, so it seems; unless there are arguments to show not just that confirmation, interpretation, or the individuation of functional properties is holistic but also that the meaning of a symbol is somehow determined by facts about how its applications are confirmed or how its tokens are interpreted or the functions that it performs. These are all possibilities that we will presently explore.

Here's our take on meaning holism. First, it's important. Second, it may be true; holistic theories have earned their keep in fields as far apart as phonology and epistemology, so why not in semantics? But, third, none of the arguments for meaning holism that we've heard about so far or that we've been able to reconstruct from the arguments for meaning holism that we've heard about so far or that we've been able to reconstruct from the discussions of the arguments for meaning holism that we've heard about so far is actually sound. Almost all of what you'll find in this book is devoted to making a case for this claim.

Here is how we are going to proceed. The chapters are intended to be largely self-contained. The first is geographical. It tries to say, relatively precisely, what the doctrine of meaning holism is and a little about how it is related to some other, large philosophical issues; issues not just about language and mind, but also about epistemology, intentional explanation, and metaphysics. Our only tendentious claim in this part of the book is that there is very probably no way of holding meaning holism in an attenuated form that isolates these broader questions from its implications. This is a theme that receives further elaboration chapter 7.

The other chapters are largely devoted to considering, in some critical detail, three different sorts of arguments that have been alleged in support of meaning holism in the recent philosophical literature: arguments that assume epistemological holism and verificationism (chapter 2), transcendental arguments that turn on the conditions under which radical interpretation, radical translation, and intentional explanation are possible (chapters 3–5), and arguments that assume that the semantic properties of an expression derive from its "conceptual role"; that is, arguments that infer semantic holism either from a certain kind of "use" theory of meaning or from a structuralist semiology (or both in case these aren't different; chapter 6).

Our tactics in going about this critical survey will be a little unconventional. Rather than construct straw holists to knock down, we've decided to go straight to the texts. After the Introduction, each chapter proceeds from the analysis of a work which, in our view, provides an especially transparent and revealing exposition of one or other line of thought that might be taken to militate for holistic conclusions in semantics. Readers considering a purchase will therefore have an opportunity to become acquainted with a variety of types of meaning holism to choose among; at a minimum, we hope to discourage impulse buying.

It bears emphasis, however, that not all the texts we discuss were actually intended to be arguments for meaning holism. Quine's "Two dogmas of empiricism," for example, seems to be mostly about *epistemological* holism and pragmatism. Block isn't a holist of any sort; he relies on the analytic/synthetic distinction to exempt him from the holistic implications to which his conceptual role semantics would otherwise commit him. And though Lewis may hold holist views, his "Radical interpretation" is certainly not intended to defend them. Scholarly exegesis is therefore not our main concern; we are using these texts for our own purposes, not necessarily for the ones their authors had in mind. In each of the texts under examination, we find considerations that could plausibly be (and often have been) alleged in aid of the meaning holist's cause. We are interested in deciding to what degree such allegations have force.

One of the reasons we chose these particular texts to write about is that they insist on connections between meaning holism and other issues that we find philosophically fascinating: Could there be a theory of radical interpretation? What's the place of compositionality in a semantic theory? What's the relation between theories of linguistic content and theories of belief content? Are normative principles constitutive of intentional ascription? Can only rational creatures mean things? Can only rational creatures think things? What's the relation between truth and coherence? Is there an a priori semantic argument against skepticism about external objects? How should we construe the relations between language and the mind? How should we construe the relations between language and the world? Part of the reason why arguing about meaning holism is fun is that it leads you, sooner or later, to all these questions. There are lots of other texts we could have chosen; but, all else being equal, we've preferred ones that lead to these questions as soon as possible.

We've already said what the bottom line of this book is going to be: we find the arguments for meaning holism that the literature in philosophy (and cognitive science) has offered so far not to be rationally persuasive. We want to distinguish *very carefully*, however, between claiming this and claiming that meaning holism *isn't true* (or, for that matter, that it *is* true). One of the authors of this book is inclined to think that meaning holism is simply preposterous; "really a crazy theory" is how he has described it elsewhere (in print). The other author is inclined to think that meaning holism is at the very least an idea of great depth and interest. But we have embarked on our joint undertaking in an atmosphere of considerable harmony despite these deeply opposed intuitions. That's because we *both* think that the available arguments for meaning holism are no good. That, and only that, is what this book will try to convince you of.

Every now and then, however, we're told that it doesn't matter whether – it doesn't even matter *that* – the arguments for meaning holism are no good. Meaning holism is, we're told, a very beautiful metaphor (we really *were* once told that, in those very words), a profound way of seeing things, a revealing picture of how the world might be, or even, heaven help us, a Form of Life. It isn't, it appears, appropriate to *argue* with metaphors, pictures, and Forms of Life; like pre-Baroque opera and beef tartare, either they grab you or they don't. What's wrong with someone who doesn't feel for meaning holism is therefore lack of sensibility. Or, worse yet, it's that his *Weltanschauung* is out of fashion. And what philosopher wants to be found wearing last year's *Weltanschauung*?

We don't know what to make of this. Anyhow, we're pretty sure it's not the way we wish to do philosophy. It seems to us that what there is no argument for, there is no reason to believe. And what there *is* no reason to believe, one *has* no reason to believe. We proceed, then, to our task of examining the arguments for meaning holism, taking what comfort we can from these chilly methodological truisms.

A lot of people read all or parts of this book in manuscript and made suggestions from which we have benefited. The following list is probably incomplete, but the omissions are inadvertent, and our gratitude to all our commentators is heartfelt: Bruce Aune, Anita Avramides, Ned Block, Paul Boghossian, Jennifer Church, Paul Churchland, Bo Dahlbom, Donald Davidson, Michael Devitt, Ray Elugardo, Richard Foley, Roger Gibson, Gil Harman, John Heil, James Higginbotham, David Lewis, Barry Loewer, Tim Maudlin, Brian McLaughlin, Christopher

Peacocke, W. V. O. Quine, Georges Rey, Mark Rollins, Michael Root, Gideon Rosen, David Rosenthal, Stephen Schiffer, John Searle, Gabe Segal, Robert Stalnaker, and Steven Stich. We are likewise indebted to colleagues and students at Rutgers University, Washington University, and The City University of New York, where much of this material was developed in graduate seminars.

We wish to express our gratitude to Stephan Chambers and Andrew McNeillie for having seen us through, Luca Bonatti for his help with the references, Catherine McKeen for her help with the index, and to Jean van Altena for copy-editing. Special thanks to Dr Jessie Rosenthal.

A version of some material from chapter 6 was published in the 1991 *Proceedings of the Chicago Linguistics Society* under the title "Why meaning (probably) isn't conceptual role."

J.F.
E.L.

1
INTRODUCTION:
A GEOGRAPHY OF THE ISSUES

ANATOMIC AND HOLISTIC PROPERTIES

This is a book about semantic holism. Semantic holism is a doctrine about *the metaphysically necessary conditions* for something to have meaning or content. We therefore commence our discussion by attempting to view semantic holism in its metaphysical context.

Many properties have the property of being, as we shall say, *anatomic*.[1] A property is anatomic just in case if anything has it, then at least one other thing does. Consider, for an untendentious example, the property of being a sibling. If I am a sibling, then there is someone whose sibling I am; someone other than me, since no one can be his own sibling.[2] My being a sibling is thus, as one says, *metaphysically dependent* upon someone else's being a sibling (and so too, of course, is my sibling's being a sibling). So the property of *being a sibling* is anatomic; I *couldn't be* the only person in the world who instantiates this property. If I could *prove* that I am a sibling, that would refute solipsism.

If a property is not anatomic, then we shall say that it is *atomistic* or *punctate*. An atomistic or punctate property is one which might, in principle, be instantiated by only one thing. (So, for example, all properties expressed by predicates like "discovered the only . . . " or "ate the last . . . " are punctate, and so

1

too, we suppose, is the property of being a rock.) One way of formulating a main issue to be discussed in this book is whether *being a symbol, being a symbol belonging to language L, having an intentional object, having intentional content, expressing a proposition, having a referent, being semantically evaluable,* and the like are punctate properties. The currently received philosophical view is that these sorts of properties are not punctate but anatomic. We propose to explore the arguments for this view.

Many anatomic properties have the property of being *very* anatomic, or, as we shall say, the property of being *holistic.* Holistic properties are properties such that, if anything has them, then *lots* of other things must have them too. The "lots of" part of this definition could bear to be sharpened, no doubt; but, for our purposes, this isn't required. Our primary concerns in this book will be with natural languages and with minds. Natural languages and minds can be assumed to be productive in all the interesting cases; minds (in any event, human minds) can grasp endlessly many different ideas, and languages (in any event, human languages) are capable of expressing endlessly many distinct propositions. The semantic properties we'll discuss will therefore generally be ones which, if they are holistic, then if anything at all has them, so too do endlessly many other things.

Consider, for an untendentious example of a holistic property, *being a natural number.* Some philosophers have brought themselves to doubt that anything has this property; to doubt, that is, that numbers exist. For all we know, it is coherent – even well advised – of them to doubt this. But nobody could coherently doubt – and, so far as we know, nobody has ever sought to do so – that if there are any numbers, then there must be quite a few. One couldn't, for example, coherently wonder whether there is only the number three.

Why not? Well, according to standard treatments, the natural numbers are defined by reference to the *successor relation*: nothing is a natural number unless there is a natural number that is its successor. No number is its own successor, so if anything is a natural number, something else must be a natural number too; the existence of each natural number is thus metaphysically dependent on the existence of other natural numbers. That is, the property of being a natural number is anatomic. So far the number case is quite like the sibling case, but now the examples diverge. For whereas every sibling is his sibling's sibling, no number is its successor's successor (or its successor's successor's successor, and so forth). So, if there are any siblings, then there must be at least two of them; but if there are any numbers, then there must be an infinity of them. So, unlike the property of being a sibling, the property of being a number is not just anatomic but also holistic.

Part of coming to see why there must be lots of numbers if there are any is coming to see that being a number is really a relational property. (It's evident on the face of it that being a sibling is a relational property; one speaks not only of *being* a sibling but also of *having* one.) Not all relational properties, however, are anatomic; a fortiori, not all relational properties are holistic. You can't be a cat owner unless there is a cat that you own, so being a cat owner is a relational property. But it's by no means obvious that you can't be a cat owner unless there are other cat owners. Patently, the cat you own needn't itself own a cat in order for *you* to own *it*. So, not very surprisingly, the relation between a cat owner and his cat is quite unlike the relation between a number and its successor; although being a cat owner and being a natural number are both relational properties, the latter is anatomic and holistic and the former is neither.

Or consider: you can't earn the average income unless there are people whose incomes are related in a certain way to yours; so earning the average income is a relational property. In fact, it's the relation a wage and its earner bear to n wage earners and their wages if and only if (iff) his wage equals the sum of their wages divided by n. But there don't have to be *other* people who

3

earn the average income in order for *you* to do so, so earning the average income is a punctate property. For that matter, there don't have to be *other* people who earn wages in order for you to earn the average income, since the relation that defines the average income is one that a wage earner can bear *to himself.* You can therefore earn the average wage in an economy in which you are the *only* wage earner. Indeed, in that sort of economy, you *can't but* earn the average wage.

Well, so be it. But why does any of this matter?

ANATOMISM AND THE THEORY OF LANGUAGE

Steamy philosophical issues can sometimes be rephrased as questions about whether a certain property is anatomic. This is a sort of ontological equivalent of the tactic of "semantic ascent"; and, like semantic ascent, it can have the salutary effect of lowering the temperature. Consider, for example, the steamy question of whether there could be a private language. To argue that there could be is at least to deny that the property of *having a language* is anatomic; correspondingly, it's at least to assert the conceptual possibility of a language with only one speaker. This doesn't get you *much* further, but it does help a little to distinguish the part of the private language problem that's about language from the part that's about privacy. (Compare Rhees, "Can there be a private language?")

As previously remarked, this book is largely about whether semantic properties are holistic. We'll see that the standard argument for meaning holism requires the premise that semantic properties are typically anatomic. Discussing anatomisity is thus a way into considering whether the connection between *being a symbol* and *belonging to a language* is internal; whether symbols can have their being only as parts of whole language systems. Since this will be our main expository tactic, we wish to alert the reader to a couple of caveats.

4

First caveat

Though questions about meaning holism can often be phrased as questions about whether some semantic property is anatomic, not just any semantic property will do for these purposes. This is just an uninteresting consequence of how "anatomic" was defined. So, for example, to claim that the property of *expressing the proposition that the cat is on the mat in L* is anatomic would be to claim that a language that has one expression that means that the cat is on the mat must also contain at least one other expression *that also means that the cat is on the mat*. This claim is most implausible; and, anyhow, no general issues about meaning holism would appear to turn on it.

The interesting and, prima facie, plausible claim is that *generic* semantic properties – loosely speaking, properties whose specification can be taken to involve variables ranging over propositions, contents, meanings, and the like – are anatomic. Examples of this claim are that *the property of expressing some proposition or other* or *the property of having some referent or other* or *the property of having some content or other* are anatomic. In particular, we'll see that it is for these sorts of properties that there is arguably an inference from semantic anatomism to semantic holism, so that if the first can be established, so too, perhaps, can the second. The reader is hereby advised that, barring specific notice to the contrary, when we talk about whether semantic properties are anatomic, it will almost always be generic semantic properties that we have in mind.

In particular, much of our discussion will be concerned with one of the following two, closely related doctrines. What we will call *content holism* is the claim that properties like *having content* are holistic in the sense that no expression in a language can have them unless many other (nonsynonymous) expressions in that language have them too. In effect, it's the doctrine that there can be no punctate languages. What we will call

5

translation holism is the claim that properties like *meaning the same as some formula or another of L* are holistic in the sense that nothing can translate a formula of L unless it belongs to a language containing many (nonsynonymous) formulas that translate formulas of L.[3] It came as a surprise to us, and we hope it will interest the reader, to discover that almost all the arguments for meaning holism that actually get proposed in the literature are arguments for *content* holism. *The* argument for *translation* holism seems to be one that assumes that meanings supervene on intersentential relations – that they are something like inferential roles – and hence that translation preserves meaning only if the inferential relations among many of the sentences in the home language preserve the inferential relations among many of the sentences in the target language. We'll consider this sort of argument in detail in chapter 6.

Second caveat

The issues about anatomism aren't by any means the only ones that philosophers have had in mind when they raise "the" meaning holism question. For example, there's the thesis, famously explored by Wittgenstein, Austin, and their many followers, that there is an internal connection between *being a symbol* and playing a role in a system of *non*linguistic conventions, practices, rituals, and performances – an internal connection, as one says, between symbols and Forms of Life.[4]

We mention this, as it were, *anthropological* holism only to put it to one side. Our excuse for doing so is as follows. Anthropological holism is distinct from semantic holism *only* insofar as it concerns the relation between language and its intentional background – that is, the relation between language and the cultural background of beliefs, institutions, practices, conventions, and so forth upon which, according to anthropological holists, language is ontologically dependent. When applied to the background itself, however, anthropological holism just reduces to semantic holism. That is, it reduces to the doctrine that intentional states, institutions, practices, and the like are ontologically dependent on one another; hence that they are anatomic. To put the point slightly differently, we have, at least for present purposes, no argument with the philosopher who holds that the linguistic is holistically dependent on an intentional background *but accepts atomism about the background*, thereby allowing, in effect, that there could be arbitrarily punctate Forms of Life. (We suppose, for example, that someone who is a "Gricean" about the relation between thought and language could coherently be an atomist about thought itself.) To put it yet another way, it might be that for anything *linguistic* to have content, there must be something *non*linguistic that has content. That's alright with us as long as the conditions for the nonlinguistic thing having content are atomistic.

Though anatomism isn't the only philosophical issue about semantic holism, it nevertheless suffices to distinguish two great traditions in the philosophy of language. The atomistic tradition proceeds from the likes of the British empiricists, via such of the pragmatists as Peirce and James. The *locus classicus* is the work of the Vienna Circle, but see also the Russell of *The Analysis of Mind*. The contemporary representatives of this tradition are mostly model theorists, behaviorists, and informational semanticists. Whereas people in this tradition think that the semantic properties of a symbol are determined solely by its relations to things in the nonlinguistic world, people in the second tradition think that the semantic properties of a symbol are determined, at least in part, by its role in a language. Languages are, inter alia, *collections* of symbols; so, if what a symbol means is determined by its role in a language, the property of *being a symbol* is anatomic. This second tradition proceeds from the likes of the structuralists in linguistics and the Fregeans in philosophy.[5] Its contemporary representatives are legion. They include Quine, Davidson, Lewis, Dennett, Block, Devitt, Putnam, Rorty, and Sellars among philosophers; *almost* everybody in AI and cognitive psychology; and it may be that they include absolutely everybody who writes literary criticism in French.

It's pretty clear that whether semantic properties are anatomic is an interesting question if you happen to be interested in the philosophy of language. The point, to repeat, is that there is a widely (if often implicitly) endorsed argument which suggests that if a semantic property is anatomic, then it is also holistic. Suppose we grant, for the moment, that this inference from anatomism to holism goes through. Then anatomism about semantic properties has whatever consequences meaning holism itself has. And, arguably, the implications of meaning holism for the philosophy of language are formidable.

Dummett, for example, maintains that:

> A thoroughgoing holism, while it may provide an abstractly intelligible model of language, fails to give a credible account either of how we use language as an instrument of communication, or of how we acquire a mastery of language. . . . The situation is essentially similar to that of a language all of whose sentences consist of single words, i.e. have no internal semantic structure; . . . it becomes unintelligible how the speakers of the language could ever have come to associate . . . senses with their unitary sentences, let alone to achieve the same association among different individual speakers; or how any one individual could discover the sense attached by another to a sentence, or decide whether it was or was not the same as that which he attached to it. In the same way, if a total theory is represented as indecomposable into significant parts, then we cannot derive its significance from its internal structure, since it has none; and we have nothing else from which we may derive it. (*Frege: Philosophy of Language*, pp. 599–600)

Dummett is, in effect, arguing from the following analogy: Sentences are interpersonally intelligible because their meanings are compositionally derived from those of their constituents and because speaker and hearer are privy to the meanings of the constituents and to the conventions that govern the derivation. This explanation presupposes that the constituents of sentences *are* meaningful – indeed, that they mean the same in the speaker's language as they do in the hearer's. Similarly, Dummett claims, if I can understand your theory (by any incremental procedure), that must be because the content of the theory is determined by the contents of its constituent sentences. (Let's assume, for expository convenience, that theories are sets of sentences.) And if I can *learn* your theory (incrementally), that must be because I can learn part of your theory by learning some of its constituent sentences, more of your theory by learning more of its constituent sentences, and all of your theory by learning all of its constituent sentences. But, again, these possibilities presuppose that the sentential constituents of a theory *have* meanings – indeed, that they can have the same meanings in your whole theory and in the approximations to your whole theory that I learn along the way.

All of this would *seem* to be false if meaning holism is true, since, as the reader will recall, meaning holism would require that if any one sentence in your theory occurs in my theory, then practically all the sentences that occur in your theory must occur in my theory. And similarly, mutatis mutandis, if "theory" is replaced by "language." If holism is true, then I can't understand any of your language unless I can understand practically all of it. But then how, save in a single spasm of seamless cognition, could any language ever be learned?

We don't wish to take a stand on whether the considerations that Dummett advances constitute a refutation of semantic holism. For one thing, occasional digressions to the contrary notwithstanding, our business in this book is not to determine whether holism is true, but only to examine the arguments that have been offered in its favor. Second, suppose Dummett is right: suppose, that is, that the standard picture of how they are learned, communicated, and so forth presupposes that the semantic properties of theories and languages are determined by the semantics of their constituent sentences in something like the way that the semantics of a sentence is itself determined by the meaning of its constituent terms. Still, offering this argument as an objection to meaning holism may underestimate the extent to which holists are likely also to be revisionists. A semantic holist might accept Dummett's analysis and reply, "So much the worse for our conventional understanding of how languages and theories are learned and communicated." Clearly Quine, Dennett, Stich, the Churchlands, and many other meaning holists are strongly tempted by this sort of revisionism.

Suffice it for present purposes that *if* you assume that properties like *having a meaning in L* and *having the same meaning as some expression in L* and the like are holistic, then a certain standard picture of how communication and language learning work would seem to be in jeopardy. The picture is that the linguistic and theoretical commitments of speaker and hearer can overlap *partially* to any degree you like: you can believe some of what I believe without believing all of it; you can understand part of my language without having learned the rest of it; and so forth. This would seem to be essential to reconciling the idea that languages have an interpersonal, social existence with the patent truth that no two speakers of the same language ever speak exactly the same dialect of that language. As Frege remarks in a related context:

> Both the nominatum and the sense of a sign must be distinguished from the associated image . . . the image is subjective, the image of one person is not that of another. . . . [Hence] the image thereby differs essentially from the connotation [that is, sense] of a sign, which latter may well be a common property of many and is therefore not a part or mode of a single person's mind; for it cannot well be denied that mankind possesses a common treasure of thoughts which is transmitted from generation to generation. (Frege, "On sense and reference," pp. 159–60)

But, if we understand Dummett correctly, he is arguing that this picture of language as public property can make sense only to the extent that *partial* consensus in usage does *not* require *perfect* consensus of usage – that is, only to the extent that semantic holism is denied.[6]

10

So much for a first sketch of how issues about semantic anatomism may connect with some other questions proprietary to the philosophy of language.

BROADER IMPLICATIONS

Reference Holism and Scientific Realism

It has recently become increasingly clear that semantic holism also has repercussions further afield. Consider the property R that a linguistic expression has iff it refers to the same thing that some expression in English does. So, for example, R is a property that "la plume de ma tante" has (because it refers to the same thing that the expression "my aunt's pen" refers to), and so too do "la penna di mia zia" and, of course, "my aunt's pen." Question: Is the property R holistic? Could languages that overlap only slightly share any of their "ontological commitments?"

Here's one reason why this question matters. Suppose that ontological commitments are holistic, so that two languages can share any of their ontology only if they share quite a lot of it. It might then turn out, for example, that no language could have an expression that refers to what the English expression "the pen of my aunt" refers to unless it also has expressions that refer to, as it might be, Chicago, the cat's being on the mat, the last game of the 1927 World Series, the day after they built the Statue of Liberty, the last of the Mohicans, *The Last of the Mohicans*, and so forth.[7] Such a result, though still of primary relevance to the philosophy of language, would nevertheless be interesting and rather strikingly counter-intuitive.

It raises the stakes, however, that the same considerations would apply if we asked about the semantic property R*. An expression has R* iff it refers to something or other that currently accepted astronomical theories refer to. Suppose that R* is anatomic, hence holistic on the assumption that anatomism implies holism. Then it might turn out that no

11

theory could refer to (for example) stars unless it could also refer to (as it might be) planets, nebulas, black holes, the center of the galaxy, the speed of propagation of light, and the location of the nearest quasar. It would follow that Greek astronomy (hence, Greek astronom*ers*) couldn't ever have referred to stars. And it would follow from *that* that (what one had naively supposed to be) the Greek view that stars are very nearby and that they ride around the heavens on glass spheres is actually *not contested* by our view that the stars are very far away and don't ride around the heavens at all. In fact, strictly speaking, it would follow that the Greeks didn't *have* any views about *stars*; we can't, in the vocabulary of contemporary astronomy, say what, if anything, Greek astronomy was about. A fortiori, it makes no sense to speak of an empirically motivated choice between Greek astronomy and ours; whereof you cannot speak, thereof you must be silent.[8]

So if the property R* is holistic, then it may well turn out that scientific theories are empirically incommensurable unless their ontological commitments are more or less identical. But notice that *the* argument for Scientific Realism is that science is progressive; in the present case, the main argument for being Realistic about our astronomical theories is that, in virtue of having embraced them, we are in a position to make more and better predictions about stars than the Greeks did. If, as now threatens, it turns out that this is *trivially* true (because Greek astronomy made no predictions about stars at all or, indeed, about anything that *our* astronomy talks about), the standard argument for Scientific Realism goes down the drain.[9]

This understanding of the implications of R*'s being anatomic is widely shared. Inferring from holism about ontological commitment to anti-Realism (or relativism or Instrumentalism) about the theoretical constructs of science has been a main tactic of twentieth-century metaphysicians. Consider, among current practitioners, Quine, Goodman, Kuhn, Feyerabend, Putnam, and many others.[10] Indeed, Kuhn's (putative) discovery of the incommensurability of scientific paradigms appears to be the only result in recent philosophy that many nonphilosophers care about. And the argument that leads first to holism and then to incommensurability depends essentially on the claim that properties like R* are holistic (a fortiori, that they are anatomic).

Meaning Holism and Intentional Explanation

Now consider the property T. An expression has T iff it *translates* some or other expression of English. So, "the pen of my aunt" and "la plume de ma tante" have T, and so too do "The pen of my aunt is on the table" and "La plume de ma tante est sur la table," "La penna di mia zia é sul tavolo," and so forth. Question: Is the property T anatomic?

Here is why *this* question matters. Suppose, once again, that there is an argument from the anatomism of a semantic property to its holism. Then it might turn out that no language can have an expression that means what "The pen of my aunt is on the table" means unless it also has expressions that mean what, as it might be, "Two is a prime number," "London Bridge is actually in Arizona," "XYZ is not H_2O," "Snow is white," and "The snark is a boojum" mean. A consequence of this would be that Chaucer, Shakespeare, and Lincoln (and, for that matter, since XYZ is quite a recent invention, Ludwig Wittgenstein) did not speak a language in which one could say that the pen of one's aunt is on the table.

If there are arguments that show that neither Chaucer, Shakespeare, nor Wittgenstein could have said of his aunt's pen that it was on the table, then presumably much the same arguments would show that none of them could ever have *thought* of his aunt's pen that it was on the table. For, consider the property T* which a belief has iff it expresses a proposition that is the content of some belief of mine. According to the present assumptions, if T* is anatomic, then it is holistic. And if T* is holistic, then (assuming that thoughts are individuated by their propositional contents) it might turn out that nobody has thoughts that are tokens of the same type as·my thought about

13

Auntie's pen unless he also has thoughts that are tokens of the same type as, as it might be, my thought that the cat is on the mat, my thought that black holes are odd kinds of objects, my thought that some presidents are wimps, or my thought that *Salome* will never sell in Omaha. This too might be considered an interesting, even counter-intuitive, result in the philosophy of mind. And once again there are implications further afield.

Lots of people, including most cognitive scientists and many riders on the Clapham omnibus, hold the following view of behavior: that higher animals act out of their beliefs and desires. According to this view, there are counterfactual-supporting generalizations that connect the mental states of higher animals with their behaviors (and with one another) *and which subsume mental states in virtue of their intentional contents.* Consider such shopworn examples as "If you see the moon *as being on the horizon,* then you will see it *as oversized"* or "If someone asks you what's the first thing salt makes you think of, you'll think of pepper" or "If someone asks you what's the first color you think of, you'll think of red."[11]

And so forth.

We emphasize that it's in virtue of *what they are thoughts about* that thoughts fall under a generalization like "If you think of a color, the first color you think of is red" – that is, it's in virtue of their being thoughts about color and thoughts about red (reading "thoughts about" de dicto). A fortiori, the generalization subsumes you and me (as it might be) only if we both *have* thoughts about color and about red.

But now suppose that holism is true about thought content. Then, since you and I surely have widely different belief systems (think of all the things you know that I don't) and since, by definition, a property is holistic only if nothing has it unless many other things do, it may well turn out that none of your thoughts has the property of bearing T* to any of mine.[12] It would follow that not more than one of us ever has thoughts about color or thoughts about red. So, at most one of us is subsumed by the generalization that if you think of a color, then the first color you think about is red. In fact, it might well turn out that, at most, one *time slice* of one of us is subsumed by this generalization since, after all, vastly many of one's beliefs change from moment to moment, and, on the present assumptions, belief individuation is holistic.

These sorts of considerations suggest that it might turn out that if T* is holistic, there are no *robust*, counterfactual-supporting intentional generalizations,[13] none that is ever satisfied by more than an individual at an instant. Many philosophers have indeed drawn this sort of inference. Since, they argue, mental properties are holistic, there couldn't really be intentional laws; and since there can't really be intentional laws, intentional explanations can't be fully factual. (See, for example, Quine, Davidson,[14] Stich, Dennett, both Churchlands, and others.) Presumably, if there aren't fully factual intentional generalizations, then there can't be an intentional science of human nature (or a scientific epistemology or a scientific moral psychology) in anything like the sense of "science" that the physical and biological sciences have in mind. "Behavioral science," "social science," "cognitive science," and the like are therefore, strictly speaking, oxymorons if semantic holism is true.

Above all, there can't be a scientific theory of *rationality*:

There are powerful universal laws obeyed by all instances of gold . . . but what are the chances that we can find powerful universal generalizations obeyed by all instances of rationally justified belief? The very same considerations that defeated the program of inductive logic, the need for a criterion of "projectibility" or a "prior probability metric" which is "reasonable" by a standard of reasonableness which seems both topic-dependent and interest-relative, suggests that . . . even in a restricted domain, for example physics, nothing like precise laws which will decide what is and is not a reasonable inference or a justified belief are to be hoped for . . . We should and must proceed in a way analogous to the way we proceed in science . . . ; but we cannot reasonably expect that *all* determined researchers are destined to

15

converge to one moral theory or one conception of reality. (Putnam, "Philosophers and human understanding," pp. 201–2)

Notice that this line of argument doesn't depend on parochial considerations about what you think intentional content *is*. All that's required is that, whatever it is, it's "topic-dependent and interest-relative" – namely, holistic.

The Autonomy of the Intentional

Our point up till now has been that the implications of meaning holism may reach far enough to jeopardize, on the one hand, a certain sort of Metaphysical Realism in the philosophy of science and, on the other hand, the likelihood that the intentional sciences might eventually produce theories whose objectivity and reliability parallel those of the physical and biological sciences. Prima facie, this makes meaning holism look like bad news from the point of view of linguists, psychologists, economists, cognitive scientists, and the like.

But, there is a more cheerful way of reading the moral; if the "constitutive principles" of intentional theories are ipso facto holistic (or normative or, maybe, holistic *because* normative; see chapter 5) in a way that those of the physical and biological sciences are not, then it may be that intentional explanations are ipso facto immune to a kind of reductive criticism with which the physical and biological sciences have sometimes seemed to threaten them. To put it the other way around, if you think of commonsense belief/desire psychology as "just another empirical theory," less articulate than, but not different in kind from, such philosophically unproblematic empirical theories as meteorology or geology, then it presumably follows that commonsense belief/desire psychology could turn out, on simply empirical grounds, to be largely or entirely *false* – just as it could turn out that much or all of our current meteorology or geology is simply empirically false. Commonsense belief/desire psychology *will* have turned out to be empirically false if, for example, it proves not to be capable of integration with the rest of our developing scientific world view. The Churchlands (and maybe Quine) think that something like this is actually in the process of happening.

But that *couldn't* happen if, in virtue of their holistic character, interpretive and hermeneutic explanations are ipso facto not in competition with theories in the empirical sciences. One might then rationally take the view that the general structure of intentional explanation is, as one says in Britain, "not negotiable" *however* biology and physics turn out. There is in this line of argument more than a hint of the Kantian strategy of buying the autonomy of the foundations of ethics at the price of accepting a priori bounds on the scope of scientific understanding – except that it is now the conception of persons as intentional systems rather than the conception of persons as moral agents whose freedom from empirical critique is to be guaranteed by transcendental argument.[15]

Whichever way you look at it, if it's true that meaning holism is incompatible with a robust notion of content identity, and hence with a robust notion of intentional law, then the connections between the holism issues and some very deep questions about our understanding of ourselves are seen to be intimate and urgent.

CONTENT IDENTITY AND CONTENT SIMILARITY

Why, then, aren't many people outside philosophy (many cognitive/behavioral/social scientists, for example) worried about the holism issues? One reason is that they may not have noticed the undesirable consequences of holism, or they may doubt that these consequences actually follow. Another reason is that it's widely supposed that even if holism precludes a robust notion of content *identity*, still it permits a robust notion of content *similarity*. (There's a third reason too, as we'll see in the next section.) Taking this for granted seems like just

17

common sense. After all, there does *seem* to be a colloquial notion of belief similarity. We do say things like "What I believe is a lot like what the President believes" or "Her world view is sort of similar to Dracula's" or "His understanding of definite descriptions is less like Russell's than like Strawson's" and so on. So maybe this colloquial sense of "similar belief" can be co-opted to provide for a robust formulation of intentional generalizations. Maybe the right generalization is: If somebody asks you something *sort of like* what is the first color you think of, then you will think of something *sort of like* red.[16]

The trouble is that we really have no idea what it would be like for this new generalization to be true (or false) and, barring some illumination in this quarter, the suggestion that appealing to content similarity may mitigate the severer consequences of semantic holism is simply *empty*. This point is so important, and so widely goes unrecognized, that we propose to spend a little time rubbing it in.

No doubt, one does know (sort of) what it is like to more or less believe the same things as the President does; it's to share *many of the President's beliefs*. For example, the President believes P, Q, R, and S, and I believe P, Q, and R; so my beliefs are similar to his. An alternative, compatible reading is: the President believes P and Q *very strongly* and I believe them equally strongly or almost as strongly, so again my beliefs are similar to his. But neither of these ways of construing belief similarity helps with the present problem. The present problem is not to make sense of believing-most-of-P, -Q, -R, -and-S or of more-or-less-strongly-believing-P; it's to make sense of believing *something-similar-to-P* – that is, believing *more-or-less-P*.

The colloquial senses of "similar belief" *presuppose* some way of *counting* beliefs, so they presuppose some notion of belief *identity*. If you have most of the beliefs that I have, then, a fortiori, there are (one or more) beliefs that we both have. And if there is a proposition that you sort of believe and that I believe strongly, then, a fortiori, there is a proposition that is the object of both of our beliefs. But precisely because these colloquial senses of belief similarity *presuppose* a notion of belief identity, they don't allow us to *dispense with* a notion of belief identity *in favor of* a notion of belief similarity. In consequence, if you're a holist and your notion of belief identity is very unrobust, so that, de facto, people can hardly ever have the same belief, then it will also turn out that, in either of the colloquial senses just discussed, people can hardly ever have *similar* beliefs. If it's never true that I believe *any* of what the President believes, then, of course, it can't be true that I ever believe *most* of what he believes. If the President and I never believe the same thing, then there is nothing that he believes as strongly as I do.

It's not, of course, incoherent to imagine a notion of "similar belief" which, unlike these colloquial ones, is compatible both with meaning holism and with there being robust intentional generalizations. The trouble is, as we remarked above, that nobody seems to have any idea what this useful new sense of "similar belief" might be. On the contrary, it seems sort of plausible that you can't have a robust notion of *similar* such and suches unless you have a correspondingly robust notion of *identical* such and suches. The problem isn't, notice, that if holism is true, then the conditions for belief identity are hard to meet; it's that, if holism is true, then the notion of "tokens of the same belief type" is defined *only* for the case in which *every* belief is shared. Holism provides no notion of belief-type identity that is defined for any other case and no hint of how to construct one. But if there is no construal of the claim that two beliefs are tokens of the *same* type in cases where belief systems fail to overlap completely, how, in such cases, are we to construe the notion of two beliefs being tokens of *almost* the same type? (One recent proposal for construing the notion of similarity of meaning will be discussed in chapter 7, q.v.)

We really do think it's hard to get out of this; the sort of unconsidered talk about similarity of intentional content that is currently so prevalent in cognitive science serves only to obscure the magnitude of the problem. For example, it might be suggested that a content holist could endorse a *physicalistic* account of belief similarity; after all, your beliefs and mine are presumably *identical* if you and I are *identical* molecule for molecule.[17] Doesn't it follow that our beliefs are *similar* if we are *similar* molecule for molecule? This notion of belief similarity would be robust because, even if no two time slices of organism are ever physically identical, there are plenty of ways, surely, that two time slices of organism can perfectly well be physically *alike*.

But, on second thought, this doesn't help at all. Even if it's granted that identity of belief systems supervenes on physical identity, it doesn't begin to follow that similarity of belief systems supervenes on physical similarity. It is, perhaps, reasonable to assume that if you are my molecular twin, then you share all my beliefs. But it is entirely gratuitous to assume that if you are my molecular cousin, some of your beliefs are ipso facto similar to some of mine. (Which ones, by the way?) No doubt there *are* indefinitely many ways in which the brains of molecular cousins are similar; but there are also *indefinitely many ways in which they aren't*, and we have no idea how to decide which similarities and differences are the ones that determine whether their beliefs are similar. Which is just to say that nobody has a better idea of how to explicate a notion of *physical* similarity that is relevant to psychological taxonomy than of how to explicate a notion of *content* similarity that is relevant to psychological taxonomy.

"Well, maybe two beliefs are similar if they participate in mostly the same inferences." There are two reasons why this too doesn't help. One is the same sort of point we've just been noticing: that if this proposal is to provide a robust notion of similar belief, it will have to presuppose a correspondingly robust notion of *identity of inference;* and that is one of the things that meaning holism appears likely to deny us. If it turned out to be a consequence of meaning holism that no two people ever have exactly the same belief, it would surely also turn out to be a consequence of meaning holism that no two people ever accept exactly the same inference. After all, *identical* inferences must have *identical* premises and *identical* conclusions. And if it is replied that, well, holism still allows that different people could accept *similar* inferences, we're back where we started – except that it's the notion of *similar inference* rather than the notion of *similar belief* that now cries out for explication.

The second problem with reconstructing similarity-of-beliefs-entertained by reference to similarity-of-inferences-endorsed is that some inferences have to count for more than others, surely. Consider the man who may be thinking about red. When *I* think about red, I am in a state from which I am prepared to make certain inferences about tomatoes. So, for example, if I think this book is red, then I'm prepared to believe that this book is the same color, more or less, as ripe tomatoes are. But my willingness to make *this* inference (and thousands like it) surely can't be *constitutive* of my having thoughts about red. If it were, Shakespeare would be out of luck; he didn't know about tomatoes.

In fact, however you individuate beliefs, it's sure to turn out that there are *vast numbers* of red things – hence vast numbers of things about red – that I know about that Shakespeare didn't; and, of course, vice versa. So now we need to know *how much* the differences between the red-inferences I endorse and the ones that Shakespeare did count as differences in our concept of red. The extent to which this sort of question lacks a principled answer is the extent to which we have no notion of similarity of content that is compatible with a holistic account of belief attribution. And it lacks a principled answer entirely; does believing that Mars is red count more or less for having the concept *red* than believing that tomatoes are?[18]

The long and the short of it seems to be that intentional explanation needs a robust notion of belief identity, and meaning holism appears to prejudice the possibility of such a

21

notion. You can't get out of this just by appealing to a notion of *similarity of content*, because all the robust notions of content similarity – or, at a minimum, all the ones that spring to mind – *presuppose* a robust notion of belief identity and hence are themselves incompatible with holism if robust belief identity is.

MEANING HOLISM AND THE ANALYTIC/ SYNTHETIC DISTINCTION

There is an alternative move that it's traditional for philosophers to make at this point – namely, to opt for a notion of belief identity after all, one that's grounded in an analytic/synthetic distinction. Beliefs are identical iff they participate in the same *analytic* inferences. (Presumably a corresponding notion of belief similarity can be introduced if it's required, some variant on "Beliefs are similar insofar as they participate in *many of the same* analytic inferences." See chapter 2 for further discussion of analyticity and chapter 6 for its relation to belief identity.) *Strictly speaking*, this way of squaring content holism with a robust notion of belief similarity might surely be accused of begging the question, since, once again, it appears that a robust notion of *accepting the same inference* (hence a robust notion of *same inference*) is being taken for granted. But we propose not to harp on this any longer. The a/s distinction has been lurking in the closet through this whole discussion, and it is now time to let it out.

Up till now, we've been considering some consequences of assuming both that semantic properties are typically anatomic and that if a semantic property is anatomic, then it is holistic. Notice that the first assumption is relatively innocuous unless the second one is also in place. It would, no doubt, be interesting and curious to show that, for example, you can't share any of my beliefs unless you share at least two of them (mutatis mutandis, that a language can't express any propositions unless it can express several, and so forth). But it's not at all obvious that drastic implications for theory commensurability, Scientific Realism, translation, intentional explanation, and the like would follow from this sort of "molecularist" semantics.[19] These seem to depend on the *holistic* claim that the conditions for content relativize to entire languages or belief systems; for example, that you can't share any of my beliefs unless you share practically all of them.

What we now want to emphasize is that the argument from anatomism to holism itself depends on the premise that no principled a/s distinction can be drawn. If this is so, then the only context in which a discussion of semantic holism is worth having is one in which the failure of the a/s distinction is taken as common ground. We remarked, in the preceding section, that if not many cognitive scientists are worried about the threat that holism poses to the concept of belief identity, that's often because they suppose that some notion of belief similarity will serve to take up the slack. In like spirit, if not many "functional role" semanticists or verificationists are disturbed by the spectre of holism, that's often because they are prepared to buy into some kind of a/s distinction.[20]

We now propose to consider how the argument from the anatomism of semantic properties to the holism of semantic properties might be supposed to run and what role in the argument the denial of the a/s distinction plays. Here's a candidate formulation.

Argument A

Premise 1: Generic semantic properties like T, T*, R, R*, being-some-or-other-belief-of-Smith's, being a formula of language L, etc. are anatomic.

Comments:

1. We want to be noncommittal about *how many* generic semantic properties are anatomic. The argument under analysis

requires only that the property of being-some-or-other-belief-of-Smith's is.

2. Premise 1 might itself be derived from, for example, some version of "inferential role" semantics – for example, from the assumption that the identity of a concept (mutatis mutandis, the meaning of a word) is at least partially determined by its role in a belief system (or language or theory). Our impression is that most contemporary philosophers who accept premises like 1 do so for this sort of reason. For example, we'll see in chapter 2 that Quine is widely read as endorsing a form of argument A in which the first premise derives from verificationist assumptions about semantics: roughly, the assumption that the content of a belief is the means of determining that the belief is true (/false), including, in particular, the inferences involved in such determinations.

Lemma: If Smith has the belief that P, he must have other beliefs not identical to P.

Comment: Instantiation.

Premise 2: There is no *principled* distinction between the propositions that Smith has to believe to believe that P and the propositions that Smith doesn't have to believe to believe that P.

Comments:

1. The standard reason for holding premise 2 is that, on the one hand, the only principled distinction anyone can think of depends on the idea that if you can't believe P unless you believe Q, then "if P, then Q" must be analytic (or, perhaps, analytic *for you*), and, on the other hand, there is no principled a/s distinction. This, then, is the precise point at which the argument from the anatomism of semantic properties to the holism of semantic properties turns on the rejection of a/s.

2. Notice, however, that what is meant by "the rejection of a/s" in this context is quite different from the rejection of the a/s distinction that Quine almost certainly has in mind in "Two dogmas of empiricism" and other of his papers in which the distinction is impugned. When Quine says "No a/s," he presumably means "No analytic sentences." On that reading of premise 2, however, argument A would appear to be inconsistent. For premise 1 requires that there be sentences other than P that must be believed if P is believed; and it looks as though the hypothetical formed by writing one of these sentences after "if P, then" must be analytic, as we've just observed.

So the reading of premise 2 that argument A really requires is "The a/s distinction isn't principled," rather than "No sentences are analytic." This reading is, of course, acceptable to conceptual role semanticists and their ilk; but it's pretty clear that Quine couldn't put up with it.[21] There is a fair amount of irony in this. Accepting semantic holism is often seen as a *consequence* of agreeing with Quine about the a/s distinction. But what Quine said about the a/s distinction is that there are no analytic sentences, and it doesn't look as if a semantic holist who endorses argument A *can* agree with *that*.

Conclusion: The property of being-some-or-other-belief-of-Smith's is holistic.

Comments:

1. The reference to Smith is inessential. If the argument is right, it shows that there couldn't be a punctate mind (a mind which can entertain only one proposition) or, mutatis mutandis, a punctate language (a language which can express only one proposition).

2. The form of argument A is: "If some a's are F, and there is no principled difference between the a's that are F's and the ones that aren't, then all a's are F." So argument A has the form of a "sorites" or "slippery slope."

25

3. As often happens when a form of philosophical argument is in the air, it's frustratingly difficult to find fully explicit instances in print. (Devitt, "Meaning holism," registers the same complaint.) Stich, however, comes pretty close:

> I want to demonstrate that . . . intuitive judgments about whether a subject's belief can be characterized in a given way . . . are often very sensitive . . . to other beliefs that the subject(s) are assumed to have. The content we ascribe to a belief depends, more or less holistically, on the subject's entire network of related beliefs.
> . . . . .
> Consider the fact that . . . intuitions [of conceptual identity and difference] . . . seem . . . to lie along a continuum. Recall, for example, the case of Mrs. T, the woman suffering from gradual, progressive loss of memory. Before the onset of her illness Mrs. T clearly believed that McKinley was assassinated. By the time of the dialogue reported in Chapter 4 she clearly did not believe it. But at what point in the course of her illness did her belief stop being content-identical with mine? The question is a puzzling one and admits of no comfortable reply. What we are inclined to say is that her belief gradually becomes less and less content-identical with mine [as the inferences we share come to overlap less and less] . . . How much physics must my son know before it is appropriate to say that he believes that $E = MC^2$? The more the better, of course, but there are no natural lines to draw. (Stich, *From Folk Psychology to Cognitive Science: The Case Against Belief*, pp. 54, 85–6)

More or less explicit versions of argument A are also to be found in Dennett ("Intentional systems"), Churchland ("Perceptual plasticity and theoretical neutrality: a reply to Jerry Fodor"), Gibson (*The Philosophy of W. V. Quine: An Expository Essay*), and maybe in Quine ("Two dogmas"). Indeed, the practically universal tendency to invoke "No a/s" as a premise when making a case for semantic holism would seem senseless except in the context of some such argument as A.

26

The status of argument A
There are plenty of reasons for doubting that argument A is sound. In the first place, one might doubt that semantic properties actually are anatomic. For example, the usual justification for supposing that they are is that one assumes some functional role (or verificationistic) account of meaning. To deny this assumption would thus be to undermine the standard argument for premise 1. Second, even if the a/s distinction is untenable, there might be some other principled way of distinguishing the propositions that you have to believe to believe P from the ones you don't. Third, as we remarked above, A is a species of sorites argument, and these are notorious for leading from true premises to false conclusions. Consider the slippery slope that runs from there being no principled difference between baldness and hairiness to the conclusion that everyone is bald (or that nobody is). Fourth, A's validity might be challenged on grounds independent of the status of slippery slope arguments. At least one version of this fourth objection merits discussion.

Weak anatomism, strong anatomism, and the a/s distinction
A number of people (Boghossian, Loewer, Maudlin; see n. 9) have suggested the following as a situation in which A's premises might be true *but its conclusion false*. Imagine that there are disjoint sets of propositions such that (1) believing any one of these sets is sufficient for being able to believe P; (2) you must believe *at least* one of these sets in order to believe P; (3) none of these sets is such that you must believe *it* in order to believe P. So someone can believe P if he believes A *or* if he believes B, and so on. It might be further assumed that there are indefinitely many such sets of sufficient-but-not-necessary conditions for believing that P, and that nobody is able to believe the proposition formed by disjoining these indefinitely many sets of propositions (perhaps because the resulting disjunctive proposition is so complicated that no mind is able to

entertain it). Then, on the one hand, premise 1 would clearly be true. And premise 2 would be true in at least the sense that there are no analytic beliefs.[22] Yet neither content holism nor translation holism would follow. Content holism wouldn't follow because it requires that there must be *many* other propositions that I believe if I believe that P (that is, it requires *a lot* of anatomism), and the current assumptions allow that some or all of the disjoint sets each of which is sufficient to be able to believe P might be quite small. So, compatible with the present account, content might be molecular rather than holistic. Translation holism wouldn't follow either, because it requires that for two people to share any belief, they must share at least one other belief, and the present model allows that what you believe is P and A, whereas what I believe is P and B. What everybody *really* wants is that meaning should be anatomic and that translation holism should nevertheless be false. This suggestion seems to do the trick.

There is, to put the point slightly differently, a quantifier-scope ambiguity lurking in the definition of "anatomic," and hence in premise 1 of argument A. What might be meant by claiming that properties like *having the belief that such and such* are anatomic – and what we have thus far been meaning in discussing the claim – is:

> *There are other propositions such that you can't believe P unless you believe them.* Call this the "long scope" or "strong" reading.

Or what might be meant is:

> *You can't believe P unless there are other propositions that you believe.* Call this the "short scope" or "weak" reading.

The proposed criticism of argument A is that, on the short scope reading of "anatomic," the premises can be true and the conclusion false.

The line of thought we are considering is framed as an objection to argument A. But it might equally be thought to show that holding anatomism while rejecting the a/s distinction need entail no pernicious consequences. As we've been seeing, on the short scope reading of "anatomic," conjoining premises 1 and 2 would *not* entail that you can't share any of my beliefs without sharing all of them, or even that your having any one belief requires your having lots of others. In short, it looked at first sight as though argument A might make semantic holism the only coherent alternative to semantic atomism. That is, it looked at first sight as though the only way to avoid argument A might be to take premise 1 to be *false*. But if, instead, you take premise 1 to be *true on the short scope reading*, then atomism is blocked, yet holism doesn't follow. Atomism is not conceded, but argument A is nevertheless defanged.

The trouble with this line of thought is that the kind of anatomism you get if you take premise 1 on the short scope reading is too weak to be worth the effort of defending. The way to see this is to ask yourself why it ever seemed important to argue that semantic properties are anatomic. We think that the answer is pretty clear: There is undeniably a pre-theoretic intuition that two people couldn't agree about *only one thing*. The intuition is that, if you and I agree that protons are very small, then there must be lots of other propositions we agree about too – for example, that protons aren't tangerines or prime numbers or mammals; that, ceteris paribus, very small things are smaller than very big ones, that there are sub-atomic particles, that positive charges are different from negative charges, and so forth. In effect, semantic holism proposes to hold onto this intuition even if the price is claiming that we can't agree that protons are very small unless we agree about *everything* else.

We're not prepared to endorse this intuition straightaway; to do so would just close the book against the possibility of semantic atomism.[23] But we don't deny its first blush force. One might even think that the very point of content attribution turns

29

upon the intuition being true; that it's only because we're guaranteed that people who share *any* beliefs must share *lots* of them that content attributions can warrant predictions "from the intentional stance." (In chapter 5 we'll examine an argument of Dennett's that's much in this spirit.) Our present point, however, is that if honoring this intuition is the motive for anatomism, then weak anatomism isn't any better off than atomism is.

The holist wants to capture the intuition that you and I can't both believe the proposition that protons are very small unless we also both believe some other propositions. But beware of the quantifier ambiguity here too. This might mean "Unless each of us believes at least one proposition other than '*Protons are very small*,'" or it might mean "Unless there is at least one proposition other than '*Protons are very small*,' that we both believe." It's clearly the second reading that is demanded by the idea that you and I couldn't agree on just one thing. (The first reading says only that neither of our beliefs that protons are very small could be punctate.) But the second reading is just *strong* anatomism; that is, it's not one to which a *weak* anatomist is entitled.

The sum and substance of this is that strong anatomism is the only kind worth having. So, from now on, we'll be understanding premise 1 according to the long scope interpretation.

The status of argument A (continued)
It's still on the cards, of course, that there may be something wrong with arguments that seek to infer semantic holism from anatomism together with the rejection of a principled a/s distinction. But though it's not clear what one should say about such arguments, the following *is* clear: If there is a principled a/s distinction, then the *inference* from anatomism to holism is blocked. A principled account of the a/s distinction would distinguish the propositions that you do have to believe to be able to believe that P from the ones that you don't (and the propositions that a language has to be able to express if it's able

to express P from the propositions that it doesn't). So far as we can see, this point is perfectly general. *Whatever* your argument for semantic holism might be – whether or not it's some version of argument A – it's going to fail if the a/s distinction can be sustained. It's only if you contemplate giving up an a/s distinction that you have to contemplate taking semantic holism seriously.

So, then, if we're going to discuss semantic holism at all, it had better be common ground that premise 2 of argument A is OK; and, specifically, that it is OK because there is no principled a/s distinction. Notice that, for our purposes, this rules out any possibility of a "molecularist" compromise between atomism and holism. A molecularist says that there are other beliefs that we must also share if we are to share the belief that P, but he denies that *all* our other beliefs have to be shared. But distinguishing between those that do and those that don't depends on invoking the a/s distinction, for believing P requires accepting the *analytic* inferences in which P figures. Molecularism is thus a closed option on the only assumption on which holism is sufficiently plausible to be worth discussing: namely, that the a/s distinction can't be sustained.

So be it. In what follows we will be seeking to undermine A and arguments like it; but (unlike Devitt, "Meaning holism," for example) we won't claim that what's wrong is that premise 2 is false. We also won't claim that what's wrong with arguments like A is that they are slippery slopes – though it may well be that all arguments from anatomism to holism *are* slippery slopes, which may well be one of the things that are wrong with them. What we'll do instead is attack the grounds that have been alleged in support of the *first* premise; we'll try to show that no good reason has yet been given as to why (generic) semantic properties are (strongly; see above) anatomic. If we are right about this, then, a fortiori, there are no good arguments for semantic holism, it being the *stronger* thesis.

One last preliminary remark about argument A: though it isn't, perhaps, really very convincing, it may nevertheless be a straw in the wind. At a minimum, if you are *independently* persuaded that the atomistic alternatives to holism have been explored *and have been shown not to work*, then arguments in the spirit of A may well suffice to produce a rational conviction that holism is true. That brings us to the next part of our story.

SEMANTIC ATOMISM

Why is almost everyone a meaning holist? There are, we think, two kinds of considerations conducive to the doctrine. The first consists of positive arguments (in the spirit of argument A, for example) that meaning holism is true. The second is a sort of intuition about the historical situation in semantics. It's the intuition that holism is the last log afloat, that the history of philosophical discussions of meaning shows that either semantic properties are holistic or there are no such properties.

Suppose you think that there is no a/s distinction and that there is a convincing argument from anatomism to holism. In consequence, you think that semantic properties must be either holistic or punctate. What is the likelihood that they are punctate? Well, if they are, then, by definition, the meaning of an expression can *not* depend on its role in a language. What else might it depend upon? The traditional nonholist answer is: some symbol/world relation – specifically, some punctate symbol/world relation, some relation that one thing could bear to the world even if nothing else did. This is the doctrine we've been calling "semantic atomism."

It's a widely held view that much of the history of the philosophy of language consists of a failed attempt to make semantic atomism work.[24] Given this view, there is an inductive argument that the only story about language that is compatible with taking semantic properties seriously is holism.[25] For example, the tradition that runs from the mentalistic empiricism of Hobbes, Locke, Berkeley, and Hume to the behavioristic empiricism of Watson, Mead, Skinner, Dewey, and Ogden and

Richards offers two different reconstructions of the mind/world relation on which content is supposed to depend. Both of these reconstructions are atomistic, and both of them fail.

The mentalistic version of this tradition holds that semantic properties inhere, in the first instance, in a certain class of mental particulars, in "Ideas" according to one use of that term. (The semantic properties of, for example, English words are derivative; to have a word that means *dog* is to have a word that is associated, in the right way, with the *dog* Idea.) These mental particulars are species of images, and what they mean depends on what they resemble.[26] To have the idea of a dog is thus (approximately) to have an Idea that looks like a dog; to have the idea of a triangle is (approximately) to have an Idea that looks like a triangle. And so forth. Since what one of one's Ideas looks like is presumably independent of what other Ideas one has, the requirements for meaning are atomistic according to this account.

According to the behavioristic version of the tradition, meaning inheres in the first instance in certain (paradigmatically verbal) behavioral gestures. To have in one's behavioral repertoire a sound that means *dog* is (approximately) to be so conditioned that dogs reliably cause one to utter that sound; to have in one's behavioral repertoire a sound that means *triangle* is (approximately) to be so conditioned that triangles reliably cause one to utter *that* sound. And so forth. Since whether one's behavioral repertoire includes a sound the utterance of which is reliably conditioned to dogs is, presumably, independent of what, if anything, the other sounds in your repertoire are reliably conditioned to, the requirements for meaning are atomistic according to this account too.

We propose to spare the reader a rehearsal of the arguments which show that meaning can't be reduced either to resemblance or to behavioral conditioning.[27] We remark only that to admit that these versions of meaning atomism are hopeless is not the same as admitting that meaning atomism is false; a fortiori, it's not the same as admitting that meaning holism is true. In fact –

or so it seems to us – the present situation in the philosophy of language includes the following open options:

1.   It might turn out that semantic properties are anatomic (so that semantic atomism is false) but that holism doesn't follow because the a/s distinction proves to be tenable. What would be left is a sort of semantic molecularism (as has been suggested by Dummett, among many others). Roughly, the smallest language that could express the proposition that P would be one that can express the propositions to which P is analytically connected.

2.   It might turn out that semantic properties are anatomic (so that semantic atomism is false) but that holism doesn't follow because, although the a/s distinction isn't tenable, there is some other principled way of grounding the distinction between the inferential relations that are constitutive of content and the ones that aren't. Once again, the upshot would probably be some sort of semantic molecularism.

3.   It might turn out that holism follows from the assumption that semantic properties are anatomic, but that semantic properties aren't, in fact, anatomic. That is, it might turn out that meaning atomism is true.

What the familiar arguments show, it seems to us, is that, if option 3 is the way it does turn out, then somebody will have to cook up a story about how symbol/world relations are constitutive of content that does *not* appeal to resemblance or behavioral conditioning. What we doubt is that the reasons that have thus far been invoked against meaning atomism show that this *could not* happen.[28]

Modesty, however, is our middle name; nothing so ambitious as a defense of meaning atomism is contemplated in the text that follows. Here is what we propose to do instead. We want to look, as carefully and exhaustively as we can, at arguments for meaning holism that reject *an als distinction* but that *do not assume that meaning atomism has been shown to be false.* We're going to try to show that none of these residual arguments is convincing. The bottom line might then be that there aren't any semantic properties; or it might be that some kind of meaning atomism is true but nobody knows *which* kind; or it might be that there really are good arguments for meaning holism, but nobody has been able to find one yet. We're noncommittal; you choose.

2

W. V. O. QUINE:
MEANING HOLISM AND
CONFIRMATION HOLISM

Quine's "Two dogmas of empiricism" is perhaps the most analyzed short philosophical paper written in the last fifty years and is the point of departure for many discussions of holism. Our treatment will therefore be relatively brief. We propose to swallow Quine's epistemology whole, confining ourselves entirely to those aspects of "Two dogmas" that are widely interpreted as bearing on the status of meaning holism. We think that the implications of Quine's epistemological doctrines for strictly semantic theses have been in some respects exaggerated; in particular, that meaning holism can be resisted even assuming – as we are inclined to do – that most of what "Two dogmas" says about the holism of confirmation (the so-called Quine/ Duhem (Q/D) thesis) is right-headed.

We commence by reminding the reader of the architecture of "Two dogmas." In effect, the paper divides into two major parts. The first part (sections 1–5) is a long argument to the conclusion that the analytic/synthetic distinction cannot be enforced, together with a rejection of the reductionist claim that there is, for each "statement" in an empirical theory, a proprietary range of (dis)confirming conditions (for example, a proprietary range of sense data statements). By definition, a reductionist holds that the confirmation conditions for a statement are knowable a priori, because they are among the statement's *analytic* implications. Quine thus takes anti-reductionism to be an immediate consequence of abandoning the a/s distinction. To claim that the a/s distinction fails is to claim, in particular, that our knowledge of confirmation relations is a posteriori. This means, for Quine, that it is *contingent* knowledge, since, like the positivists before him, Quine assumes that "a posteriori" and "contingent" are co-extensive (compare Kripke, *Naming and Necessity*).

Except for the very last paragraph of section 5 (which will presently be the object of much of our discussion), the moral of this first part of "Two dogmas" is clear; the consequence of assuming that there is no a/s distinction is confirmation holism: "Our statements about the external world face the tribunal of sense experience not individually but only as a corporate body" ("Two dogmas," p. 41). This, of course, is the part of "Two dogmas" that has received most of the critical attention. But we don't propose to get involved either in the squabble about whether Quine really did *show* that the a/s distinction is untenable or in the squabble about whether the failure of the a/s distinction really implies the Q/D thesis that confirmation is holistic. Our strategy is rather to grant all this and to ask what the implications for semantics are.

The second (and much the shorter) part of "Two dogmas" (section 6) spells out what Quine takes to be the pragmatist implications of confirmation holism for the philosophy of science: "As an empiricist I continue to think of the conceptual scheme of science as a tool, ultimately, for predicting future experience in the light of past experience . . . in point of epistemological footing the physical objects and the gods differ only in degree and not in kind. Both sorts of entities enter our conception only as cultural posits" ("Two dogmas", p. 44). Whereas our official position is that we concede both the failure of the a/s distinction and the truth of confirmation holism, we are officially neutral about pragmatism; it turns out to be largely independent of the semantic issues that we want to raise. It is worth a brief digression to emphasize that this is so; you *can* coherently buy Quine's confirmation holism *without* buying his pragmatism; prima facie, they are independent in both directions.

That a pragmatist might accept an a/s distinction (and hence be a localist about confirmation) is just a way of saying that a pragmatist can be what Quine calls a "reductionist" (that is, what is usually called a "verificationist"[1]), which, of course, pragmatists typically *have* been (see Peirce, for example). Indeed, one of the things that's so *surprising* about "Two dogmas" is precisely the idea that you can have a *non*-reductionist pragmatism (that is, a pragmatism without an a/s distinction, hence a pragmatism that is holist about confirmation). Given the history of pragmatism, you might have supposed that its connection to reductionism is internal.

That a confirmation holist doesn't have to be a pragmatist – indeed, that he can be an ontological Realist[2] – also seems clear. In fact, if the Q/D thesis is the claim that it is a posteriori (rather than a priori) what confirms what, then the Q/D thesis is a doctrine that a Realist clearly ought to embrace. The reason is this: from the Realist perspective, *what confirms what* is a matter, not of linguistic convention, but of what is actually (for example, causally) connected to what *in the world*. If the pinkness of the litmus confirms the acidity of the fluid, that is not because "is acid" *means* (as it might be) "turns litmus pink," but rather because *being acid* and *being a cause of pinkness in litmus paper* are lawfully connected properties of acids. But if confirmation relations depend on how things are in the world, then presumably our knowledge of confirmation relations must be a posteriori – hence the Q/D thesis.

Or, rather, hence the Q/D thesis according to one of its formulations.[3] As will become increasingly clear, we think that "the" Q/D thesis is really a galaxy of nonequivalent (but closely interrelated) doctrines and that "Two dogmas" uses various versions of the thesis as its polemical purposes require. For example, we'll see that Quine has an important use for a formulation of the Q/D thesis according to which you can hold onto any statement, if confronted by recalcitrant data, by making compensatory adjustments elsewhere in your theory. This isn't the same claim as that confirmation relations are ipso facto a posteriori, but it's hard to see how the first could be true unless the second were too. Since Quine assumes the equivalence of the a priori with the semantic, revising a *non*empirical relation would presumably involve equivocation.

Since we think that most of the epistemological doctrines that cluster together in the Q/D galaxy are probably right, we will not insist on the differences between them. Sooner or later, somebody will doubtless write a doctoral dissertation that sorts them all out.

Squeezed in between the long first part and the short second part of "Two dogmas" is the following paragraph:

> The idea of defining a symbol in use was, as remarked, an advance over the impossible term-by-term empiricism of Locke and Hume. The statement, rather than the term, came with Frege to be recognized as the unit accountable to an empiricist critique. But what I am now urging is that even in taking the statement as unit we have drawn our grid too finely. *The unit of empirical significance is the whole of science.* ("Two dogmas," p. 42; our emphasis)

If there is a holist semantic thesis in "Two dogmas," this would appear to be it.

We say "If there is" because it would be natural, given both its position in the text and the occurrence of phrases like "unit accountable to an *empiricist critique*" and "unit of *empirical* significance" (our emphasis), to wonder whether this passage isn't itself just a reiteration of the Q/D thesis – that is, of holism about *confirmation*. Certainly it's *at least* that. However, three considerations at least *suggest* that it's worth taking seriously the view that a semantic thesis is at issue: first, the reference to Frege[4] (who, presumably, really was talking about the units of meaning rather than the units of confirmation); second, the critical tradition according to which "Two dogmas" is a *locus classicus* for semantic holism;[5] and third, since reductionism is explicitly viewed as both a semantic and an epistemological doctrine in "Two dogmas," it's natural to construe its denial there as both an epistemological and a semantic doctrine too. It is quite plausible (though, as we will see, by no means inevitable) to suggest that, just as "Two dogmas" offers the Q/D thesis to oppose (say) Carnap's localism about confirmation, so too it offers semantic holism to oppose Carnap's localism about meaning.

We propose, then, for purposes of argument, to just drop the "empirical" and read Quine as claiming that "the unit of *significance* is the whole of science" (mutatis mutandis, the whole of a belief system). The question then arises as to how this claim is related to the text it immediately follows: that is, "What does confirmation holism have to do with semantic holism?" to put this question in a nutshell.

There is an obvious suggestion – one which we take to be congenial to the critical tradition in Quine scholarship. (See, for example, Dummett, *Frege: Philosophy of Language*; Gibson, *The Philosophy of W. V. Quine*.) Quine is a verificationist;[6] that is, he accepts the identification of the meaning of a statement with its means of confirmation; as Quine puts it, paraphrasing Peirce, "The meaning of a statement is the method of empirically confirming or infirming it" ("Two dogmas," p. 37).[7] Conventional wisdom is that, if you put verificationism together with the Q/D thesis, you get semantic holism and that *that* is the argument for semantic holism that Quine intends in "Two dogmas."[8] Whether or not this is the intended argument, it's fallacious. Or so we claim.

Here, to a first approximation, is the way the verificationist argument for semantic holism is supposed to go. The Q/D thesis says that confirmation is holistic; that is, that every statement in a theory (partially) determines the level of confirmation of every other statement in the theory.[9] Verificationism says that the meaning of a statement is determined by its confirmation relations. The invited holistic inference is that every statement

41

in a theory partially determines the meaning of every other statement.

Now the first thing to say about this first approximation is that it's unclear – not just in our reconstruction, but in the literature at large – precisely what the force of the conclusion is supposed to be. The metaphor that often goes with semantic holism is as follows: A theory is a sort of network, in which the statements are the nodes and the semantically salient relations among the statements are the paths. The meaning of a statement *is* its position in the network and is hence defined with respect to the *totality* of the nodes and paths (since the identity condition for networks is itself holistic). If you take this metaphor dead seriously, then any change in the theory changes the semantic value of all the statements that the theory entails; and, strictly speaking, only identical theories can have any of their entailments in common.

That's *a* reading of the conclusion of the "Two dogmas" argument; but there are reasons to think that it can't be a doctrine that Quine intends. For one thing, as we shall presently have reason to emphasize, among Quine's preferred formulations of the Q/D thesis is that you can hold onto any statement, come what may, in the face of recalcitrant data. But this claim would seem to be literally unintelligible barring a notion of trans-theoretic statement identity of precisely the sort that semantic holism appears to preclude.[10]

Second, consider the role of observation statements in confirmation. On the one hand, they must be trans-theoretically identifiable if the *public* character of scientific confirmation is to be preserved. If observation statements are to *decide among* theories, then what your observation statements mean must not depend on which theory you hold. But, on the other hand, it's a truism that if they don't enter into confirmation relations with other statements, observation statements won't confirm anything except themselves. But the Q/D thesis entails that if they do enter into confirmation relations with *any* other statement in a theory, they enter into confirmation relations with *every* other statement in the theory. And Peirce's thesis says that confirmation relations are constitutive of semantic identity. It presumably follows that if theories differ in any of their entailments, they can't agree (or disagree) about which observation statements are true.[11]

Formulating a reasonable version of semantic holism (one that is compatible with the Q/D thesis, to say nothing of being compatible with Realism about semantic properties) is, in fact, no small problem. However, it's not *our* problem. For our purposes, we're content to leave the claim that "Every statement in a theory partially determines the meaning of every other statement" largely unexplicated, with the proviso that it be so construed as to entail semantic holism in at least one of the senses we specified in chapter 1: either that the metaphysically necessary conditions for content preclude punctate theories (minds/languages) or that only identical languages can contain intertranslatable statements, or both.

So now we have an argument on the table which infers semantic holism from verificationism together with the Q/D thesis. And the question arises as to what to do about it. Various options suggest themselves. For example, if you are persuaded that the argument is valid, but you don't like semantic holism, it would be reasonable for you to say, "Well then, so much the worse for verificationism (or for the Q/D thesis or for both verificationism *and* the Q/D thesis)."[12] Given the tribulations to which verificationism, in particular, has been subject over the years, this would not be a wildly unreasonable reaction.

However, though we claim to be as anti-verificationist as the next guy, this is not the course that we propose to follow. Instead, we want to argue that, appearances to the contrary notwithstanding, *even* the conjunction of confirmation holism and verificationism is compatible with the denial of semantic holism (in either of the senses mentioned above). (So this might be a good time to remind the reader that it's not, in our view, entirely obvious that this argument really does occur in "Two dogmas.")

Let's construct an argument, in the spirit of "Two dogmas," to show that a theory (language/belief system) couldn't contain *only* the statement that it's raining:

Premise 1: The statement that it's raining (R) is partially confirmed by the statement that the streets are wet (S). (Metereological platitude.)

Premise 2: Confirmation relations are ipso facto semantic. (Peirce's thesis.)

Premise 3: Statements are individuated by their semantic properties; or, as we will sometimes say, they have their semantic properties essentially. (Truism.)

Lemma: R is individuated, inter alia, by its relation to S.

Conclusion: Any theory that contains R must contain S. A fortiori, no theory could contain just R.

Since this form of argument is clearly independent of the particular choice of examples, and since the Q/D thesis guarantees, at a minimum, that each statement in a theory bears on the confirmation of many, many others, semantic holism follows.

What, if anything, is wrong with this argument? We want to claim that preserving such appearance of validity as it may have depends on being very careful *not to say what a statement is* (and, in fact, in "Two dogmas" Quine *is* very careful not to say what a statement is). So far as we can see, there are only the following three possibilities, none of which does what the argument needs: Statements are *formulas* or they are *propositions* or they are *formulas together with their conditions of semantic evaluation*. We propose to consider these options in turn.[13]

(1)   Statements are formulas.
That is, they are morpho-syntactically individuated expressions which have both their semantic properties and their linguistic affiliations *contingently.*[14] It follows that one and the same statement can have many different meanings ("The duck is ready to eat") and that one and the same statement can occur in many different languages ([Empedikliːs liːpt]). If this is the intended reading of "statement," then, for example, premise 1 of the holism argument is equivalent to: "It's raining" is confirmed by "The streets are wet."

Problems:

1.1   This can't be the intended reading; in fact, it's inconsistent with the truism that premise 3 expresses. Formulas precisely do *not* have their semantic properties essentially.

1.2   Formulas as such don't enter into confirmation relations (or entailment relations and the like). It makes no sense to ask whether the form of words "The streets are wet" tends to confirm the form of words "It's raining," since that depends entirely on what these forms of words *mean.*[15] In a language in which "It's raining" means that it's raining and "The streets are wet" means that the streets are wet, the answer is "Yes"; presumably, if a token of the first were true, then, likely enough, a corresponding token of the second would be too. But in a language in which the one means that Chicago is in Indiana and the other means that the cat is on the mat, the answer is presumably "No" (though no doubt it's an empirical issue).

1.3   To identify statements with formulas contradicts (or trivializes) the Q/D thesis under at least one of its preferred formulations: You can hold onto any statement, if confronted by recalcitrant data, by making compensatory adjustments elsewhere in your theory.

That this *is* a preferred formulation of the Q/D thesis is no accident. Duhem's holism flows in large part from his analysis

45

of the logic of experimental confirmation. It is not enough, in order for a scientific theory to have testable consequences, that it entail an experimental hypothesis. It must also warrant a host of "auxiliary" hypotheses which will be assumed by the experimental design, auxiliary hypotheses about the operation and the acuity of the experimental apparatus, for one kind of example. The confirmation holism comes in with the recognition that, in principle at least, recalcitrant data can always be accommodated by retaining the experimental hypothesis and abandoning some or all of the auxiliary apparatus. In short, it is largely because auxiliary assumptions are required to generate experimental predictions from experimental hypotheses that no "statement, taken in isolation from its fellows, can admit of confirmation or infirmation at all" ("Two dogmas," p. 41). And it is largely because, in principle, these auxiliary assumptions are always at risk that "our statements about the external world face the tribunal of experience not individually but only as a corporate body" ("Two dogmas," p. 41). (It is precisely at this point in "Two dogmas" that Quine acknowledges his debt to Duhem. See his n. 17.)

But if this is the argument for the Q/D thesis that "Two dogmas" intends, then the formulation that emphasizes the scientist's options about which hypotheses to forfeit is close to the heart of Quine's confirmation holism. And our present point is that it's hard even to make sense of this formulation of the Q/D thesis on a reading that takes "Two dogmas" to mean "formula" when it says "statement."

Here's a slightly different way of putting the issue. The Duhem analysis of experimental confirmation turns upon the thought that one might *give up some hypotheses* (the auxiliary ones) while *holding onto others* (the experimental ones). But, as we remarked a few pages back, this formulation appears to presuppose exactly what semantic holism denies: that there can be a principled, trans-theoretic way of individuating statements, hypotheses, and the like. At first thought, one might seek to reconcile semantic holism with the Q/D thesis by supposing that

46

when the Q/D thesis says, "You can save any hypothesis if you're willing to pay the price," what it means by "hypothesis" is "formula." Since formulas don't have their meanings essentially, semantic holism allows that their individuation can be principled and trans-theoretic; in particular, that they can be individuated morpho-syntactically.

But second thoughts suggest that this won't do; when the Duhem analysis talks of "hypotheses," it can't be just forms of words that it has in mind. For, consider:

1.3.1 What is it for a *form of words* to be confronted by data (recalcitrant or otherwise)?

1.3.2 It's only epistemologically interesting that you could hold onto "Burning is the liberation of phlogiston" even in the face of Lavoisier's results if "Burning is the liberation of phlogiston" means that burning is the liberation of phlogiston. It's no news that you could hold onto it in the face of those results if it means that Greycat has whiskers.

1.3.3 If statements are just formulas, you don't have to "make compensatory adjustments elsewhere" in order to hold onto them; if a formula that you like gets into trouble, use it to mean that two and two is four and leave the rest of the theory alone.

We conclude that reading "statement" as "formula" precludes a substantive reading of the Q/D thesis.

1.4 If statements are formulas, then translation holism looks to be trivially false. For, clearly, otherwise different languages *can* contain the same *formulas*: English and German both contain [Empedikliːs liːpt]. And, if it is possible for there to be a language which contains only one *morpho-syntactically* well-formed form of words, then content holism is false too – even if, in such circumstances, the form of words wouldn't *mean* anything.[16]

47

We conclude that statements can't be formulas.

(2) Statements are propositions.
According to this account, statements are trans-theoretical (trans-linguistic) entities, entities that can be expressed by the formulas of more than one theory. (In particular, they're the sorts of things that the "that" clauses in "the fact that P" or "the belief that P" are said to name.) So questions like "How do you spell the statement that P?" or "What's the first word in the statement that P?" are nonsensical, though the question "How do you state that it's raining in German?" is perfectly OK.

This would perhaps be the natural way to read "statement" if the present discussion were about confirmation rather than meaning, since it's natural to say things like "That the streets are wet confirms (suggests/shows/makes it seem likely, and so on) that it's raining." Moreover, this reading of "statement" secures the truism that statements have their conditions of semantic evaluation necessarily. It's a nonaccidental property of the proposition that it's raining that it's true iff it's raining.

Problems:

2.1 Though, as we remarked, we aren't primarily interested in *ad hominem*s, it's worth remarking that this clearly can't be what Quine means by "statement." It's precisely because Quine is suspicious of language-independent meanings, propositions, and the like that he's suspicious of the a/s distinction. Indeed, suspicion of one is really just suspicion of the other. So the idea that statements are propositions, in the sense of language-independent meanings, flies in the face of the first part of "Two dogmas."

2.2 Translation holism is a constraint on the expressive power of *languages, theories*, and the like (roughly, of systems of symbols). It says, for example, that if L can express one of the statements that English can express, then L can express practically all the statements that English can express. But if statements are propositions, the putative Quinean argument for holism doesn't have anything like this consequence. The argument does perhaps show that there are internal relations among *propositions*; for example, if there is the proposition that it's raining, then, according to the argument, there must be the proposition that the streets are wet. But from the fact that there being the proposition that P necessitates there being the proposition that Q, it does not follow (at least, it doesn't follow without further argument) that a language can't *express* the proposition that P unless it can also express the proposition that Q.

This is a perfectly general point, worth stressing outside the present context. Here's a bad argument for content holism about concepts:

> The concept *cat* is partially constituted by its connection to the concept *animal*; nothing could *be* the concept *cat* unless its applies only when the concept *animal* applies. So no mind entertains the concept *cat* unless it entertains the concept *animal*. So a mind that entertains the concept *cat* can't be punctate.

This argument is a non sequitur if you read "concepts" the way philosophers usually do: namely, as abstract objects which individuals can *share*.[17] Reading "concepts" that way, there is no obvious inference from "There wouldn't be the concept A but that there is the concept B" to "Entertaining the concept A requires entertaining (being able to entertain, being able to learn to entertain, grasping, and so forth) the concept B." In fact, barring further argument, assumptions about necessary relations among concepts don't appear to have any *psychological* consequences at all;[18] nor, for precisely parallel reasons, would they appear to constrain the expressive power of languages in which the concept can be articulated.

2.3   We take this to be the really crucial consideration: If statements are propositions, then statements have their contents essentially; propositions are individuated by reference to their contents. So, if contents are means of confirmation (as per

49

Peirce's thesis), then statements have their means of confirmation essentially. But the Q/D thesis is (inter alia) the idea that statements have their confirmation conditions *contingently*; according to the Q/D thesis, it's *contingent* what confirms what. So you can't consistently hold both Peirce's thesis and the Q/D thesis if you also hold that statements are propositions. (More of this sort of argument in the next section; it shows that statements can't be formulas together with their conditions of semantic evaluability either.) So Quine couldn't hold that statements are propositions even if he were a friend of propositions – which, of course, he's not.[19]

So statements can't be propositions.

(3)   Statements are formulas together with their associated conditions of semantic evaluability.[20]
This seems to us to be the most interesting candidate. In particular, it allows a substantive construal of the Q/D thesis, which now says that you can hold onto a form of words, come what may, *without equivocation*; and this is an interesting claim, one that isn't at all self-evident.

So then, what do you get if you conjoin the Q/D thesis with Peirce's thesis on this construal of "statement?" Presumably something like this: Statements have their conditions of semantic evaluation essentially; Peirce's thesis says that what it is for a statement to have the conditions of semantic evaluation that it does is for it to have the confirmation relations to other statements that it does (at a minimum, conditions of semantic evaluation supervene on confirmation relations); so statements have their confirmation relations to one another essentially.

Much of this may seem to be in the spirit of "Two dogmas," but it can't be what Quine (or anyone else who accepts the Q/D thesis) has in mind either.

3.1   A formulation of the Q/D thesis that is very close to its core is this: Confirmation relations are a posteriori; it's *a matter for scientific discovery* what confirms what,[21] and we change our estimates of confirmation relations to accommodate the evidence, just as we do our other theoretical commitments. Indeed, as we've already seen, the heart of Quine's argument against what he calls "reductionism" (the doctrine that statements are analytically connected to their confirmation conditions) is, to all intents and purposes, that it *can't* be a matter of meaning that "The streets are wet" confirms "It's raining," because we might simply *discover* that it doesn't. But if confirmation relations among statements are revisable and if meaning is construed in terms of confirmation, then statements don't have their semantic properties essentially. So statements can't be formulas *together with their conditions of semantic evaluation*. (This is the same argument that showed that statements can't be propositions; see above.)

The reader might well be wondering whether there is *any* version of Peirce's thesis that can be squared with the idea that confirmation relations are revisable. After all, Peirce's thesis just *is* the claim that confirmation relations constitute semantic relations and are therefore not contingent. Quite so. The arguments we have been considering amount to a dilemma:

If statements as such are just formulas, you can't make sense of talk about confirmation relations holding among them.

If statements as such are semantically interpreted, then the Q/D thesis says that they have their confirmation relations contingently and Peirce's thesis says that they have their confirmation relations essentially.

It looks as though what the Q/D thesis and Peirce's thesis say about statements are mutually inconsistent. We conclude that, questions about semantic holism to one side, there must be something deeply wrong with "Two dogmas," since it is explicitly committed to both principles.

It is, prima facie, inadvisable to try to run an argument for semantic holism (or, indeed, for anything else) which takes both the Q/D thesis and Peirce's thesis as premises. You could try the following, however. The Q/D thesis requires confirmation conditions to be *a posteriori*; but, strictly speaking, it does not require them to be *contingent*. It is thus compatible with the Q/D thesis that confirmation relations should be (not linguistically but) *metaphysically* necessary. On the one hand, *if P confirms Q, then it's necessary that P confirms Q*; but, on the other hand, since metaphysical necessities are presumably known a posteriori, only inquiry would allow us to determine when a confirmation relation holds.

Given his empiricism (to say nothing of his anti-essentialism), it isn't easy to imagine Quine opting for this markedly unepistemological reading of "confirmation condition"; but at least it does square the Q/D thesis with Peirce's thesis. Notice, however, that it doesn't help with the argument for semantic holism. On the contrary, semantic holism *clearly* would not follow from confirmation holism according to this account. For, though what a statement means now depends on what confirms it, what confirms it does *not* depend on the theory it's embedded in. On the present assumptions, it could perfectly well turn out that the embedding theory for P might be *entirely wrong* about what the confirmation conditions of P are, in which case P's role in the theory (including what the theory says about P's confirmation conditions) would be simply *irrelevant* to what P means. The moral is that to get semantic holism from confirmation holism, you need to relativize what a statement means in a theory to what *that theory* says about the confirmation conditions of the statement.[22]

3.2 A second, relatively minor reason not to suppose that what Quine means by "statement" is *formula with its conditions of semantic evaluation* is that this interpretation would fail to secure the *immanence* of confirmation. (See *Philosophy of Logic*, pp. 19–20; we are extending Quine's usage from languages to theories.) Immanence is the idea that because confirmation is defined over sorts of entities whose connection to a particular theory (/language) is essential, it need not be possible to construe such questions as whether two theories agree about confirmation relations. This is, pretty clearly, a thesis that Quine wishes to maintain. But immanence fails on the present proposal, just as it does on the proposal that statements are formulas. There is no obvious reason why the formula "It's raining" couldn't, by accident, turn out to be a Swahili sentence that is true iff it's raining; in which case, English and Swahili would have a statement in common.

So statements can't be formulas together with their conditions of semantic evaluation. So, apparently, there is nothing that statements *can* be, consonant with the use to which the "Two dogmas" argument for semantic holism wants to put them. So the argument is unsound.

What's gone wrong? We think it's this: The strategy we've been attributing to "Two dogmas" is to infer semantic holism from confirmation holism. In order to do so, it must take for granted that the X's that enter into confirmation relations (in particular, the X's to which the Q/D thesis applies) are the very same X's that semantic theories are about; they're the very same things whose conditions of semantic evaluation semantic theories specify.[23] The trouble is, however, that whereas the natural objects of semantic interpretation are linguistic entities like formulas, the natural bearers of confirmation relations are trans-linguistic entities like propositions. So, even though confirmation holism is quite likely true, and even though verificationism is assumed for the sake of argument, there is no sound inference from those premises to semantic holism, because confirmation holism and verificationism are true *of different things*.[24]

We conclude this section by reminding the reader that, since we don't think that verificationism *is* true, the previous argument is a little on the hypothetical side. But we sense, in the philosophical community at large, some sympathy for the idea that, well, maybe verificationism is sort of *a little* true;[25] at least, it might be true enough to buy you a semantics from which meaning holism can be inferred. So it seemed to us worth stressing that the (putative) Quinean argument has troubles that run deeper than the odd false premise. It is – ineliminably, in our view – a fallacy of equivocation.

ANOTHER ARGUMENT FOR MEANING HOLISM

We're almost done with the discussion of meaning holism in "Two dogmas." But before we pack up the chapter, it's worth mentioning a curious subsidiary argument that Quine suggests both in "Two dogmas" and in "Epistemology naturalized" (see p. 72): namely, that "Russell's concept of incomplete symbols defined in use" implies *statement* holism; that is, it implies that "the primary vehicle of meaning . . . [is not] . . . the term but in the statement" ("Two dogmas," p. 39). This suggestion is worth considering in the present context, because a demonstration that the unit of meaning is no smaller than a whole statement (or sentence) might be a lemma on the way to demonstrating that the unit of meaning is no less than a whole theory (or language). Also, it's possible to wonder how the statement-as-semantic-unit story is to be squared with the widely prevalent idea that sentences (and, hence, the statements that they are used to make) have *compositional* semantic structure; that is, that the meanings of sentences are derived from the meanings of their lexical constituents.

Unfortunately, Quine doesn't say how the argument from definitions-in-use to statement holism is supposed to run; and it's not easy to guess what he could have had in mind. For one thing, statement holism is presumably a *modal* claim, something like that no expression *could have a semantic value* except as it functions as part of a sentence. The least Quine would appear to need to get this modal conclusion would be the corresponding modal premise: namely, not just that (some) terms *are* defined in use but that all terms *have to be*. It is, to put it mildly, unclear that Russell's remarks on definite descriptions warrant any such claim.

In fact, it's not clear whether the (presumed) facts about definitions-in-use warrant *any* claim about *meanings*. Let's suppose that some words are defined with respect to their sentential contexts, just as Russell thought. It remains open – and crucial – *which aspects* of their sentential contexts these words are defined with respect to. In particular, it depends on whether words that are defined in use are ipso facto defined relative to *semantic* properties of their contexts.

Consider, for example, [kriːks], which means one thing in "The door . . ." but something quite different in "The . . . flow." Do these considerations show that [kriːks] is not a "unit of meaning" (that is, that the unit of meaning is not [kriːks] but, as it might be, [kriːks]-in-a-sentence-about-doors)? Well, perhaps; but also perhaps not. Maybe the right story is that the units of meaning are [kriːks]$_{verb}$ in the one case and [kriːks]$_{noun}$ in the other. If this *is* the right story, then it suggests that the sentence is the unit of *syntax*; that is, that words couldn't have the *syntactic* properties they do if they did not occur as constituents of sentences.

This suggestion seems plausible enough; on the face of it, syntactic properties look to be ones that words have in virtue of their relations to the sentences that contain them.[26] By contrast, it is *by no means* obvious that their *semantic* properties are ones that words have in virtue of their relations to sentences that contain them. And it is also not obvious that the questions "What's the unit of semantic analysis?" and "What's the unit of syntactic analysis?" have to get the same answer.[27]

FACTS ABOUT MEANING?

So much for the arguments for semantic holism in "Two dogmas"; we can now say what the rest of this book will be about. Since it appears that the arguments usually attributed to

55

"Two dogmas" are deeply flawed, the question arises as to whether there are other arguments that are more convincing. In the course of discussing this question, it will often turn out that whether Quine is right about the a/s distinction is crucial to the direction that the polemics take. We propose, if only because it is the more conservative policy, not to appeal to the a/s distinction in the evaluation of holistic theses about meaning; in effect, we will assume that Quine *is* right and that the a/s distinction cannot be sustained.[28] So then, if there is something wrong with semantic holism, it is *not* that only the statements that S is *analytically* related to are constitutive of what S means.

We want to emphasize, however, that conceding this is conceding very much less than that (for example) there are no facts about meaning or that there are no truths that hold "in virtue of meaning alone" or that the notion of a semantic rule is unintelligible or (a fortiori) that there can be no such thing as a semantic theory. It's perfectly possible to be eliminativist about an *epistemologically based* a/s distinction but not about semantics as such and, indeed, not about the a/s distinction as such.

To see what's at issue, imagine somebody who holds a reductionist theory of meaning; for example, somebody like Skinner, who holds that for "dog" to mean *dog* in a certain speaker's mouth is for the speaker to have the habit of uttering "dog" when there are dogs around. Perhaps it needn't be said that we think this sort of theory is unlikely to work. But there are *some* lines of argument against which it's defensible; and here's one. Look, someone might say, if Skinner were right, then you could have a situation in which a speaker has two responses ("dog" and "shmog," as it might be) that are conditioned to *exactly the same stimuli*. But then it would follow that these responses would be *synonymous* for that speaker. So then the following sentence would be *analytic* in the speaker's language (assuming he has the logico-syntactic apparatus to frame it): "Whatever is a dog is a shmog." But Quine showed in "Two dogmas" that there are no such things as synonyms or analytic sentences. So Skinner's semantics *must* be wrong. A priori! In fact, *all* semantic theories must be wrong, a priori, except for the nihilistic theory which says that there are no semantic properties.[29]

What has gone wrong this time? We take it that, strictly speaking, Quine in "Two dogmas" did *not* show, or even argue, that there are no semantic facts, or even that there are no analytic truths.[30] Rather, what we are conceding is that if there *is* sense to be made of meaning and the associated notions, it can't be reconstructed by reference to *statements that a speaker assents to*. Or, equivalently for these purposes, if Quine is right in "Two dogmas," then what you mean can't be reduced to what inferences you are prepared to accept.

For example, it can't be that whether you mean that John is a bachelor by your utterance of "John is a bachelor" depends on whether, if you are prepared to utter "John is a bachelor," then you are prepared to utter "John is an unmarried man," or on whether you are prepared to accept the inference that if "is a bachelor" applies to John, then "is an unmarried man" does too. Because, Quine argues, what inferences you are prepared to accept (and/or what you are prepared to utter given that you are prepared to utter . . .) depends not only on what you intend your words to mean, but also on how you take the (non-linguistic) world to be. And there is no principled way to separate the respective contributions of these factors. Knowing which inferences someone accepts doesn't tell you which of them he accepts a priori; so it doesn't tell you which of them is analytic.

Quine's rejection of analyticity, insofar as it's actually argued for (and insofar as we are proposing to concede it), is a rejection only of the possibility of an *epistemic* criterion for "true in virtue of meaning." In principle, at least, everything else remains wide open. For example, it's left open that you might be able to reduce semantic relations to resemblance relations (the way Hume wanted to) or to conditioning relations (the way Skinner wanted to) or to nomological relations (the way

Dretske wants to) or to nonepistemic intentional relations of being appeared to (the way we gather phenomenologists want to) – or to other relations as yet undreamed of. Any of these reductions would imply corresponding notions of synonymy/analyticity (Ideas that resemble the same things are the same Ideas; words that are conditioned to the same things are synonyms, and so forth). And, since none of these notions of synonymy/analyticity is epistemic, none of them is in jeopardy of the sorts of considerations that Quine offers in "Two dogmas."

On this view, the only doctrine that *can't* be held, consonant with Quine's rejection of the a/s distinction, is the following conjunctive one: Some inferential relations are constitutive of semantic relations, *and* which they are can be determined by applying an epistemic criterion like aprioricity or unrevisability. Inter alia, meaning holism remains open; and so too does a reductionistic atomism (and so too, of course, does semantic nihilism).

What we now want to know is: What can someone who *isn't* a verificationist say on behalf of the first of these options?

3

DONALD DAVIDSON:
MEANING HOLISM AND RADICAL INTERPRETATION

The most interesting of the arguments for holism to be discussed in this chapter and the following two pursue a common strategy. The idea is to show that certain principles of charity are constitutive of content ascription. It's purported that these principles are intrinsically holistic, so the holism of the intentional is entailed.[1]

All the arguments we'll be looking at are more or less transcendental in style; but it is characteristic of the ones to be considered in this chapter that they have premises that are simultaneously epistemological and metaphysical. The basic idea is that it is metaphysically constitutive of facts about content that they must be accessible to someone in the epistemological situation of a *radical interpreter* and that radical interpretation is impossible unless principles of charity are invoked. Our primary sources for this discussion will be Donald Davidson's "Truth and meaning," "Reply to Foster," and "Radical interpretation."

MEANING THEORIES, TRUTH THEORIES, AND RADICAL INTERPRETATION

Philosophers have traditionally disagreed not only about what the right theory of meaning is for a natural language (for

English, as it might be), but even about what kind of theory a theory of meaning for a natural language ought to be. Correspondingly, a traditional project in the philosophy of language is to provide a general, abstract characterization of meaning theories for natural languages; to make clear, in particular, what form they should take and what conditions of adequacy they should be required to satisfy. A recurrent theme in Davidson's writings is the claim that a Tarski-like truth theory is the appropriate form for a meaning theory, and much of Davidson's philosophy of language is an attempt to elucidate the conditions of adequacy for meaning theories that take this form.

A (finite) theory T is a truth theory for language L iff, for each sentence E of L, T entails a *T-sentence* of the form:

E is true-in-L iff P.

Call a truth theory *extensionally adequate* iff all the T-sentences it entails are true. Then the first proposal that might suggest itself is that being an extensionally adequate truth theory suffices for being a successful meaning theory.

It would be surprising if such a simple suggestion worked; and, in fact, a moment's reflection shows that it can't. In particular, you could achieve extensional adequacy by pairing each sentence of L with any materially equivalent sentence regardless of what it means. The classic example is a truth theory for English which entails, inter alia, the T-sentence W.

W: "Snow is white" is true in English iff grass is green.

All else being equal, this theory is extensionally adequate. But it could scarcely claim to capture the meanings of the sentences it describes; for example, interpreting English speakers in accordance with W is quite compatible with misunderstanding their utterances of "Snow is white."

A more plausible proposal is this: Call a T-theory *materially adequate* if it is extensionally adequate and if, in each T-sentence, the condition that P *translates* E is satisfied. This is, in effect, Tarski's "Convention T." So now, a truth theory for English that entails W can't be materially adequate since "Grass is green" does not translate "Snow is white."

If, however, the philosophical project is to make clear what a successful meaning theory for a natural language *is*, the claim that it is a materially adequate truth theory is arguably not very interesting. Intuitively, the requirement that P must *translate* E is doing all the work; and "translates" is as much in need of explication as "meaning theory." What is wanted, then, is a characterization of "adequate meaning theory for L" which does not itself essentially employ unelucidated semantic notions like "translates," "means," "is synonymous with," and so forth.

Moreover, Davidson wants success for a meaning theory to be so defined that the adequacy of a meaning theory for L can be ascertained by a "radical" interpreter – a fortiori, by an interpreter who doesn't know L. "But we cannot assume in advance that correct translation can be recognized without pre-empting the point of radical interpretation. In empirical applications we must abandon th[is] assumption" ("Radical interpretation," p. 134). Davidson apparently holds that if success for a meaning theory is defined as material adequacy, radical interpretation would be impossible.[2]

So the situation seems to be this: Davidson says at one point that his program is to "take truth as basic and to extract an account of translation or interpretation" ("Radical interpretation," p. 134). The obvious prima facie objection to this project is that, whereas notions like *means that* and the like are intensional, the truth of a T-sentence requires only equivalence of truth value (extensional equivalence) between the formula mentioned on the left and the formula used on the right. It is thus reasonable to wonder how a theory constrained only to issue in true T-sentences could hope to reconstruct the semantic relations.[3] Clearly, some *further* constraint must be placed on

61

the truth theories that are to count as successful meaning theories.[4] We will call this "the extensionality problem." Davidson is, of course, intensely aware of this problem. As far as we understand, (at least) three different (though compatible) suggestions can be found in the papers under consideration. Since, as we'll see, each of these proposals can be construed as having holistic implications, all three will be discussed in what follows.

Suggestion 1: Exploit the fact that natural languages exhibit compositional semantic structure; in particular, that the same expressions can recur with the same meanings in (indefinitely) many formulas. This is the main strategy contemplated in "Truth and meaning."

Suggestion 2: Require that the T-sentences in favored truth theories be laws. This is the strategy contemplated in the "Reply to Foster" and in note 11, added to "Truth and meaning" in 1982.

Suggestion 3: Require the favored truth theory for L to entail T-sentences according to which most of the sentences that speakers of L hold true *are* true. This is one version of Davidson's "principle of charity" and is the main strategy contemplated in "Radical interpretation."

We turn to a detailed consideration of these three suggestions after a preliminary remark on the course that our discussion will pursue. As will become clear, the issues raised by suggestions 2 and 3, unlike those raised by suggestion 1, are intimately concerned with the question of radical interpretation. We shall therefore proceed as follows. Having first completed our discussion of suggestion 1, we will then indulge in a longish digression (the section called "Interlude") in which we will consider the general question of how theories of radical interpretation might constrain theories of meaning. Our reading of Davidson in this section will depart considerably from standard Davidson exegesis (see Evans and McDowell (eds), *Truth and Meaning: Essays in Semantics*; Platts, *Ways of Meaning: An Introduction to a Philosophy of Language*; Platts (ed.), *Reference, Truth and Reality: Essays on the Philosophy of Language*; Lepore (ed.), *Truth and Interpretation: Perspectives on the Philosophy of Donald Davidson*), but we hope to illuminate, in ways which we think the standard literature fails to do, the relations between, for example, Davidson's holistic views about radical interpretation and his metaphysics. Having explored these background issues, we will then return to discuss solutions 2 and 3 to the extensionality problem.

SOLUTIONS TO THE EXTENSIONALITY PROBLEM

The Compositionality Solution

If extensional adequacy is all that is required of successful truth theories, what is wrong with a truth theory for English that entails W? In "Truth and meaning" (p. 25; see also "Radical interpretation," p. 134), Davidson says that the fact that T-sentences like W are true serves to remind us of the hopelessness of trying to distinguish successful truth theories just by looking at their *theorems* (at the T-sentences they entail). Rather, the relevant question is *how* the T-sentences are derived. The theory must derive T-sentences by exploiting the linguistic structure of the formulas whose truth conditions they specify. In particular (for any sentence except an idiom), *the theory must exhibit the semantic properties of the sentence as determined by the semantic properties of its lexical parts together with its syntactic structure.* It is, for example, because the meaning theory must arrive at the truth conditions of "Snow is white" *and every other sentence of the object language* in this way that we can expect the right-hand side of the T-sentence to interpret the left-hand side. It is therefore this "holistic" constraint on successful

63

truth theories that is the key to the connection between truth and meaning.

Thus, Davidson suggests (in a footnote added to "Truth and meaning" (op. cit.)) that no extensionally adequate truth theory for English could both entail W and exhibit compositional structure for all the English sentences that contain "snow" or "white." Roughly, this is because, if a theory that entails W respects compositional structure, it has to assign the wrong truth conditions to other sentences in which "snow" and "white" occur – in particular, to sentences in which they occur with demonstratives, like "This is white" and "This is snow." For example, it would have to claim that "This is white" is true iff this is green.

Suppose, then, we assume that the interpretation of "This is white" and "This is snow" is somehow given independent of, and prior to, the interpretation of "Snow is white." (We'll see presently that Davidson's account of radical interpretation can be construed as rationalizing this sort of assumption.) Then compositionality can be appealed to in order to fix the interpretation of "Snow is white" relative to the interpretation of the corresponding demonstrative sentences. In short, "Snow is white" has the truth conditions it does because "This is white" and "This is snow" have the truth conditions they do and because a successful truth theory is required to honor the structural relations among the sentences it analyzes.

One moral is that we can have an extensional theory of meaning after all, so long as the structural relations among formulas are respected in the derivation of T-sentences. "The present thought is rather to expect to find a minimum of information about the correctness of the theory at each single point; it is the potential infinity of points that makes the difference" (Davidson, "Reality without reference," p. 225). Or, as Evans and McDowell (eds) put it: "The fact that each axiom of a truth theory has its impact upon an infinite number of T-sentences does indeed have the consequence that it is difficult for counterfeit theories to pass the test" (*Truth and Meaning*, p. xv). A second moral is holistic. "Snow is white" has the truth conditions it does because it belongs to a language that contains "This is white" and "This is snow" (and indefinitely many other sentences in which "is white" and "is snow" occur.

Clearly, however, this is a good argument for semantic holism only if the appeal to compositionality really is required to rule out T-theories that entail theorems like W; and it's possible to doubt that it is. Indeed, on reflection, it's hard to see how it could be. If it's really only because of the structural similarity between "Snow is white" and "That's snow" that the former means that snow is white (and not that grass is green or that 2+2=4), then it would seem that there is an a priori argument against the possibility of a noncompositional language. The expressions of such a language, according to this argument, *could not* have determinate truth conditions.

We doubt that there could be such an argument. Consider the following thought experiment. Suppose there is a child who has (to all appearances) mastered the entire nonrecursive apparatus of English. So he can say things like "It's raining," "Snow is white," "Grass is green," "That's snow," "That's green," "That's frozen," "Everybody hates me," "I hate spinach," and so forth, but not "Snow is white and grass is green" or "Everybody hates frozen spinach," and so forth. We take it that, assuming that everything about this child's speech dispositions in respect to this nonrecursive part of the language is exactly like that of the corresponding normal adult, it is *very* plausible that when the child says "Snow is white," he means that snow is white. Thus far, the compositionality argument for holism is not in jeopardy, since we assume that the child has (for example) both "Snow is white" and "That's snow" in his idiolect, and hence that his idiolect meets the compositionality condition for determinate content.

But now consider a child who is *just like* this one in his speech (and inferential and, generally, cognitive) dispositions except that, whenever child 1 would use "Snow is white" to say that snow is white, child 2 uses the unstructured expression

"Alfred"; and similarly, whenever child 1 would use "That's snow" to say that that's snow, child 2 uses the unstructured expression "Sam"; and whenever child 1 would use "That's cold" to say that that's cold, child 2 uses the unstructured expression "Mary"; and so forth.

We want to insist that these children are required to be otherwise identical in all relevant respects. Thus, if having certain stuff around prompts child 1 to say "That's snow," the same stuff on the same occasion prompts child 2 to say "Sam." If the first child infers from "That's snow" to "That's cold," then the second child infers from "Sam" to "Mary." And so forth. Indeed, to make the case stronger, we can even imagine that child 2 can pass a sort of Turing test that goes like this: Put him in a box and let him communicate with an interrogator via a translator who speaks both the child's dialect and the nonrecursive part of English. Then, barring tasks that require the comprehension or production of recursive sentences, let it be that the translated verbalizations of child 2 are *indistinguishable* from the verbalizations of child 1. *Nevertheless*, if compositionality is a necessary condition for content, then there is an a priori argument that child 2 couldn't mean anything determinate by what he utters. We take it that it is just obvious that such an argument couldn't be sound.[5] After all, whether the child means anything by his utterances presumably depends on the intentions with which he utters them. What a priori argument would show that a child couldn't utter "Sam" with the intention of thereby saying that snow is white?

We think these considerations make it seem really very implausible that compositionality is *necessary* to solve the extensionality problem. Presumably the T-sentence *"Alfred" is true iff snow is white* is to be preferred to the T-sentence *"Alfred" is true iff grass is green*; but this can't be a consequence of some feature of *"Alfred"*'s compositional structure because it has none.[6]

There are some persuasive considerations which suggest that appeal to compositionality (together with considerations about token reflexives) is also not sufficient to solve the extensionality problem. There are two related problems. First, the proposal that invokes the truth conditions on "That's snow" to rule out W as the T-sentence for "Snow is white" works only because "snow" and "grass" are not coextensive. Consider, however, any pair of coextensive but not synonymous atomic predicates "F," "G." Then, a T-theory which, as it were, swaps the truth conditions on the expression ". . . F . . ." for the ones on the expression ". . . G . . ." will be extensionally adequate even if some of the expressions in which "F" and "G" occur contain demonstratives. Of course, one could still appeal to certain compositionality considerations to distinguish the semantics of "F" from the semantics of "G," since they will not, in general, substitute *salve veritate* in *intensional* (for example, counter-factual or propositional attitude) contexts. But if the compositionality solution to the extensionality problem must appeal to *these* contexts, then it seems to be implied that *there could not be an entirely extensional language whose sentences have determinate truth conditions* (contrary, it goes without saying, to the widely held view that, really there couldn't be any other kind of language whose sentences do). And if it is replied that, well, at least the test does work for intensional languages, the answer to *that* is that if *translation* is not a concept that is at the disposal of semantic metatheory, then neither is *intensionality*, and for the same reasons. So, even if the compositionality solution to the extensionality problem can be saved by applying that solution only to intensional languages, the metatheoretic characterization of "successful meaning theory" is debarred from exploiting the fact that this is so.

The second problem is closely related. It is, in effect, that if one of the theorems of a theory has a *logical consequence* that is expressible in the vocabulary of that theory, then that logical consequence is also a theorem of the theory. If, for example, LT is a logical truth expressible in the vocabulary of the truth theory of English, then, since Q is a logical consequence of the paradigmatic T-sentence T, Q is also a T-sentence entailed by

67

T "Snow is white" is true in English iff snow is white

Q "Snow is white" is true in English iff snow is white and LT

that theory. (See Lepore and Loewer, "What Davidson should have said.") Notice that appealing to the truth conditions for "This is snow" won't help with this problem, since there is, so far, nothing to choose between " 'This is snow' is true iff this is snow" and " 'This is snow' is true iff this is snow and LT."

By the way, the present "logical truth" problem is not just a special case of the "extensional equivalence" problem discussed above. "Extensional equivalence" is concerned with the possibility that the *object* language contains equivalent but nonsynonymous expressions, hence expressions which T-sentences cannot distinguish (assuming they achieve only extensional adequacy). By contrast, the present point depends on the expressive power not of the *object* language but of the *meta*language (of the truth theory itself). The worry is that the logical apparatus that the metalanguage requires in order to generate the correct T-sentences will automatically generate indefinitely many incorrect ones (including, for example, Q).

In "Semantics for natural languages" and "Radical interpretation," Davidson suggests that one could avoid troublesome T-sentences like Q by making it part of the definition of a successful theory that its T-sentences follow from its axioms by a "canonical proof" ("Radical interpretation," p. 138; "Semantics for natural languages," p. 61). Davidson says that the canonical proofs would allow one to move from biconditional to biconditional only via the base clauses of the truth definition. The derivation of the T-sentence with "and LT" appended would be ruled out because it requires additional logical apparatus. The prima facie difficulty with this move is that what Davidson has in mind is a strictly syntactic notion of canonical proof. There aren't actually any proposals that we know of for a *theory-neutral* notion of canonical derivation, so we don't know what is to count as a canonical derivation when the syntax varies from truth theory to truth theory.

But, whatever sense can be made of the notion of a canonical *derivation*, there is surely no sense to be made of the notion of a canonical *axiom*; and the logical truth problem infects the axioms as well as the derivations. Q does not depend on appending "and LT" to the right-hand side of a T-sentence that is independently derivable. It could be worked in earlier. (See Quine, "Review of Evans and McDowell *Truth and Meaning*," p. 226.) One could, for example, take

(x) (x satisfies "is white" iff (x is white and LT))

as an axiom and then derive Q from it *by a canonical proof.*[7]

Our provisional conclusions are these: It is most unlikely that compositionality is necessary for solving the extensionality problem, and there are technical reasons (the problem of co-extensive object language expressions and the logical truth problem) suggesting that it isn't sufficient either.

Suppose, however, that all these difficulties can somehow be accommodated. Then we have an argument that the distinction between a theory which entails W and a theory which entails T can be sustained if (and maybe only if) L contains sentences in which "snow," "white," "grass," and "green" occur in constructions with demonstrative (or other "token-reflexive"[8]) expressions. This appears to be a holistic conclusion; it's a special case of the general holistic thesis that, for any expression to have even reasonably deterministic content, there must be other contentful expressions that belong to the same linguistic system as it does.

However, this conclusion seems premature. In the first place, though the present concessive assumptions give us an argument that you can't have a language *none* of whose sentences are token-reflexive, there is no argument so far that you can't have a language *all* of whose sentences are token-reflexive. (Quine has speculated, in effect, that we all start out speaking such languages; we assume that this speculation is at least coherent.) So we have, as it were, holism insured in one direction only: having sentences that aren't token-reflexive is contingent on having sentences that are, but (so far) having sentences that are token-reflexive is contingent on nothing. We have, that is, no argument from compositionality to a holist thesis about the latter.[9] If, however, you can have a language that contains only token-reflexive sentences, what argument shows that you can't have a language that contains only one sentence, so long as *it* is token-reflexive? In short, even if an appeal to compositionality really is required to choose the right reading for "Snow is white," we still have no argument against the possibility of a punctate language.[10] (In fact, for reasons that will presently become clear, we doubt that the interpretability of standing sentences depends on their being compositionally related to token–reflexive sentences. See note 28 and the discussion that precedes it.)

As far as we can tell, compositionality is neither necessary nor sufficient to solve the extensionality problem, and it wouldn't entail holism even if it were.

Interlude: The Status of Radical Interpretation Theories

In the following sections, we will turn to the discussion of approaches to the extensionality problem that arise from considerations of the preconditions for radical interpretation.[11] But before we do so, we need to consider the nature of radical interpretation theories and the architectural role they play in Davidson's philosophy of language.

We have seen that a crucial problem for Davidson is to find rational grounds for deciding which of the indefinitely many T-theories that are extensionally adequate representations of L is to be identified as the correct meaning theory for L (or meaning theor*ies* assuming semantic indeterminacy; for ease of exposition, we will drop this caveat in what follows). As we have also remarked, Davidson takes the view that there are further considerations that can be appealed to in making this choice:

roughly, a successful meaning theory is an extensionally adequate truth theory that meets further evidential constraints.

Viewed in this context, a radical interpretation (RI) theory seeks to do two things. First, it must specify the kinds of empirical evidence that a successful meaning theory may be required to account for. In this context, "empirical evidence" includes *any contingent propositions that the radical interpreter may legitimately appeal to to warrant his interpretation.* We emphasize that these constraints must be substantive – they must entail that many true contingent propositions are *unavailable* to the radical interpreter – or there will be no content to the insistence that his epistemological situation is "radical." Second, since different ways of constraining the evidence will lead to different T-theories being selected, an RI theory must *justify* the imposition of one set of evidential constraints in preference to others.

Notice, in particular, that the justification of the evidential constraints that an RI theory imposes must be a priori; "bootstrapping" is not allowed. To see what this means, let E be a set of constraints that is proposed for choosing among T-theories. Then it might be supposed that E is itself justified "empirically," by appeal to the fact that the truth theories it chooses for given languages are, in fact, correct meaning theories for those languages. That, however, would presuppose some independent way of assessing the correctness of these truth theories. The usual technique in linguistics, where this sort of problem arises in practice, is to appeal to independent knowledge of an informant's intuitions. This is equivalent, for present purposes, to assuming that the linguist knows the language he is trying to model, and it therefore violates the constraints on *radical* interpretation, which include, by stipulation, that the theorist has no access to linguistic intuitions about the adequacy of the T-sentences that his theory generates.[12] So, then, what evidential constraints can reasonably be placed on the selection of truth theories, and how can these constraints be justified? Davidson's answer is that the favored T-theory is to be selected on the basis of "evidence plausibly available to an interpreter," where an interpreter is "someone who does not already know how to interpret utterances the theory is designed to cover" ("Radical interpretation," p. 128). Thus, "[the evidence] must . . . be evidence we can imagine the virgin investigator having without his already being in possession of the theory it is supposed to be evidence for" ("Belief and the basis of meaning," p. 143). This is less than fully transparent, since the notion of an "interpreter" is thus far uncashed, and we are not told in what, precisely, the virginity of the investigator consists. Davidson is never very explicit about this, but some suggestions of Quine's are relevant. Accordingly, Quine's view of interpretation, as well as Davidson's, will be at center stage for the next several pages.

Imagine someone in the position of a child exposed to a first language or of a field linguist exposed to an entirely alien language. The evidence relevant for the selection of a translation (/interpretation) theory is whatever data about the behavior of the informants it might reasonably be supposed that the child or the field linguist does, or could, have access to.

> A child learns his first words and sentences by hearing and using them in the presence of appropriate stimuli. . . . What I have said of infant learning applies equally to the linguist's learning a new language in the field. If the linguist does not lean on related languages for which there are previously accepted translation practices, then obviously he has no data but the concomitances of native utterance and observable stimulus situation. ("Epistemology naturalized," p. 81)

Consider also the following passage from Quine's recent book *The Pursuit of Truth*:

> Critics have said that the thesis [of indeterminacy of translation] is a consequence of my behaviorism. Some have said that it is a *reductio ad absurdum* of my behaviorism. I disagree with this

second point, but I agree with the first. I hold further that the behaviorist approach is mandatory. In psychology one may or may not be a behaviorist, but in linguistics one has no choice. Each of us learns his language by observing other people's verbal behavior and having his own faltering verbal behavior observed and reinforced or corrected by others. We depend strictly on overt behavior in observable situations. . . . There is nothing in linguistic meaning beyond what is to be gleaned from overt behavior in observable circumstances. (pp. 37–8)

Assume, then, the proposal is that the evidence for choosing a translation manual (or, mutatis mutandis, a T-theory) is whatever data about his informant's behavior the field linguist (or the child) may be supposed to have available. The next question for an RI theory to address is: What *justifies* this proposal? It may be that the answer to this question seems so glaringly obvious as to be not worth reciting. However, we propose to harp on it because, as will become clear in later chapters, quite a lot of Davidson's and Quine's philosophy depends on the assumption that nothing *can be* a language unless its radical interpretation is possible;[13] that is, nothing can be a language unless the correct T-theory for it could be selected by the sorts of observations plausibly available to the child or the linguist. We want to suggest that it is, in fact, *not* reasonable to endorse this principle. On the contrary, on this understanding of radical interpretation, it is entirely conceivable that the radical interpretation of perfectly kosher languages (like, for example, English) isn't possible.

As far as we can see, there are two standard ways of justifying the identification of "evidence for choosing a T-theory" with evidence about the informant's behavior plausibly available to the child or the linguist. The first is to remark that, after all, the child and the linguist do succeed in choosing the right meaning theory on the basis of the evidence available to them. A fortiori, it must be *possible* to choose a meaning theory on the basis of this evidence. So the argument might go.[14]

So articulated, however, this justificatory argument is fallacious. There is no reason at all to suppose, about either the child or the linguist, that his choice of a T-theory is determined *solely* by the available observations of the informant's behavior plus, say, the general canons of theory construction and confirmation to which he adheres.[15] Let's consider the field linguist and the child in turn.

The Field Linguist

We remarked above that, as a matter of fact, real linguists generally exploit the intuitions of their informants (or they learn the language under study and become their own informants). So field linguists aren't really in the epistemological situation that we suppose to define the radical interpreter. Our present argument, however, stresses a different consideration: beyond dispute, real field linguists – those who really do reliably end up with confirmed theories of the languages they are studying – invariably approach the analysis of the alien tongue with a background of very powerful theoretical assumptions about what the languages they encounter in the field can be like, given that the alien is a conspecific (which, of course, the field linguist takes for granted). These background assumptions are, in general, bootstrapped in the sense suggested above; the linguist's evidence for accepting them is their previous successes in interpretation (plus their face empirical plausibility plus their coherence with the linguist's assumptions about the cognitive psychology of his conspecifics and about how language learning works and about the laws of linguistic change and about what linguistic universals there may be, and so forth – whatever considerations the linguist believes may constrain the variability of natural languages, to put the point succinctly). Learning about this sort of thing is part of the linguist's professional apprenticeship; unlike the investigator that Davidson imagines, real linguists lose their virginity in graduate school.

It's entirely implausible to suppose that these background

74

assumptions play no essential role in the linguist's selection of T-theories. Our point is not just that they function in the "context of discovery" to provide the linguist with hunches about which T-theory to try to fit to the data (though this is surely true). It's that they also function in the "context of justification" as part of the corpus of empirical constraints to which the preferred T-theory is required to conform. So what we have is, at most, that the available observations of the informant's behavior *plus the background assumptions* reliably lead to the choice of a best T-theory for the alien tongue. From this it does *not* follow that radical interpretation is possible; namely, that the choice of a best T-theory can be made on the basis of *just* the observational evidence together with whatever general constraints there may be on theoretical inference as such.

It might be supposed, however, that this appeal to the working linguist's background of theory *must* be dispensable in principle. After all, what about the *first* linguist; surely he had no independently certified background theory to rely on; surely he had to proceed with just inductive methodology together with his observations of the informant's behavior. We do not propose to raise large questions in epistemology; suffice it to remark that to reject foundationalism in the philosophy of science is precisely to reject the idea of a "first scientist" in favor of the idea that science begins *in media res*. Neurath's ship didn't "start" anywhere; it always was at sea. This steady-state picture of the physical sciences is, ironically, one we owe to Quine more than anyone else. Why doesn't it also apply in linguistics?

In case this all seems a bit abstract, consider, for example, Davidson's own idea that some T-sentences (and hence the theories that generate them) are ruled out by the consideration that they are noncanonically derived. Question: Where does the linguist get his notion of a canon? Not from the identification of meaning theories with T-theories; for the notion of a T-theory per se offers no reconstruction of "canonical derivation." And not from the observational evidence about the informant's linguistic behavior; since for Davidson this is largely exhausted by evidence about what sentences the informant "holds true." So it must be that if the linguist has and essentially employs a notion of canonical derivation, it is part of a (presumably empirical) background theory with which he approaches the selection of T-theories. So, even on Davidson's view, it seems that the evidence that constrains the linguist's selection of a T-theory must exceed the evidence available to radical interpreters as such.

We pause to remind the reader just what our argument is supposed to show. Take Quine. He has two related uses for his famous thought experiments about translation. One is to show that interpretation is possible only if principles of charity are invoked; the other is to show that the empirical evidence underdetermines the choice of a translation manual. *We have no objection to either of these conclusions.* (Not, at least, for present purposes.) For all we know, it may be true both that interpretation (/translation) is empirically underdetermined (a fortiori, that it is empirically underdetermined from the epistemic position of a radical interpreter) and that there is no interpretation (/translation) without charity (a fortiori, that there is no *radical* interpretation without charity). What we're objecting to is a certain sort of transcendental argument; for example, one which seeks to *infer* that there is no translation without charity from the following assumptions: first, that radical translation without charity is impossible; second, that radical translation must actually occur whenever the translation of an alien language succeeds; and third, that field linguists do in fact succeed in the translation of alien languages. Our point is that this sort of argument seems to depend on an unargued identification of the epistemic position of real translators with the epistemic position of radical interpreters. Indeed, it depends on this identification being *necessary.* By contrast, we claim that it is prima facie implausible that real translators are ipso facto radical interpreters. So, prima facie, the transcendental argument for charity fails.

The Child

Now consider Quine's suggestion that radical interpretation be construed in terms of the child's epistemic situation. It may be that the child too approaches the language learning situation with a body of (perhaps innate[16]) background assumptions about what the character of a conspecific's dialect can be. He differs from the linguist in that his background assumptions aren't justified by bootstrapping.[17] In fact, they aren't justified *at all*. A fortiori, his choice of a T-theory on the basis of the observational evidence together with these assumptions *does not yield justified true belief*, and thus does not yield *knowledge* (which we suppose to require *at least* justified true belief). But then, there is no reason to suppose that children (or anybody except, maybe, a few linguists) *do* have knowledge of their language in *that* sense. What is truistic is only that children know their language in the sense that they are able to talk it, hence that they have whatever true beliefs about the language that talking the language may require.[18]

We digress to forestall an accusation of lack of charity. Like all empiricists, Quine is himself a sort of nativist; he doesn't really think that the child's epistemic situation is fully characterized when one specifies the available observational data. After all, the child must somehow *generalize* his data if he is to learn from them; and the principles of generalization must ultimately be given, rather than learned, if regress is to be avoided. Under pressure of this sort of argument, Quine is prepared to endow the child with an innate "similarity space"; responses trained to old stimuli generalize to new ones in proportion to their propinquity in this space. (Similarly, Skinnerian accounts of learning commence by postulating the "intact organism" with its innate dispositions to generalize in some directions and not in others; Humean accounts of learning commence by postulating associative mechanisms which are "intrinsic to human nature," and so forth.)

The first thing to be said about this proposal is that, quite independent of the issues about radical interpretation, it's unclear just what it is intended to concede. That's because it's unclear to what extent – if at all – the requirement that an innate endowment be expressible as a similarity space (or, mutatis mutandis, as a generalization gradient or a principle of association) actually constrains the innate information that a child may be supposed to have. Presumably that would depend on what sorts of properties the *dimensions* of the innate space are allowed to express. If, for example, the dimensions of a similarity space can express parameters of grammatical derivations, then, as Paul Churchland has remarked, there is no obvious reason why we can't imagine "a way of representing 'anglophone linguistic hyperspace' so that all grammatical sentences turn out to reside on a proprietary hypersurface within that hyperspace" ("Some reductive strategies in cognitive neurobiology," p. 84). That is, barring restrictions on the dimensions of the space, the hypothesis that language learning is mediated *solely* by an innate similarity space is very likely compatible with the hypothesis that the grammar of English is innate.

An *empirically motivated* proposal for restricting the dimensions of innate "similarity spaces" would be a major breakthrough in the psychology of learning. Almost certainly, what Quine has in mind, however, is to placate empiricist scruples by allowing the dimensions of the innate similarity space to express only psychophysical properties of proximal stimulations. If this is the right exegesis, then Quine needs an argument that the interpretation of, say, English is possible from the epistemic position of an investigator whose data are restricted to observations of the informant's behavior and who generalizes these observations along psychophysical parameters. For reasons that have been familiar since Chomsky's "Review of B. F. Skinner's *Verbal Behavior*," it seems most unlikely that such an argument will be forthcoming (though, of course, it's an empirical issue).

How much does all this affect the status of Quine's story about radical interpretation? Not much, we think. There are two possibilities. Suppose that information corresponding to the child's innate similarity space is *not* assumed to be at the disposal of the radical interpreter. In that case, Quine can no longer argue from the fact that languages are learned by children to the possibility of their radical interpretation; for all one knows, the child's innate endowment may play an *essential* role in mediating his learning of his language. So, suppose that information corresponding to the child's innate endowment *is* assumed to be at the disposal of the radical interpreter. Then the force of the requirement that a language be radically interpretable depends entirely on *what the innate information is supposed to be*. In the limiting case, the interpretation theory for the language is itself innate – hence available to the radical interpreter – and the requirement that the language be radically interpretable is empty; the radical interpreter can "learn" the language from no data at all. In this respect, the point about the child really is just like the point about the linguist; to take seriously the possibility that they bring a rich background of theory to their appointed tasks is to jeopardize either the argument that radical interpretation is possible or the force of the requirement that languages be radically interpretable or both.

To repeat the moral: It's plausibly true that linguists and children choose the right T-theory on the basis of, inter alia, the observational evidence available to them. It does not follow that this evidence is adequate to choose a truth theory. So it does not follow that radical interpretation is possible.

Notice that we are *not* claiming that the observational evidence available to the child and/or the field linguist (hence, by stipulation, the evidence available to the radical interpreter) is *in fact* inadequate for the warranted choice of a T-theory. We're only claiming that it's far from obvious that it is adequate; certainly that it's not true a priori that it has to be adequate, hence that no a priori argument should be ceded the princople that, insofar as the sentences of a language have determinate content, the language is ipso facto susceptible of radical interpretation. As we understand it, Davidson's transcendental argument for charity has the form: "But that the informant is supposed to believe mostly truths, language learning from the epistemological position of the radical interpreter would not be possible; language learning from the epistemological position of the radical interpreter *is* possible; so, it must be assumed that the informant believes mostly truths." But, as far as we can see, there is no clear reason to accept the second premise, so the transcendental argument for charity fails.

Nothing is Hidden

We suggested that there are at least two lines of argument which have been proposed for identifying the evidence for a T-theory with the child or the linguist's observational evidence. The second depends on the metaphysical principle that "Nothing is hidden." If there is any fact of the matter at all about what the interpretation of a language is, then the evidence which selects a meaning theory for that language must in principle be *publicly accessible* data. Some such line of thought has been central in analytic philosophy at least since Wittgenstein's discussion of private languages in the *Philosophical Investigations*.[19] And, of course, it will be acceptable to anybody who thinks that the intentional supervenes on the physical, since physical facts are publicly accessible facts par excellence.[20]

The problem with this line of argument is that, though it may show that the evidence that determines the choice of a T-theory can't be "hidden" *in principle*, it doesn't begin to show that it can't be hidden from the child/linguist/radical interpreter. Suppose God knows everything about the world that can be said without using intentional (with a "t") or semantic concepts. Then it follows from the principle that nothing is hidden that God knows everything he could need to know to warrant his choice of a correct T-theory for, say, English. But, of course, this assumption has God knowing a lot of things that radical interpreters qua radical interpreters don't know. Not only does he know (as Chomsky has emphasized in related contexts) things that go on in people's heads (under, of course, neurological or other nonintentional descriptions), but he also knows *what laws there are and what counterfactuals they support.*

For example, we're about to see that even Davidson thinks that which meaning theory is correct for L depends on which truths about L-speakers are laws. But, of course, it can't simply be assumed that if a law or a counterfactual is relevant to a justified choice of a T-theory for a language, then the application of general principles of warranted theoretical inference to the observational evidence available to an arbitrary linguist/child/radical interpreter would lead to knowledge of that law or counterfactual. Remember, in particular, that no such conclusion follows from the fact that children and linguists do succeed in learning languages. Children may not make *warranted* choices of T-theories; and linguists who arrive at warranted T-theories may have not only the observational evidence to go on, but also independently confirmed background theories.

In short, if you read the principle "Nothing is hidden" metaphysically (as a supervenience thesis), then it's probably true; but nothing follows about radical interpretation. If you read it epistemologically ("Nothing relevant to the choice of a T-theory is hidden *from a radical interpreter*"), then to assume it is to beg the question. A way to put this point is that the metaphysical doctrine of the supervenience of the semantic/intentional upon the public/physical couldn't, by itself, be enough to justify a choice between extensionally equivalent T-theories. It certainly doesn't help to distinguish theories that say that "Snow is white" means that snow is white from theories that say it means that grass is green. What would suffice to choose, presumably, would be the supervenience principle *together with an inventory of the facts on which the intentional/semantic actually supervenes* (say, a complete nonintentional description of the actual world, laws included). But, it goes without saying, this inventory isn't available to anybody *except* God.[21]

It might reasonably be suggested that the way to proceed is now to redefine RI: to *liberalize* the contingent information presumed available to the radical interpreter so that it is allowed to include more than what their informants make available to children and field linguists. To construct an argument for charity, one would then have to show that radical interpretation *is* possible from the epistemic position of this revised sort of radical interpreter if (but also only if) charity is exercised toward the informant. And one would have to show that the possibility of radical interpretation, in this revised sense, is presupposed by the possibility of actual interpretation. That is, one would have to develop a transcendental argument for charity based on the revised notion of radical interpretation. This returns us to where we started: we have no proof that such an argument couldn't be constructed; but also we know of no reason to suppose that it could. We remind the reader that our brief throughout is only that there are no good arguments for semantic holism *so far*.

We think – and we think it's important – that no case has been made for the claim that appeals to the epistemological conditions that define the radical interpreter have an interesting role to play in the philosophy of language. (For the same reasons, we think that Quine has no case that appeals to the epistemological conditions for radical translation can play an interesting role in the philosophy of language.) For purposes of proceeding with the argument, however, we now propose to suppress these qualms. Suppose, then, that we put to one side the general issue as to whether warranted constraints on intentional attribution can be generated by appeals to the possibility of radical interpretation. The theory of radical interpretation that Davidson actually uses when he discusses the problem of choosing among extensionally adequate T-theories amounts to not much more than that the data for interpretation are mainly observations of informants "holding true" some or other sentence in their language in some or other context. "The evidence available is just that speakers of the language to be interpreted hold various sentences to be true at certain times and under specified circumstances" ("Radical interpretation,"

82

p. 135).[22] The idea that the conditions for radical interpretation are defined by access to such observations together with general canons of theoretical inference is supposed to help to solve the extensionality problem (that is, the problem of saying what conditions over and above extensional adequacy a correct T-theory must satisfy). The project is now to understand why Davidson thinks that this is so.

According to the present assumptions, the data for radical interpretation are formulable as what we'll call *singular hold true* (SHT) sentences. A typical example of the species is:

> E: Kurt belongs to the German speech community, and Kurt holds true "Es regnet" on Saturday at noon, and it is raining near Kurt on Saturday at noon.

The process of selecting a T-theory appeals to this evidence to confirm what we'll call *generalized hold true* (GHT) sentences. The GHT-sentence that corresponds to E is:

> GE: $(x)(t)$ (if x belongs to the German speech community then (x holds true "Es regnet" at t iff it is raining near x at t))

Apparently, Davidson assumes that the inference from SHT-sentences to GHT-sentences is relatively unproblematic; it requires only whatever canons of rationality are deployed in nondemonstrative inferences from singular data sentences to universal generalizations in cases where issues of intentionality (/semanticity) don't arise.

Finally, in certain critical cases, GHT-sentences about an expression are used to license an inference to a T-sentence for that expression.[23] And, ceteris paribus, a truth theory is warranted as a meaning theory iff it entails all the T-sentences which are licensed in this way (and meets the usual conditions of simplicity, conservatism, and so forth; we generally won't mention considerations of adequacy that apply to all empirical theories qua empirical). It is in the course of fleshing out this account of what it is for a T-theory to be warranted as a meaning theory that Davidson invokes the considerations that lead from radical interpretation to holism. So, in a certain sense, this entire apparatus can be viewed as a transcendental argument in which holism is deduced from the possibility of radical interpretation.

After this long interlude we are, finally, in a position to consider the two ways in which Davidson hopes to use his account of radical interpretation to solve the extensionality problem.

The Nomologicity Solution

In a footnote to his discussion of the "compositionality" solution of the extensionality problem (in a 1984 republication of "Truth and meaning"), Davidson remarks that the T-sentences of the favored T-theory are offered as warranted empirical generalizations about the speakers of L and so must be not only true but also lawlike.[24] This is sufficient to distinguish between W and T, since the former, though true, does not support appropriate counterfactuals. Presumably the thought is that "Snow is white" would be true in nearby worlds where grass isn't green, so long as snow is white in those worlds; this is a way of saying that the truth value of "Snow is white" depends on the color of snow and is independent of the color of grass.

We want to reserve some of our comments on this proposal. Roughly, we approve of the idea that the solution to the extensionality problem may somehow exploit appeals to law contexts, though we're about to see that the idea that T-sentences themselves could be laws is not plausible. We propose first to clear up this point and then to turn to what will be our main contention: namely, that even if it is assumed that the exigencies of solving the extensionality problem show that T-sentences are laws, there is no warranted inference from the nomologicity of T-sentences to the holism of content.

T-sentences aren't laws. How could they be, compatible with the conventionality of language?[25] The thought that language is conventional *just is* the thought that it can't be a law that a formula means what it does. (It might be a law that anyone who is following the conventions of English means *grass is green* by "Grass is green." But that wouldn't make the corresponding T-sentence itself a law.)

Here is another way of putting the same point. We just remarked that, to be a law, a T-sentence would have to support counterfactuals. For example, for it to be a law that "John is tall" is true in English iff John is tall, it would have to be the case that all the nearby worlds in which "John is tall" is true are worlds in which John is tall and vice versa. But there is no reason to believe that this *is* the case, since there is no reason to doubt that there are nearby worlds in which John is not tall but "John is tall" means something true all the same (for example, worlds in which "John is tall" means that snow is white). If you think this is implausible, consider sentences like "Particles of like charge do not repel each other." The nearest world in which this sentence is true is surely one in which the conventions of English are different from here, not one in which the laws of physics are different.

Various replies might be considered:

1. The quoted formula in a T-sentence is individuated by reference to its meaning, so there is *no* possible world in which "Snow is white" doesn't mean that snow is white.

Clearly, however, this way of individuating quoted formulas is not available to an unquestion-begging elucidation of notions like "correct meaning theory."

2. A T-sentence says what "Snow is white" means *in English*; a language in which "Snow is white" didn't mean that snow is white wouldn't *be* English.

Very well, but this makes T *conceptually* necessary, rather than nomologically necessary. Moreover, in reply to the worry that the use of "in English" in T-sentences is itself question begging, Davidson remarks that "Speakers belong to the same speech community if the same theories of interpretation work for them" ("Radical interpretation," p. 135). But, of course, if "in English" is explicated by reference to "successful interpretation theory," it mustn't also be that "successful interpretation theory" is explicated by reference to "in English."

If, however, these considerations show that T-sentences can't be laws, it seems that GHT-sentences can't be laws either, and for the same reasons. Suppose it's the case that (ceteris paribus) English speakers hold "It's raining" true iff it's raining in their vicinity. Surely there are nearby worlds in which this biconditional fails, because, intuitively speaking, in those worlds "It's raining" means not that it's raining but that the cat is on the mat. GHT-sentences fail to support counterfactuals in just the crucial cases where the corresponding T-sentences fail to support them.

So something has gone wrong. But we needn't assume that what's wrong is the idea that a warranted inference from SHT-sentences to T-sentences would have to establish the nomological necessity of some generalization. All we've argued is that if there *are* laws involved in warranting these inferences, the laws can't be the GHT-sentences or the T-sentences. This needs to be explored, because appealing to nomologicity to solve the extensionality problem is attractive, and Davidson's argument from nomologicity to holism doesn't depend on its being the T- or GHT-sentences that are nomological, but only on there being *some* counterfactual-supporting generalization that the SHT-sentences warrant.

What kind of laws *might* SHT-sentences support, consonant with the requirement that the conventionality of semantic relations be respected? Sentences like L offer, we think, the most plausible candidates:

L: For some relation R, and for any person S, *if S bears R to the pair consisting of* ⟨*"It's raining," it's raining*⟩ (that is, the pair consisting of the expression type "It's raining" and the situation type in which it's raining in S's vicinity), *then S holds "It's raining" true iff it's raining in S's vicinity.*[26]

In effect, this account says that the SHT-sentences available to an interpreter of English provide him with evidence that English speakers are in some state such that it's a law that anybody who is in that state holds true "It's raining" iff it's raining in his vicinity.

The most natural way of thinking of R is as a relation that S might be in as a consequence of his learning history. For example, if only Skinner had been right, we could take R to be a relation that S is in iff it is nonvacuously true of S that he has by and large been rewarded for uttering "It's raining" when and only when it was raining in his vicinity. But it is equally alright to think of R as, for example, the relation that S is in by virtue of being in a certain neurological or functional condition. Just choose R to be any relation you like such that it is counterfactual-supporting that bearing R to ⟨"It's raining," it's raining⟩ is sufficient (ceteris paribus) for someone to mean that it's raining by his utterances of "It's raining."[27] Notice that L is consonant with the conventionality of semantic relations: that Smith holds true "It's raining" iff it's raining in his vicinity will be deducible from L only via contingent premises that are not themselves laws; in particular, only via the premise that Smith bears R to ⟨"It's raining," it's raining⟩.

Second, L secures the desired counterfactuals. The main objection against T-sentences and GHT-sentences being laws was that there are nearby worlds in which Smith holds "It's raining" true even though it's *not* raining in his vicinity. This is because, intuitively speaking, "It's raining" doesn't mean *it's raining* in those worlds; perhaps it means that the cat is on the mat. Presumably, some of these worlds are *quite* nearby, since all that's required to get to them is that you change some of the conventions of English. However, there is no corresponding problem for the assumption that L is a law; in the nearby worlds in which it's false that "It's raining" means that it's raining, it won't be the pair ⟨"It's raining," it's raining⟩ that Smith bears R to, but rather the pair, as it might be, ⟨"It's raining," the cat is on the mat⟩. If L is nomologically necessary, then the nearest worlds in which Smith bears R to ⟨"It's raining," it's raining⟩ but "It's raining" doesn't mean that it's raining are those in which the laws of psychology that operate here are suspended.

Finally, it's not so unreasonable to suppose that the relevant SHT-sentences really are evidence for L. The SHT facts are supposed to be that Smith goes about uttering "It's raining" in, and only in, rainy situations. What would explain this? Well, that he is in some psycho-neuro-functional condition such that, in virtue of being in that condition, he holds "It's raining" true when, and only when, it's raining. Which is, of course, exactly what L says.

So far, the idea that nomologicity comes into interpretation via L-sentences, rather than GHT-sentences or T-sentences, can be viewed as a friendly amendment to Davidson's views. It is quite compatible with his claim that SHT-sentences are the evidence for interpretation and with his idea that appeals to the nomologicity of the generalizations that SHT-sentences support figure in the solution of the extensionality problem. However, it is *not* clearly compatible with idea that interpretation (as practiced by the child or the linguist) can be construed as *radical* interpretation.

The problem is this: A radical interpreter is, by stipulation, somebody who arrives at a true and justified interpretation using SHT-sentences as evidence (plus principles of logic plus the general methodology of empirical theory construction plus "transcendental principles" like charity). But, now, what forced us to the view that nomologicity comes into interpretation via L-sentences rather than via GHT-sentences or T-sentences — that is, what convinced us that GHT-sentences and T-sentences aren't themselves laws — was respect for the principle of conventionality; and the problem for Davidson is that the principle of conventionality is, on the one hand, contingent and, on the other hand, substantive in the sense of being concerned specifically with natural languages. So, by definition, the principle of conventionality is not something that a radical interpreter can know about.

Field linguists know about conventionality because they bootstrap. That English is conventional is the obvious explanation of why foreigners don't say "dog" when they mean *dog*. As for children, there is some evidence that they don't know about conventionality at all; until quite late in their ontogenetic careers (well after they have become fluent speakers), they believe, in effect, that T-sentences are laws. It's only when they are told about there being lots of languages other than English that they understand that there are nearby worlds in which "Snow is white" is true even though snow isn't white. (See Piaget, *The Language and Thought of the Child*.) This may really be a case where learned performances are mediated by the assimilation of *false* theories (see the note on Hume above). Specifically, the theory that the child accepts is compatible with all *his* evidence, but incompatible with some relevant counterfactuals, these latter being accessible to God and to field linguists, but not to children learning English.[28]

We think these considerations about how law statements might come into interpretation are interesting for assessing Davidson's construal of RI theory. They point to a picture of what an interpreter is like that is far richer than Davidson's RI theory allows. Correspondingly, they caution against taking seriously the argument scouted above: that, since children and linguists are successful interpreters, *radical* interpretation has to be possible. Of course, we haven't argued that radical interpretation *isn't* possible; only that the facts about children and linguists don't *show* that it is. We take the situation to be that it's *open* whether radical interpretation is possible, and that the heart of the issue is how the extensionality problem is to be solved.

At this point, it is still on the cards that the solution to the extensionality problem is that the generalizations that SHT-sentences support are nomological. We're interested in the question of whether this sort of solution works and whether it's holistic. (It might be that the solution to the extensionality problem has to be holistic for reasons that don't turn on whether radical interpretation is possible.) Since, for these purposes, it might as well be the T-sentences and/or the GHT-sentences for which nomologicity is claimed, we propose to forget about L-sentences in the discussion that follows.

Our first point, then, is that the nomologicity solution of the extensionality problem doesn't work – or not, at least, without considerable elaboration. There are cases in which the assumption that T-sentences are laws doesn't choose between correct meaning theories and merely extensionally adequate truth theories. Consider truth rule T_1, according to which "Water is wet" means that water is wet, and truth rule T_2, according to which "Water is wet" means that H_2O is wet. Since "Water is H_2O" is (at least) nomologically necessary, if T_1 is a law, so too is T_2, and vice versa.[29] The same considerations hold for *any* T-theory derived from the correct one by interchanging nomologically equivalent expressions. The point is that, not surprisingly, a solution to the extensionality problem based on appeals to law contexts does not, in and of itself, slice truth conditions thinner than nomological equivalence. And this doesn't appear to be thin enough, since, prima facie, "It's a law that" is less opaque than "means that."

Our second, and more urgent, point is this: the nomologicity approach to the extensionality problem is not holistic; it's compatible with semantic atomism. This is so even if you assume what we have been seeing that there is no good reason to assume: namely, that the evidence for interpretation must be exhausted by SHT-sentences.

Let's see how the inference from SHT-sentences to GHT-sentences (or T-sentences) would go on the assumption that the latter are laws. Arguably, if GHT-sentences are laws (or if T-sentences are; to simplify the exposition, we assume it's the

GHT-sentences that are supposed to be laws, but nothing turns on this), then they must support counterfactuals. So if the evidence for interpretation is the available SHT-sentences, then the available SHT-sentences must somehow warrant GHT-sentences *as* counterfactual-supporting. How is this to be insured? Presumably by appeal to the heterogeneity of the (actual and possible) SHT-sentences on which the inference to a GHT-sentence may be based. In effect, it's *because the method of differences is employed in the inference from SHT-sentences to GHT-sentences* that it is reasonable to suppose that the latter are counterfactual-supporting when they are evidenced by the former.

This view of the way in which SHT-sentences warrant GHT-sentences is in Davidson's spirit, and is perfectly reasonable as far as it goes. Our present point is just that *none of this implies that the nomological solution of the extensionality problem leads to content holism.*[30] The reason is this. We can employ the method of differences on SHT-sentences *either* by keeping the quoted formula fixed and varying the context of utterance or by keeping the context of utterance fixed and varying the quoted formula. In effect, we can either see if Kurt holds true "Es regnet" when it isn't raining or see if Kurt holds true "Es schneit" (or whatever) when it is. If the latter maneuver were essential to warranting counterfactual-supporting GHT-sentences, then the inference from SHT-sentences to GHT-sentences would ipso facto fail for punctate languages. We couldn't, for example, know that GE supports counterfactuals unless there were many other formulas (that is, many other formula *types*) in the same language that contains "Es regnet."[31]

No doubt, if you do have more than one sentence type in your language, then (if the language is compositional) you can apply the method of differences across types. But the premise that the argument for content holism needs is that you *can't* employ the method of differences *unless* you have more than one sentence type in your language; that is, that you can't employ it just "across tokens." There may, of course *be* an argument that

91

applying it just across tokens wouldn't be enough to justify a GHT-sentence for the corresponding type. But, so far as we know, Davidson gives no such argument, and it is by no means obvious how one could do so. Prima facie, all that the method of differences needs to certify GE is SHT-sentences in which "Es regnet" is held true in a variety of circumstances and not held true in a variety of others (always when it's raining, never when the sun is out). There is no reason to suppose that this condition can't be satisfied even if "Es regnet" is the only thing that Kurt knows how to say. To put the point slightly differently, there doesn't seem to be anything about what is required to certify a GHT-sentence as counterfactual-supporting that is incompatible with the following possibility: there is a language for which there is a correct T-theory, and that T-theory entails only one T-sentence, and that T-sentence is inferred from a GHT-sentence, which is a law.[32] But if this is possible, then the nomological approach to the solution of the extensionality problem offers no comfort to the semantic holist. On the contrary, if taking GHT-sentences to be laws solves the problem of extensionality, then the solution to the problem of extensionality is compatible with semantic atomism.

We take the discussion to have secured the following. First, the nomologicity solution to the extensionality problem is compatible with the impossibility of radical interpretation. It's compatible with the "Nothing is hidden" thesis that the knowledge that a certain GHT-sentence is a law might be accessible to God but not to interpreters whose evidence is restricted to SHT-sentences. Second, even if you assume that a GHT-sentence somehow can't be a law unless its being so is epistemically accessible to a radical interpreter, meaning holism still doesn't follow. The kind of inference required from SHT-sentences to a certain GHT-sentence being counterfactual-supporting could be available even if all the informant's hold-trues were tokens of the same type (that is, even if the target language were punctate).

The Charity Solution

Davidson thinks – and this is one of his most characteristic doctrines – that, ceteris paribus, a GHT-sentence licenses the corresponding T-sentence, but only if a "constitutive principle" of intentional ascription is presupposed: namely, that truth conditions must be assigned to formulas of L under the constraint that most of the sentences held true by a speaker of L *are* true.[33] This principle is supposed to imply content holism on the intended interpretation, which is that "most of the sentences" means a lot of them.[34]

We are going to argue that this picture of how GHT-sentences license T-sentences is misconceived; that appeals to the principle of charity (POC) actually play no essential role in the inference, and that the version of POC that's in play in these arguments is, in any event, not holistic. If this is right, it's important for some of the larger metaphysical theses that Davidson holds. For example, it's primarily on the grounds that POC is constitutive of intentional ascription, but *not* of physicalistic ascription, that Davidson denies the possibility of homonomic, exceptionless psychophysical laws. So questions other than semantic holism are now at issue. (See his "Mental events," "The material mind," and "Psychology as philosophy.")

However, though we deny that POC is presupposed in inferences from GHT-sentences to T-sentences, we do think the following is true: if you are prepared to infer from something of the form "L-speakers hold S true in circumstance C" to "S is true (in L) iff C," then you cannot coherently deny that if an L-speaker utters S in C, then what he says is true. If, in short, your grounds for holding that *"It's raining" means that it's raining* are just that people say that it's raining when and only when it's raining, then you can't deny that people who say that it's raining just when it's raining are saying something true. We admit all this, but we don't think that it follows that POC plays a constitutive (or, indeed, any) role in interpretation.[35]

93

We have two points to make. The first will be familiar from our discussion of the "nomologicity solution" in the last section. Suppose that charity is required to get from a GHT-sentence about E to a T-sentence about E. All this means is that most of the informant's utterances of E are required to be true; and this is compatible with the assumption that the subject never utters – indeed, never can utter – tokens of any type other than E. This connects, in obvious ways, with our remark in the preceding section that the requirements that the method of differences imposes on interpretation could be satisfied in a punctate linguistic repertoire. (You could, of course, just stipulate that POC isn't satisfied unless it applies across types as well as tokens; this is presumably the version of POC that its proponents have in mind. But, barring a supplementary argument that only a POC that is satisfied across types can cope with the extensionality problem, that would be to invoke holism by stipulation. So far, no such supplementary argument is on offer.)

The second point is a little more intricate. If you think that what ground T-sentences are just unelaborated GHT-sentences, then you might reasonably wonder what principle of inference could ever get you from one of the latter to one of the former. After all, as Davidson points out, "Kurt . . . may be wrong about whether it's raining near him . . . and [this is] a reason not to expect generalizations like GE to be more than generally true" ("Radical interpretation," p. 136). But if the fact that a sentence is generally held true in a certain circumstance doesn't, in and of itself, warrant the inference that the sentence *is* true in that circumstance, one might reasonably wonder how the inference from a GHT-sentence to the corresponding T-sentence could possibly be defended. Answering this question is, in fact, what POC is for; and it's precisely because the present picture makes the inference from a GHT-sentence to a T-sentence look so *very* nondemonstrative that POC seems to play such an essential role in interpretation. And it's the fact that POC seems to play such an essential role in interpretation that makes interpretation look so very different from everyday empirical theory confirmation.

However, there is an alternative picture. Whether or not T-sentences are laws, we saw above that if they are inferred from GHT-sentences, then the GHT-sentences they are inferred from must be counterfactual-supporting.[36] We take it that, plus or minus a bit, this amounts to saying that GHT-sentences are laws; after all, laws are presumably counterfactual-supporting generalizations that are confirmed by their instances, and, on the present assumptions, GHT-sentences are counterfactual-supporting generalizations that are confirmed by SHT-sentences.

But now, why do we need a POC to get from "It's a law that GHT" to the corresponding T-sentence? Why not just say that if a GHT-sentence is a law, then the inference to the corresponding T-sentence is thereby licensed? *Davidson himself never offers any grounds for accepting a T-sentence except that the corresponding GHT-sentence is warranted;*[37] so if you think that warranted GHT-sentences all alone license the corresponding T-sentences, you will never come out accepting a T-sentence that Davidson doesn't accept or failing to accept one that he does.

The current issue is *not*, then, about which T-sentences are licensed; it's only about what principles of inference are used to license them. We're claiming that no case has been made that POC is so used. Notice, in particular, that the injunction to prefer the interpretation of a language L that accommodates the maximum of observed SHT-sentences (consonant with the usual systematic constraints on simplicity and the like) is not itself a form of POC. It's just an instance of the perfectly general methodological principle that always prefers the theory which is maximally compatible with the data, ceteris paribus. In effect, an interpretation that infers T-sentences from SHT-sentences identifies the truth conditions of a formula with the conditions under which its tokens are reliably observed to be held true,[38] all else being equal. And an interpretation that, all else being equal, identifies the truth conditions of a formula with the circumstances in which its tokens are reliably observed to be held true is *thereby* guaranteed to make the observed SHT-sentences turn out true, all else being equal. No further *methodological* injunction to do so is required. In particular, no independent principle of charity is required; all that's needed is the truism that a good theory had better comport with the data.

Here's another way to put the same point. Under interpretation, sentences that are *held* true keep turning out to *be* true. *Pace* Davidson, this need not be because interpretation is a special sort of project, one that is methodologically constrained by a POC. It may be for the much more boring reason that the truth conditions of an expression are *constituted* by the circumstances under which speakers are disposed to hold its tokens true (as, for example, causal theorists of content hold to be the case). This is equivalent to saying that a nomologically necessary GHT-sentence is metaphysically sufficient for the truth of the corresponding T-sentences (ceteris paribus). If this is wrong, Davidson needs an argument to show that it is; an argument to show, in effect, that the conditions for T-sentences being true don't reduce to the conditions for GHT-sentences being laws. Lacking such an argument, we have no reason to believe that the methodology of interpretation amounts to anything other than the routine methodology of empirical theory construction.

So, then, to summarize: Davidson says, in effect, that arguments from GHT-sentences to T-sentences are enthymemic, with POC as the suppressed premise (or presupposition). We suggest that, where a GHT-sentence is a law, no further principle is required to license the corresponding T-sentence; the truth of a GHT-sentence satisfies a *metaphysically sufficient condition* for the truth of the corresponding T-sentence. We now want to make a number of points about this proposal.

First, some things Davidson says suggest that he thinks that a meaning theory can't make room for error unless it endorses POC. However, as far as we can see, POC solves no problem about error that is unsolved on the assumption that nomologically necessary GHT-sentences directly license the corresponding T-sentences. In fact, both sorts of theories accommodate errors by appealing to ceteris paribus clauses. On the Davidson story, POC must be interpreted so that "it makes sense to accept intelligible error and to make allowance for the relative likelihood of various kinds of mistake" ("Radical interpretation," p. 136). Clearly, nobody could hold POC in a form that requires *everything* the subject says to be true by the interpreter's lights.[39] On the alternative story, the ceteris paribus clause comes in the GHT laws;[40] in effect, the GHT laws say that ceteris paribus S's hold true E iff P. Here, as elsewhere, a ceteris paribus clause allows a law to hold even though there are counter-instances (even though S's sometimes hold E true when it's not the case that P). The counter-instances to nomologically necessary GHT-sentences include the cases where what is held true is false.

Second, it might be thought that even if you don't need POC to get you from nomologically necessary GHT-sentences to T-sentences (because, to repeat, you don't need *anything* to get you from nomologically necessary GHT-sentences to T-sentences; the nomological necessity of the corresponding GHT-sentence is all the license a T-sentence need have), still, you will need POC to warrant all the (indefinitely many) *unlicensed* T-sentences that the favored T-theory generates; that is, the ones that govern the *non*token-reflexive sentences of the object language. A moment's reflection will convince you that this is confused.

Suppose we have a confirmed GHT-sentence that says that "This is snow" is held true iff this is snow and another one that says that "This is white" is held true iff this is white, and suppose we assume that this situation licenses the corresponding T-sentences for "This is snow" and "This is white." Then, given compositionality (that is, given the assumption that "snow" and "white" mean the same thing in "Snow is white" as they do in "This is snow" and "This is white"[41]), it will *follow* that "Snow is white" is true iff snow is white.[42] No appeal to POC is required to make this inference.

The preceding argument shows that compositionality will license assignments of truth conditions to nontoken-reflexive sentences all by itself in at least some cases; so that, in those cases, no appeal to POC is required for interpretation. But it might be thought that this won't work for the interpretation of *intentional* contexts; indeed, it might be thought this precisely because one holds the view that intentional contexts are ipso facto not compositional (as does Davidson; see his "On saying that," for example). But this might suggest that appeals to POC *can* play an essential role in the interpretation of *in*tentional (for example, belief) contexts, where, by assumption, appeals to compositionality break down. It's worth a couple of paragraphs to run this down, since, in doing so, one sees very clearly why, in cases where compositionality can't help a radical interpreter, POC can't help him either.

Suppose it's nomologically necessary that *x is F iff x is white*, so that for any GHT-sentence that supports the T-sentence " 'This x is white' is true iff this x is white," there will be an equally well-supported T-sentence " 'This x is white' is true iff this x is F." Now consider the T-sentence for "Sam believes that snow is white"; namely:

"Sam believes that snow is white" is true iff Sam believes that snow is white.

Notice that if this is well supported by the data about the indexical utterances, so too will be the "bad" T-sentence

"Sam believes that snow is white" is true iff Sam believes that snow is F.

Notice, too, that appealing to POC doesn't get you out of this. Interpreting Sam as believing that snow is white and that snow is F *both* make what Sam believes true. Hence, so far, POC doesn't do anything that compositionality can't.

However, consider sentences with *iterated* belief contexts like "Bill believes that Sam believes that snow is white." Here again we have two possible T-sentences, namely:

"Bill believes that Sam believes that snow is white" is true iff Bill believes that Sam believes that snow is white

and

"Bill believes that Sam believes that snow is white" is true iff Bill believes that Sam believes that snow is F.

Now, suppose that what Sam believes is, in fact, that snow is white (and not that snow is F). Then, adopting the first of these T-sentences will make Bill's belief about Sam's belief true, whereas adopting the second will make it false. So POC mandates the choice of the first T-sentence *ceteris paribus*. Thus there is something for POC to do in the theory of interpretation, after all. What's going on here is that "believes that" is more opaque than "is nomologically coextensive with," so inferences that substitute on the basis of the second in contexts governed by the first aren't guaranteed valid. Appeals to POC will therefore buy more than appeals to compositionality in languages that have iterable intentional (or more generally, intensional (with an "s")) expressions that are more fine-grained than "it's nomologically necessary that . . ." if there happen to be properties necessarily coextensive with the properties that the atomic predicates of such a language pick out.

However, though this is the kind of case in which it serves the radical interpreter well to follow a policy of making the informant's beliefs true, it's also the kind of case in which his epistemic position precludes his doing so (save by accident). POC enjoins the interpreter to make what Bill believes about what Sam believes true. By assumption, he can do this if (but only if) he interprets Bill as believing that Sam believes that snow is white. But how is he to know that this *is* the interpretation of Bill's belief that complies with POC? Answer: If he's to comply with POC, *the interpreter must know what Sam believes*. But now, how is he to know that? We just saw that POC does not prefer the hypothesis that Sam believes that snow is white to the hypothesis that Sam believes that snow is F. And the reader will remember that, by Davidson's stipulation, a radical interpreter's data can include no detailed information about the informant's beliefs; all it includes is information about which sentences the informant holds true.

The moral is that there *are* cases in which POC could help the interpreter; they are the cases in which his job is to understand beliefs about beliefs. But, in the nature of radical interpretation, radical interpreters are prohibited from appealing to POC in such cases, because their data about the informant's holding true sentences are required to be specified in *nonintentional* terms; hence, although they can include the information that Sam holds true "This x is white" iff this x is white, they can't include the information that Bill holds true "This x believes that P" iff this x believes that P. To use such information would be to use the truth of one semantic/intentional ascription to "bootstrap" the interpretation of others and would thus fail to count as *radical* interpretation.[43]

We've been able to think of only one other way in which appeals to charity might be required in the radical interpreter's epistemic situation; we mention it now in a spirit of comprehensiveness. Suppose there are expressions which (1) don't appear in token-reflexive utterances (or don't appear in them often enough to matter) and (2) which are *syntactically* atomic. Well, by assumption, the interpretation of these expressions can't be fixed by their behavior in token-reflexive utterances; and since they are syntactically atomic by assumption, their interpretations can't be determined compositionally from the interpretations of their parts. We don't know whether there are such expressions, but we don't see why there couldn't be. Very theoretical terms like "proton" would be among the likely candidates. The suggestion is that it is in the radical interpretation of *these* sorts of expressions that appeals to charity somehow play an ineliminable role.

We're prepared to view this as an open possibility, subject, however, to the following two caveats. In the first place, it's not at all clear how appealing to charity would help. The obvious suggestion for radically interpreting theoretical terms would be more or less reductive; one might suppose that "there are quasi-constitutive belief connections between every theoretical and mathematical term and some relatively observational terms of the kind that would turn up in occasion-[that is, token-reflexive] sentences" (Vermazin, "General beliefs and the principle of charity," p. 117). However, we've seen that most token-reflexive utterances will turn out true *whether or not* charity is assumed. So, given "constitutive connections" between theoretical and observational sentences, the truth of most of the latter is guaranteed *without* appeal to charity. (This is why reduction is so often prescribed as a cure for skepticism about unobservables.) It remains open that some argument might show that charity is required to interpret theoretical sentences on the assumption that they do *not* bear constitutive relations to observation sentences. But we don't see how such an argument would go.

The second point is that, as a matter of fact, it's exactly where people's beliefs fail to make close contact with observables that we *don't* assume that what they believe is overwhelmingly likely to be true. We would, for example, boggle at a translation scheme that made most Greeks have false beliefs about whether they had hands; this surely is the point of Moore's reply to the skeptic. But we are perfectly willing to swallow a translation scheme that makes most of the Greeks wrong about how far away the stars are and about whether matter is made of atoms. If there's *anything* that's right about the kind of linguistic empiricism that says that the semantic status of token-reflexive sentences is special, it's precisely that token-reflexive sentences and *not* theoretical sentences are the ones that we're inclined to insist that translation treat as true.

This is, in fact, a way of seeing the difference between a principle of *charity* and a principle of *humanity*. (See Grandy, "Reference, meaning and belief," p. 443.) We don't require the Greeks to have been right about the stars. That's because we can see that most of the *observational* consequences of their false astronomical theories were *true*; even false theories save lots of the appearances if they're any good at all. So we can explain why the Greeks were content to hold the false astronomical theories that they did. So we don't insist on translating them as holding true astronomical theories.[44]

The long and the short of it is that we can't find a substantive role for POC to play in Davidson's account of the confirmation of empirical truth theories; specifically, it doesn't appear to be "constitutive" of the attribution of intentional (/semantic) content according to that account. If this is right, then the argument that interpretation is holistic *because* charity is constitutive of interpretation has not been made good, even on the assumption that interpretation must be possible from the radical interpreter's epistemic position.

In conclusion, the strategy of the arguments considered in this chapter was to infer meaning holism from proposed solutions to the problem of choosing among extensionally adequate T-theories under the conditions of radical interpretation. But, even assuming that the conditions for radical interpretation do constrain the selection of meaning theories, this strategy can be successful only if the proposed solutions actually work. We've argued that the extensionality problem resists all the solutions we've surveyed; hence, barring further candidates, the strategy fails. And we have also argued that, in the second and third of the three proposals considered, the principles invoked to solve the extensionality problem do not in fact imply holism; specifically, they are compatible with the languages for which they choose T-theories being punctate. (Compositionality is trivially incompatible with atomism; but we found no argument that you can't choose a meaning theory for a noncompositional language.)

It remains open that, though the three proposals fail severally, they might nevertheless succeed collectively. What if we require charity and compositionality and nomologicity of the T-sentences all at once? Would *that* rule out deviant T-sentences? So far as we can tell, it wouldn't. But we won't argue for this claim at length. Suffice it to recommend the following quick consideration. A main problem for Davidson was to rule out T-sentences that are just like T except that, instead of reading " 'Snow is white' is true iff snow is white," they read ". . . iff snow is F," where "F" and "white" are nonsynonymous but coextensive as a matter of nomological necessity. But notice that even a simultaneous appeal to charity, compositionality, and nomologicity won't make this deviant T-sentence go away. Compositionality doesn't help, because if "(x) (x is white iff x is F)" is nomologically necessary, then it's guaranteed that "This is F" is true iff "This is white" is true. Requiring T-sentences to be laws doesn't help, because " 'Snow is white' is true iff snow is F" *will* be a law if T is a law and it's a law that x's are F iff they are white. And charity doesn't help, because a policy of making what the speaker says come out true will make "Snow is F" come out true whenever "Snow is white" does, given the assumption that "F" applies to all and only what "white" applies to. So charity, nomologicity, and compositionality are simultaneously satisfied, and we *still* haven't got rid of the deviant truth rule.

Maybe the moral is that if what you want is a meaning theory, you have to *say* that what you want is a meaning theory. The most that asking for a truth theory seems to get you is a theory of truth. Disappointing, no doubt, but perhaps not very surprising.[45] But however that may be, it appears that there is, so far, no reason to accept radical interpretability as a constraint on possible languages, no adequate solution to the extensionality problem within the framework of RI theory, and no reason to believe that if there were an adequate solution to the extensionality problem within the RI framework, it would serve to ground an argument for meaning holism.

4

DAVID LEWIS:
MEANING HOLISM AND THE
PRIMACY OF BELIEF

The arguments for holism considered in the previous chapter were simultaneously epistemological and transcendental. What made them epistemological was the assumption that it's metaphysically constitutive of content that a language (or an intentional state) must be *radically* interpretable; "radical interpretation" is defined by reference to the epistemic situation of the interpreter. What made them transcendental was that they purported to show that radical interpretation would be metaphysically impossible except that holistic principles of interpretation are in force.

In the present chapter, the approach is still transcendental – it still turns on the conditions for the possibility of intentional interpretation – but epistemological considerations seem to play a less central role. No longer do we assume a radical interpreter who knows, besides the canons of nondemonstrative inference, only what sentences his informant holds true and under what conditions he holds them true. In his place, we are invited to imagine a radical interpreter who is given *all* the physical facts about the informant (that is, all the facts about the informant under their physical descriptions) and whose problem is to redescribe the informant in intentional terms.[1]

It should be obvious by now that my problem of radical interpretation is not any real-life task of finding out about Karl's

105

beliefs, desires and meanings. I am not really asking how *we* could determine these facts. Rather: How do the *facts* determine these facts? By what constraints, and to what extent, does the totality of physical facts about Karl determine what he believes, desires, and means? (Lewis, "Radical interpretation," p. 110)[2]

THE "BEST-FIT" ACCOUNT OF INTENTIONAL ASCRIPTION

The crux of Lewis's proposal is that we should understand intentional ascription as a kind of *constraint-satisfaction* problem; roughly, the intentional state that Karl is correctly said to be in is the one that best accommodates the physical facts together with the principles that constrain intentional ascription. We'll see in a moment more of what this amounts to. But the connection with holism – in case the reader is wondering – is that, on analysis, the constraining principles turn out to be holistic. In fact, they include some of the very holistic principles that Davidson's version of the transcendental argument from radical interpretation to meaning holism is supposed to underwrite.

By saying that intentional ascription is viewed as a constraint-satisfaction problem, we mean this: there is a set of simultaneous and (more or less) independent demands that the ascription of an intentional state is required to satisfy. The *correct* intentional ascription is the one that provides a best fit to these demands. "Best fit" is a technical term in this context, and it remains to be defined. Among the relevant considerations is that the various demands on intentional ascription may be weighted and contextualized. If, for example, we have a choice between an intentional ascription that makes Karl a believer of falsehoods and one that makes him a teller of lies, there may be some a priori preference for one over the other; and this preference may be absolute or may hold only in specified circumstances; and so forth. In short, a best-fit model requires that the various constraints on intentional ascription be *comparable*, but the procedures by which they are to be compared are left open.

There is, moreover, no guarantee that these procedures, whatever they are, will yield a *unique best* intentional ascription in every case – or, indeed, that they will yield *any* intentional ascriptions in every case. So it is left open that even the totality of physical facts may underdetermine intentional ascriptions. The metaphysical claim is just that if there *is* a fact of the matter about Karl's intentional state, then the fact is a matter of which intentional ascription is the best fit to the physical facts and constraining principles. The analogy to the way in which Lewis understands the concept of a law of nature is instructive: "What makes [a regularity] a law, I suggest, is that it fits into some integrated system of truths that combines simplicity with strength in the best possible way" (Lewis, "A subjectivist's guide to objective chance," p. 122). So we are to think of ascriptions of nomologicity to regularities as simultaneously and independently constrained by empirical data together with demands for simplicity and strength; for a regularity to be nomological *just is* for it to belong to the system of regularities that optimally satisfies these simultaneous demands.

In the case of distinguishing regularities from laws, the ruling constraints are economy and power. So, then: "What are the constraints by which the problem of radical interpretation is to be solved? Roughly speaking, they are the fundamental principles of the theory of persons. They tell us how beliefs and desires and meanings are normally related to one another, to behavioral output, and to sensory input" (Lewis, "Radical interpretation," p. 111). Thus the picture is: we have these constraints (where they come from we will discuss in a moment); we think of candidate radical interpretations (/intentional ascriptions) as being confronted with these constraints together with the data as physicalistically described; and we define "Karl's intentional state" to be that state which, when ascribed to Karl, best satisfies the demands that the constraints and the data jointly impose.

Lewis suggests several principles which he takes to constrain intentional ascription and which "must amount to nothing more than a mass of platitudes of common sense. . . . Esoteric scientific findings that go beyond common sense must be kept out on pain of changing the subject" (ibid., p. 112). What is most relevant to our present purposes is that these "platitudes" include principles of charity that constrain relations among Karl's intentional states (for example, relations of coherence) or that impose requirements that "most" of Karl's states must meet (for example, most of his beliefs must be true). By assumption, such principles could not be satisfied unless Karl has a plurality of propositional attitudes. So holism is deducible from the constraints on intentional ascription according to Lewis's account, just as it is according to Davidson's.

We'll look at the details of the argument presently; for the moment, however, we want to make some comments about the general picture. (These are not, by the way, comments with which we are at all sure that Lewis would disagree.)

In the first place, it's not clear that anything of metaphysical interest – or, indeed, that anything at all – would follow *just* from conceding that intentional ascription should be viewed as a problem of constraint satisfaction. The pertinent consideration is that *just about any problem* can be viewed as a problem of constraint satisfaction (as, indeed, recent discussions of connectionism have made clear). For example, Holmes has the following constraint-satisfaction problem, to which it may be that Moriarty is the best solution: "The criminal is someone who is not more than 5'11" and not less than 5'6" tall; he owns a brown spotted dachshund that sheds; he has a working knowledge of ichthyology, and his sister was born not far from Leeds." Moriarty is the solution to this problem because he is 5'8" tall and owns the right kind of dog and knows a *little* ichthyology, and, though his sister was born quite a distance from Leeds, no other candidate satisfies the constraints as well as Moriarty *on balance*.

But, of course, the fact that Moriarty is the best solution to the problem tells us nothing about the metaphysical, ontological, or other status of Moriarty. Nor, from the fact that identifying the criminal is finding the solution to a problem in which many conditions must simultaneously be satisfied, does anything follow about whether *being a criminal* is in some sense a *holistic* concept. For example, someone might argue that the *concept* criminal is holistic in the sense that, on the one hand, criminality is a legal property, and, on the other hand, legal properties are anatomic; no one could have them in a world in which he was the only agent. So it's conceptually necessary that Robinson Crusoe couldn't commit a crime; call this the "private criminal argument." Our point is that knowing that finding the criminal is a constraint-satisfaction problem throws no light at all on whether the private criminal argument is sound. Mutatis mutandis, if there are holistic implications of the "best-fit" account of intentional ascription, that can't be because it *is* a best-fit analysis; rather, it must be because of something intrinsically holistic about the parameters to which intentional ascriptions are to be fitted.

We want to pause to rub this in, because the idea that it is metaphysically revealing to claim that intentional ascription is a best-fit problem seems to be becoming widely endorsed – to no very good end, so far as we can tell.

It's a harmless truism that the problem of finding the x that is the best fit to F can be construed as the problem of finding the x that is the best fit to the properties that define F-ness. So we can, if we like, think of Holmes's problem as finding a best fit to the *defining* property of the criminal qua criminal; that is, to the property of *having perpetrated the crime. This* way of describing the problem really does tell us something about the metaphysical status of the criminal; it tells us something about *what kind of thing a criminal is.* (The criminal must be a perpetrator; so he can't be a rock.) That, however, is because the constraint to be satisfied is a defining property, not because the problem is one of constraint satisfaction. Notice that if you were in a tortuous frame of mind, you could say, "Being the

109

criminal *just is* being the best fit to *perpetrator of the crime*; that's *all there is* to being the criminal." This sounds metaphysically interesting – but again, only because the property being fitted is supposed to be a defining property; likewise in "All there is to being what Karl believes is being the best fit to principles of charity" or in "All there is to being a law is being the best fit to principles of power and economy." The appeal to "best fit" isn't actually doing any metaphysical work; it isn't telling us anything about what kinds of things laws and beliefs *are*. What does the metaphysical work is the assumption that rationality is constitutive of intentionality and that power and simplicity are constitutive of nomologicity.[3]

Our second preliminary point is this. Lewis has these more or less analytic constraints on intentional ascription, and his picture is that the goal of radical interpretation is "satisfying all six of our constraining principles or balancing them off as best we can" (Lewis, "Radical interpretation," p. 117). But then the constraints on *radical interpretation* can't be the whole story about what constrains *intentional ascriptions*; not even if we agree (as perhaps we oughtn't) that to allow "esoteric scientific findings" to constrain them would be to "change the subject" in content attribution. After all, it's patent that commonsense intentional ascription is constrained by commonsense intentional psychology, and this includes not just principles of charity and the like, but also a plethora of utterly *contingent* intentional platitudes such as that people don't like to be stuck with pins; people generally see what is before their eyes when their eyes are open and the lights are on; people who believe P and believe Q generally believe P and Q, and so forth. Consonance with this lore is as plausibly required of everyday intentional ascription as consonance with the injunction that what people assert is generally to be rendered as true (to cite one of Lewis's principles). If we are going to think of intentional ascription as a species of best-fit problem solving, then the received body of Grandmother-psychology should surely be counted among the parameters requiring to be fitted.

No doubt it is merely *contingent* that the right intentional attribution is a best fit to Granny's constraints; whereas (we're supposing) it is *necessary* that the right intentional attribution is a best fit to Lewis's constraints, since these constraints are supposed to *constitute* the intentional. But, so what? The problem was supposed to be *not* "What properties do intentional states *necessarily* have?" but "What are the constraints on putative solutions to problems of intentional ascription?" As we've seen, Lewis says that: "Roughly speaking, [these constraints] are the fundamental principles of our theory of persons. They tell us how beliefs and desires and meanings are normally related to one another, to behavioral output, and to sensory input" (Lewis, "Radical interpretation," p. 111). Well, it's true that interpretation is constrained by what we know about how beliefs, desires, inputs, outputs, and meanings are normally related to one another. But it's *not* true that what we know about how beliefs, desires, inputs, outputs, and meanings are normally related to one another is anything like exhausted by, on the one hand, our fundamental theory of persons and, on the other hand, scientific exotica. For example, part of what we know about how beliefs, desires, and behaviors are normally related to one another is that people don't, generally speaking, like getting stuck by pins; hence that they try to avoid situations in which they believe that pins are likely to stick them. But this isn't a fundamental principle of our theory of persons; it isn't exotic; and it certainly isn't analytic. It looks to be just a bit of applied, contingent, Granny-psychology.[4]

The significance of these considerations will be clear to the reader who followed the argument in the preceding chapter. Lewis in effect makes it true *by stipulation* that *radical* interpreters start with no knowledge of contingent intentional truths. (By contrast, radical interpreters are allowed to know about the constraints on interpretation, because these are supposed to be constitutive rather than contingent; they, as it were, define the radical interpreter's project.) Like Davidson, Lewis appears to subscribe to a residual foundationalism according to which interpretation is an exception to the rule that empirical theory construction always begins *in media res*.[5]

But if, as we've been suggesting, the constraints that are stipulated to define radical interpretation underdescribe the constraints that operate in *real* interpretation, the question arises once again why radical interpretation should even be supposed to be possible. Imagine defining a "radical geologist," whose task it is to recover all the truths of empirical geology given all the geological facts as physics describes them, together with a budget of analytic geological platitudes ("Mountains are bigger than hills, ceteris paribus," and so forth). Is there any reason to suppose that this project can be carried out? Or that it is of the slightest epistemological or metaphysical interest?

The same questions arise if the issues are framed in terms of supervenience. Given the physical facts, the principles by which the intentional supervenes on the physical are required to entail not just the satisfaction of Lewis's constraints, but *all* the intentional truths, including the intentional truths of Granny-psychology. There is no reason to doubt that Lewis's constraints, taken alone, would wildly underdetermine the formulation of these principles.

With these caveats, however, we can endorse the idea that radical interpretation is a species of constraint satisfaction (as we've seen, doing this doesn't commit one to anything much); and we can, for the sake of argument anyhow, endorse the view that among the constraints to which intentional ascription is subject are such holistic principles of charity as: Maximize the *coherence* of the beliefs ascribed and maximize the *truth* of the beliefs ascribed (both from the ascriber's point of view, of course, and both ceteris paribus).

Let's see where this leaves us. Davidson, as we read him in the previous chapter, offered a transcendental argument for charity grounded in claims about the epistemological situation of the radical interpreter. Lewis, as we read him in this chapter, considers that the principles of charity constrain the possibility of intentional ascription because they (implicitly, partially) define the notion of a belief system. The difference is important for assessing the polemical situation. It suffices as an argument against Davidson to undermine his assumption that intentional ascription must be understood by reference to the radical interpreter's epistemic situation. For, if that idea is wrong, then the fact that intentional ascription *from that epistemological position* requires charity would not imply *any* constraints on intentional ascription per se. But, clearly, you can't argue that way against Lewis. When you clear aside the stuff about best fit, it becomes obvious that Lewis – unlike Davidson – doesn't offer a *fancy* argument that interpretation is constrained by charity. Rather, he offers the following plain and simple argument: "That charity constrains belief interpretation is entailed by our concept of a person (that is, by our concept of a believer); like it or lump it." There is now *no question* whether belief is holistic; of course it is, *by definition*. (There may, however, now be a question about whether there are any believers. We'll return to this at the very end of the chapter.)

Against so short an argument, the polemical options are a little thin. Either you must dispute the claim that the connection between belief ascription and the putative holistic principles is conceptually necessary, or you must dispute that the putative principles of interpretation are holistic. Well, we have already conceded the second, and, in order to avoid a squabble about what is and what is not "part of our concept of a person," we also propose to concede the first. Clearly, belief holism follows from these concessions. The question arises, however: *What has belief holism got to do with meaning holism?* In particular, how do you get from the (for the sake of argument, uncontested) premise that there are holistic constitutive conditions for *believing* to the desired conclusion that there are constitutive holistic conditions for being in an intentional state (that is, for being in a state that's semantically evaluable)?

113

Here's one way. Assume that:

The conditions for content attribution *inherit* the conditions for belief attribution; hence, if the former are holistic, then the latter must be too.

This claim is what we call the *primacy of belief thesis*. Our polemical relation to the primacy of belief thesis is this: if it is true, then we concede that semantic holism probably follows (because it is not implausible that the conditions on *belief* attribution *are* holistic). In fact, as we're about to see, the primacy (of belief) thesis is so strong that, once you've accepted it, you can get semantic holism *without* invoking the role of charity in interpretation – indeed, without invoking the theory of interpretation at all. However, we know of no very convincing argument for the truth of the primacy thesis, and we can think of some plausible reasons why it might not be true. The rest of this chapter will be devoted to elaborating this theme.

We pause only to be explicit about the exegetical situation. Lewis's "Radical interpretation" does *not* endorse – or even mention – the primacy thesis, and we are *not* claiming that Lewis accepts it. (Unlike Lewis, Davidson is explicitly committed in this area; we'll discuss his version of the primacy thesis as we go along.) We do claim, however, that if Lewis doesn't accept the primacy of belief thesis, then the arguments for his constraints on interpretation are merely parochial. They may apply to *belief* interpretation, but they don't show that *interpretation* as such is similarly constrained. Without the more general conclusion Lewis's analysis of radical *belief attribution* would provide no argument for the holism of radical interpretation. And, to get the more general conclusion, one needs the primacy thesis.

We are about to doubt, however, that the primacy thesis is true.

114

Primacy and Functionalism

Considered in the context of radical interpretation, the primacy thesis licenses one to infer the constitutive principles of content attribution from the constitutive principles of belief attribution. But there is a broader philosophical context in which the primacy thesis allows one to dispense with talk of constitutive principles of *attribution* entirely and infer holism from the conditions for belief *individuation*. Here, even the appearance of epistemological argument is eschewed, and the governing considerations are overtly metaphysical.

Suppose we assume, in accordance with the current consensus in the philosophy of mind, that beliefs (and the rest of the propositional attitudes) are functionally individuated. It is, in fact, not so clear what this assumption actually amounts to, but there is a contrast case that philosophers rely on: the case in which the membership of an individual in a kind is determined by its microstructure (or "hidden essence"). So compare *being water* with *being an airfoil*. The rough idea is that *all* that counts for whether something is water is that its microstructure should be H_2O. So, on the one hand, things that look and behave arbitrarily much like water but have the wrong microstructure (Putnam's XYZ, for a famous example) are nevertheless *not* water; and, on the other hand, things that look and behave very differently from paradigmatic water (like ice, steam, and fog, for example) nevertheless *are* water since they are H_2O. (What they aren't, of course, is water "in the liquid state.")

By contrast, whether an individual belongs to the type *airfoil* depends very little – maybe not at all – on its microstructure and almost entirely on what macro-level laws subsume it. Very roughly, you are an airfoil if you are a (semi- – sails count) rigid object passing through a liquid or gaseous environment in such a fashion that the operation of Bernoulli's law generates lift at one or more of your surfaces. The functionalist idea in the philosophy of mind is that beliefs are more like airfoils than like water. That is, for something to be a belief state is for it to have certain macroscopic relational properties, properties that depend on the macroscopic laws that it obeys. To an adequate first approximation, according to this functionalist account, to be a belief state is to play a certain kind of role in the etiology of an organism's behavior.

It may be that holism does *not* follow just from the assumption that believing that so-and-so is a macroscopic, relational, functional property. (Though functional properties are typically holistic, we're not going to argue that the connection between being functional and being holistic is internal.) However, there is a very natural further assumption about belief individuation from which the holism of belief content does follow: namely, that a specification of the causal role that beliefs play in the etiology of behavior would make essential reference to[6] their causal interactions with *other content-bearing states.*

For example, you might reasonably suppose that it's a defining property of beliefs that, in the course of contributing to the etiology of behavior, they interact with desires according to the axioms of some decision theory or other. It would then follow that nothing can be a belief state unless it (normally) interacts with volitional intentional states. It would also follow that nobody could *have* a belief unless he (normally) has volitional intentional states of the appropriate kind. Similarly, you might reasonably suppose that it's a defining property of beliefs that they interact with one another in ways that lead to the formation of new beliefs (ceteris paribus, the beliefs that P v Q and that not-P interact to produce the belief that Q, and so on). This assumption too entails the conceptual impossibility (since these are supposed to be *defining* properties of belief) of a believer with a punctate mind.

We aren't, we hasten to say, actually endorsing such typically functionalist claims about belief individuation as that etiological relations to other intentional states (or, indeed, to "inputs and outputs") are defining properties of beliefs. In fact, the arguments for functionalism about belief individuation strike us as pretty weak. Standardly, they amount to remarking that the possibility of multiply realized intentional systems – silicon Martians and the like – rules it out that beliefs have hidden microstructural essences and then asking, rhetorically: what, except macrostructural relations, could the defining properties of believing that P be?[7]

Anyhow, for present purposes, we take no stand on the question of whether the arguments for functionalism are convincing. Our point is just that, given the primacy thesis, *any* reason you may have for belief holism is ipso facto a reason for holism about mental content per se. These include, but aren't exhausted by, considerations of the sort that Davidson and Lewis offer to show that belief *attribution* is holistic. Metaphysical arguments that belief *individuation* is holistic would do equally well. If only for this reason, we think that the decisive issue about holism is not whether some or other principle of charity is analytic of belief, but whether there is any license for inferring meaning holism from belief holism. This issue is not widely discussed, however, either by philosophers who are holists about belief attribution or by philosophers who are holists about belief individuation. We propose to consider it at some length here.

Two Prima Facie Arguments for the Primacy Thesis

Let's consider, as a test case, the principle of rationality (to which Davidson and Dennett, though not Lewis, are explicitly committed as one of the putative constitutive principles of intentional attribution). It says, roughly, that you can't both believe P and believe not-P, all else equal (the caveat includes, for example, cases where the contradiction is insufficiently obvious), and that, ceteris paribus, if you believe P, you must believe many of its consequences (the caveat includes, for example, cases where the consequence is insufficiently obvious).[8] It's notorious that this is hard to spell out, but we don't propose to worry about that here. Our question is: What is the generality of this constraint? What, other than *belief* attribution, is it a constraint *on*?

We want to rub it in that, at first blush at least, it's not plausible that the principle of rationality constraints *content* attribution as such. For example, it's not plausible that it constrains the attribution of meanings to forms of words. You surely could have a sentence, say, of English, that *means* that P and not-P. In fact, it's not plausible that the principle of rationality even constrains propositional attitude attributions as such, since it's perfectly OK to want P and to want not-P, *even* if the contradiction is obvious; ambivalence is the human condition. So it looks like rationality constrains not semantic evaluability as such but, in particular, *belief attribution*. But now, if that is so, and assuming that belief is holistic because it is constrained by the rationality principle, what licenses the inference from belief holism to semantic holism?

When Davidson and Lewis discuss interpretation, they invariably have in mind the process of assigning propositional attitudes to agents and/or the process of assigning meanings to speakers' utterances. Now you might hold, in the first case, that *all propositional attitude ascription presupposes belief ascription* in the sense that no creature can have any propositional attitudes unless it has some beliefs. This is the principle that Davidson sometimes calls "the centrality of belief."

Not only does each belief require a world of further beliefs to give it content and identity, but every other propositional attitude depends for its particularity on a similar world of beliefs. In order to believe the cat went up the oak tree I must have many true beliefs about cats and trees, this cat and this tree, the place, appearance, and habits of cats and trees, and so on; but the same holds if I wonder whether the cat went up the oak tree, fear that it did, hope that it did, wish that it had, or intend to make it do so. Belief – indeed, true belief – plays a central role among the propositional attitudes. ("Rational animals," p. 475; see also "Thought and talk," pp. 156–7)[9]

And, in the second case, you might hold that *no creature can produce interpretable utterances* (in effect, can perform speech acts) *unless some belief ascriptions are true of it.* The upshot would be that you get an internal connection between the conditions for semantic evaluation and the conditions for belief ascription. Putting the two arguments together, you get belief as a prerequisite for both mental and linguistic content, so the primacy thesis is vindicated.

Let's consider these two lines of argument for the primacy of belief, starting with the purported centrality of belief.

First argument
We find it unclear whether Davidson's centrality thesis is true – whether, for example, a creature could have desires that so-and-so without having beliefs about so-and-so. Difficult issues about the relation between attitudes and actions are involved.

Perhaps the most obvious way of arguing that you can't have desires without beliefs would be to suppose that, on the one hand, it's conceptually necessary that desires (can, sometimes) eventuate in behavior, and that, on the other hand, it's conceptually necessary that desires eventuate in behavior *via decision-theoretic interactions with beliefs.* It's only the second conjunct that has the holistic implications.[10] So, then, *is it* conceptually necessary that the causation of behavior by desires is mediated by beliefs? We don't doubt that wants really do typically have their behavioral effects decision-theoretically. What we wonder is whether it is certifiably *necessary* that they do.

For example, is the following (approximately Rylean) view of the relation between desires and actions not even *coherent? Desires are a species of behavioral dispositions, so that "ceteris*

119

paribus, if X desires that P, then X performs action A" is *semantically necessary for certain choices of P and A.* According to this view, it may be that a creature couldn't have desires (it couldn't have the appropriate behavioral dispositions) unless it had beliefs; but if so, that would be *contingent* (for example, it would be because, de facto, having beliefs is required to discharge the ceteris paribus clause). So it looks as though if the Rylean view is so much as coherent, the centrality thesis can't be necessary.

Or consider this case. There is a certain state S of a creature that is normally triggered by dehydration and that normally and reflexively (N.B. reflexively rather than decision-theoretically) causes the creature to perform a certain sort of behavior. The creature has no beliefs about the utility of the behavior that being in S causes it to perform; that is part of what it means to say that the behavior is produced reflexively. But in "ecologically valid" circumstances – roughly, in the circumstances in which the organism is normally found – the consequence of the behavior is that the creature ingests liquid, and hence that its dehydration is relieved. Assume that the preceding exhausts the functional role of S vis-à-vis the production of the creature's behavior, so that at no point in the performance of its function does S interact with beliefs. Question: Is it therefore conceptually necessary that S is *not* a state of thirst (that is, not an intentional state, not a desire for liquid)? We're inclined to doubt that this is conceptually necessary.

However, modal intuitions are notoriously unreliable, and we admit that these matters are obscure; so it's just as well that we don't have to resolve them here. The centrality of belief entails that you can't have any *propositional attitudes* unless you have beliefs. But what the meaning holist requires is that creatures can't have any *semantically evaluable states* – can't have any states with content – unless they have beliefs. Who says that the only semantically evaluable states are propositional attitudes? (We'll return to this below.)

Second argument
Davidson thinks (and maybe he thinks it's necessary) that the primary evidence for radical interpretation consists in observations of sentences being held to be true. But, of course, holding true is itself a propositional attitude; in fact, it's just the overt manifestation of *believing* something to be true. And *what* the informant believes to be true when he holds that S is true is not just that the form of words S expresses *some truth or other*. He also holds true *the proposition that S expresses*. To visibly hold true the form of words "The cat is on the mat" is to believe that the cat is on the mat and to say what you believe. So anything that Davidson would count as evidence that a speaker means that such and such would also count as evidence that the speaker believes that such and such; Davidson's view is explicitly that information about forms of words held true provides the crucial evidence for *both* meaning attribution and belief attribution. So the epistemological conditions for ascribing contents to what the informant says are inextricably linked with the epistemological conditions for belief attribution. Davidson has a perfectly general way of putting this point:

> A speaker who holds a sentence to be true on an occasion does so in part because of what he means . . . by an utterance of that sentence, and in part because of what he believes. If all we have to go on is the fact of honest utterance, we cannot infer the belief without knowing the meaning and have no chance of inferring the meaning without the belief. (Davidson, "Belief and the basis of meaning," p. 142)

If this is right, then the conditions for belief attribution are inextricably linked with the conditions for meaning attribution, and the latter must be satisfied whenever the former are.

We take the moral of these reflections to be that as long as you assume that the *objects* of radical interpretation are either *propositional attitudes* (so that what get assigned conditions of semantic evaluation are Karl's intentional states) or *meaningful utterances* (so that what get assigned conditions of semantic evaluation are the speech acts that Karl performs), the primacy thesis isn't utterly implausible. On the former assumption, the primacy thesis follows from the principle that only believers can have *any* propositional attitudes (a principle that we take to be not worse than moot), and on the latter, it follows from the weak assumption that the conditions for the interpretability of speech acts include the conditions for attributing beliefs.

We are therefore prepared to concede, for purposes of argument, not only belief holism, but also this much of the primacy thesis: that there are no propositional attitudes and no speech acts without beliefs. If all this is assumed, then the question about whether belief holism entails meaning holism is effectively the question of whether anything except speech acts and attitudes can be semantically evaluated in the first instance. (Signboards are neither speech acts nor propositional attitudes and yet, plausibly, they can be semantically evaluated. But it seems clear that their intentionality is, in John Searle's term, "derived"; that is, that the conditions for their semantic evaluation must somehow "trace back to" the conditions for semantically evaluating beliefs and intentions.) The question is whether anything other than speech acts and attitudes can have "original" or "underived" intentionality. Only if the answer to this question is negative does the holism of belief imply the holism of content and interpretation.

MENTAL PARTICULARS

As we remarked in chapter 1, the traditional philosophical view – the one that was practically ubiquitous until the second half of this century, barring occasional Direct Realists like Reid – was that, in the first instance, semantic properties inhere in a certain class of mental particulars – namely, in mental representations. It was from what Locke and Descartes called "Ideas" and Hume called "impressions" that propositional attitudes, utterances, and the rest were supposed to derive their intentionality. We digress, briefly, to remind the reader what such theories are like.

Plus or minus a bit, Hume's theory was that semantic properties inhere, in the first instance, in mental images. The conditions for the semantic evaluation of a mental image, according to this view, are determined by certain of its intrinsic features; in effect, mental images are satisfied by what they resemble. The relevant consideration, for our present concerns, is that neither Hume's theory about content nor his (associative) theory of mental processes postulates an internal connection between the conditions for semantic evaluability and the conditions for belief. Hume's account of belief, like his account of content, makes essential reference to intrinsic features of mental representations. But the belief-making features of a mental representation, its "force and vivacity," are orthogonal to its representation-making features, the latter being, in effect, geometrical.[11]

Analogously, what a mental image resembles (hence means) does not depend on what role it plays in mental processes – or, indeed, on its playing any role in mental processes at all. For Hume, the causal role of a mental image depends on *what it's associated with*, and an Idea can be associated with practically anything compatible with its having the content that it does. In consequence, the conditions for a creature's mental representations being semantically evaluable are metaphysically independent of the conditions for their having the causal role that they do. Hume is, to put it mildly, not a functionalist about content.

Nobody now thinks either that the content of a mental representation depends on what it resembles or that what someone believes is a matter of the force and vivacity of the mental representations that he entertains. And most people (with the exception of connectionists) don't suppose that the causal roles of mental states supervene on their associative relations. But none of these details of the Humean account is essential to understanding why it is that the primacy thesis can fail when mental representations are supposed to be the primary objects of semantic interpretation. The crucial points are the following.

First, it's not implausible that the essential properties of beliefs constrain their functional roles vis-à-vis other mental states (see above); whereas, plausibly, the conditions for a mental representation to be semantically evaluable constrain (not what it resembles, of course, but) its causal relations to things-in-the-world. Modern cognitive theories assume that mental representations *have* functional roles qua constituents of propositional attitudes. But (barring further argument) a mental representation's having the content that it does needn't be supposed to depend, conceptually or metaphysically, on its having the functional role that it does – or, indeed, on its having any functional role at all.

Second, it's plausible that the conditions for a mental representation being tokened – unlike, notice, the conditions for a sentence token to be held true (or, more generally, for a speech act to be performed) – do not themselves invoke intentional notions like belief, desire, and intention. Tokening a mental representation (informally speaking, having a thought occur to one) isn't (or needn't be) an *action*, and hence need not be inextricably connected to believing in the ways that speech acts and other actions are.

We will spell this out a bit in just a moment; suffice it for now to remind the reader of the architectural situation. The holism of *belief* doesn't entail the holism of *content* unless there is an argument for the primacy thesis (that is, for the case that satisfying the conditions for semantic evaluability entails satisfying the conditions for belief). We thus asked what defense of the primacy thesis might be proposed; and the best answers we could think of depended on assuming that the bearers of underived intentionality are either speech acts or (token) belief states. In the latter case the primacy thesis holds trivially; in the former it holds via the consideration that speech acts are actions, and that the concept of action invokes the concept of belief.

The present line of reply is that we might avoid the inference from belief holism to meaning holism by assuming that the objects in which semantic properties inhere in the first instance are neither propositional attitudes nor speech acts but mental representations. For, plausibly, neither what is required for mental representations to be semantically evaluable nor what is required for mental representations to be tokened (hence to play a causal role in mental life) invokes the having of beliefs. The basic idea is simply that *meaning holism* would not follow from *belief holism* if the primary bearers of meaning were *not beliefs*.

What might a mental representation story look like, assuming, on the one hand, that mental representations are the bearers of underived semantic evaluability and, on the other hand, that – *contra* Hume – mental representations can't be images in the general case? There are a number of possibilities; here, in outline, is a familiar one.

Mental representations are typically sentence-like expressions. To say that they are sentence-like is to say that there is a distinction between complex representations and simple ones and that the semantic properties of the former depend, in a regular way, upon the semantic properties of the latter (the semantics of mental representations is thus "compositional"). The semantic properties of the elementary representations are in turn supposed to be determined (not by what they resemble but) by the character of their causal (and/or nomological) relations to the things they denote and the properties they express. There are a number of suggestions about how this might work, though none of them is fully satisfactory. (See, for example, Dretske, Fodor, Millikan, Stampe, etc.) We spare the reader extended exegesis.

The point that bears emphasis for our present purposes is that mental representations differ from (for example) English sentences in the following ways. First, while a "Gricean" analysis' is perhaps plausible for the latter, it is out of the question for the former. Whatever bestows semantic evaluability upon mental representations, it can't be that they are used to express beliefs or intentions. Mental representations aren't "used" at all; and we typically have no beliefs or intentions with respect to them.

Second, in standard formulations of mental representation theory, the conditions for a mental representation to play a causal role in mental life do not invoke notions of belief, desire, and the like. This point could perhaps do with a little spelling out. The idea is that the causal role of a mental representation token in mental life is determined entirely by its nonsemantic properties. (Theories according to which mental processes are computational have it that the causal role of a mental representation is determined by the same syntactic properties on which its compositionality depends. Architecturally, these sorts of accounts of mental processes are just like Hume's, but with computation replacing association; in both cases, the conditions for having a causal role in mental life are orthogonal to the conditions for content.) The theory of mental processes is thus supposed to be articulated entirely in nonintentional vocabulary – a fortiori, without essential appeal to notions like belief and intention. In short, though mental representation theory makes tokenings of mental representations the vehicles of thought in something like the way that speech act theories make performances of speech acts the vehicles of communication, still, the analogy is misleading in a crucial way. Because performances of speech acts *are* acts, the theory of communication inextricably invokes – indeed, presupposes – notions like believing and intending; whereas, because mental representation tokenings aren't actions, the theory of mental processes doesn't.

Notice that this way of denying the primacy thesis does *not* require also denying the Sellarsian doctrine that mental content is parasitic on linguistic content; for example, that we "think in English." Maybe thinking that the cat is on the mat is just saying to oneself "The cat is on the mat." However, if it is, then "saying to oneself" must differ from "saying" *tout court*. For saying *tout court* is normally the consequence of deciding what to say; that is, of decision-theoretic processes which invoke beliefs and desires. Whereas, saying to oneself can't presuppose

126

believing or desiring, since, according to the present account, believing and desiring are themselves species of saying to oneself. Davidson at one point takes seriously the suggestion that thoughts are "like silent utterances" ("Belief and the basis of meaning," p. 144); but if that were true, thoughts would be actions. Which they aren't.

So, then, to summarize: the species of mental representation theory we have in mind (including Hume's) tells one kind of story about the difference between believing and, as it might be, wanting and quite a different kind of story about the difference between believing that P and, as it might be, believing that Q. The former story is bona fide functionalist: believing and wanting are both modes of entertaining mental representations, but they differ with respect to the causal (associative/computational) roles that the mental representations play (that is, with respect to how the representations interact with inputs, outputs, and one another). By contrast, the difference between believing that P and believing that Q invokes the semantic properties of mental representations, and these are supposed to be grounded in mind/world relations *rather than* functional roles. The point is that there is no primacy thesis anywhere in sight. The functional analysis of *belief* may be such as to make believing holistic; for example, it may be that it is essential to beliefs that they enter into decision-theoretic or confirmation-theoretic processes. But, the (putative) holism of belief need not imply meaning holism, because the notion of believing is not *primitive* in the theory of intentionality. What's primitive are mental representations with their causal relations to each other and the world; and, by assumption, the semantics of mental representations is atomistic.

The bottom line is that the inference from belief holism to meaning holism – to any holistic claims about intentionality *as such* – needs the primacy thesis. Hence, if you are going to run an a priori argument in which the inference to meaning holism depends essentially on the primacy thesis, you need an a priori argument *against* the idea that the aboriginal bearers of semantic properties are mental representations. The mental representation story is perhaps not the only way out of the primacy thesis; but it is an obvious and venerable way.

So, then, how plausible is the mental representation story? Is it an option that can be closed off, thereby protecting the inference from belief holism to meaning holism? This is a question over which a lot of philosophical ink has already been spilled; for present purposes, we restrict ourselves to replying to a couple of objections that we frequently hear.

First, it's plausible that using mental representation theory to avoid the primacy thesis depends on assuming a naturalistic semantics for the mental representations. Their semantic evaluability will have to be grounded in some nonintentional (presumably mind/world) relations: resemblance relations if one follows Hume, causal/nomological relations if one follows Dretske. Philosophers who agree with Quine that "Brentano was right about the irreducibility of . . . intentional [/semantic] discourse" (Quine, *Pursuit of Truth*, p. 71) will take a dim view of the prospects. (Davidson actually offers an a priori argument for irreducibility (see "Mental events"); but that argument can't be invoked here since it has the holism of the intentional as a premise.)

Reply: We are glad to leave this point moot, if only for the following reason: it doesn't *seem* that Intentional Realism could be squared with Brentano's thesis anyhow; but if one can't be a Realist about the intentional, it's hard to see why it *matters* whether content is holistic.

Second, it might be objected that, if the bearers of meaning are mental representations in the first instance, then the theory of *interpretation* has no interesting relation to the theory of *content*. After all, mental representations are never, as a matter of fact, objects of anyone's interpretive activity; the de facto objects of interpretive activity are propositional attitudes, speech acts, and the like. Moreover, the content of mental representations is supposed to depend on (say) causal or nomic relations between things-in-the-world and neurological states, to which real interpreters normally have no access and which are inaccessible to radical interpreters by definition.

Reply: We think that the mental representation theorist should simply bite this bullet; indeed, something like this was implicit in the discussion in the preceding chapter. It's plausible, *independent of issues about mental representations*, that there isn't any interesting connection between the epistemological situation of the interpreter and the facts on which content metaphysically depends. This is not, of course, to deny the supervenience of the intentional on physical facts; it's only to deny that the intentional supervenes on physical facts *to which interpreters as such have access*. God knows what mental representations mean; and, no doubt, God is a physicalist. But God has access to neurological and causal (and counterfactual) truths that mere mortal interpreters don't. (As we remarked, in practice even Lewis's radical interpreter is denied access to many of the physical facts. For Lewis's radical interpreter, the "available physical facts" and the "available behavioral facts" turn out to be pretty much the same.)

Nor, of course, does the idea that underived intentional content inheres only in mental representations deny that interpretation really does take place. The claim is just that the semantic properties of the things we interpret (speech acts and intentional attitudes) are derivative from the semantic properties of hidden things (hidden, that is, from us but not from God), hence that the inferences on which interpretation depends are quite generally contingent. (Inferences from the informant's behavior to his beliefs, for example, must be contingent if the identity of a belief is constituted not by the character of its behavioral expression but by the semantics of the mental representations tokened by the believer; see the discussion in the "Interlude" section of chapter 3.) Interpretation theorists invariably take for granted that what we interpret must be what has intentionality in the first instance. But this assumption is not obvious and wants argument.

Third, there's the following objection: "The strategy is to

129

make the evaluability of propositional attitudes parasitic on the evaluability of mental representations, which, in turn, is assumed not to be holistic. So propositional attitudes aren't holistic qua intentional. But if propositional attitudes are typically functional and functional states are typically holistic, why does it matter whether propositional attitudes are holistic in virtue of their semantic evaluability?"

Reply: Suppose that belief is holistic qua functional but not qua intentional. Now, of course, if there is no analytic/synthetic distinction, there will be no matter of fact about which of the functional properties of beliefs are its defining properties, because there will be no matter of fact about which of the properties of *anything* are its defining properties. But the holism problem about "believes that P" wasn't that we were unable to define it; the problem was *metaphysical*, not semantic.

Perhaps the easiest way of seeing the point is to resuscitate the airfoils. If there are no definitions, then there are no facts about which are the defining properties of airfoils. But, of course, it wouldn't follow that there are no airfoils or that there are no laws about airfoils or that there is no science of airfoils or that there is no principled difference between being an airfoil and not being one. (A striking difference between being an airfoil and not being one is that the former is a property that all and only airfoils can have. Why should this difference not count as principled?) All that follows is that "airfoil" can't be defined. Whereas, if there are no facts about meaning, it's not just that there is no definition of "believes that P"; it's that there is *no such state* as believing that P. Content enters twice, as it were, in the case of "believes that P," but only once in the case of "is an airfoil." The content of the claim that something is a belief (/airfoil) is what a correct definition of "belief" (/"airfoil") would have to preserve. But in the belief case, content also enters in because (prima facie) the objects of beliefs *are* contents (contents are what beliefs *have*). So, if there are no contents, then there are no beliefs.

The moral is that the holism of the functional threatens only

130

the *definability* of intentional states, but the holism of content threatens their very existence. There is no obvious reason why the empirical posits of a respectable theory must be definable; reflection on the history of science suggests that they usually aren't. Existence, by contrast, is plausibly a desideratum sine qua non.

This answers a question that Devitt raises in "Meaning holism." Devitt remarks that irreducibly functional – hence, presumably, holistic – concepts are ubiquitous in the *non*intentional sciences. So why, he asks, should psychologists care if beliefs prove to be holistic? The answer is that you can have functionalism about X's without functional *definitions* of X's (for example, you can have it as a metaphysical doctrine about the supervenience basis for being X). So functionalism *as such* does not require that there be semantic facts. Intentional Realism, however, does, since if there are no semantic facts, there can be no intentional states. And, as we keep seeing, meaning holism is widely taken to be a lemma on the way towards eliminativism about the semantic.

Finally, various things that Davidson and Lewis have said suggest the following sort of objection. Since the semantics of mental representation is supposed to be atomistic, it follows that intentional attribution as such is *not* constrained by constitutive principles like the rationality principle. But this can't be right; to allow, for example, the attribution of arbitrarily irrational propositional attitudes would be to "change the subject"; it wouldn't *be* intentional states that such ascriptions attribute. To put it the other way around, if we find ourselves ascribing contents to Karl in a way that violates the rationality principle, we *thereupon* revise our estimate of the content of Karl's mental states.

First reply: If this is to cut any ice, it had better be more than an epistemological point; the point had better be that even God would revise his content attributions rather than violate rationality. Is this metaphysical claim backed by more than a brute exercise of modal intuition?

Second reply: Let's suppose that the point *is* metaphysical and not just epistemological. Still, it does *not* follow from the atomistic account of the semantics of mental representation that rationality principles can be flouted in *attitude* attribution. We agree (for purposes of argument) that you can't both believe P and believe not-P, and that you can't both wish it were the case that P and believe that it's the case that P, and so forth. Indeed, we're prepared to agree (again for purposes of argument) that these principles are *constitutive* of believing, wishing, and the like, so that further argument that radical interpretation must respect them would be otiose. But what follows? Not that a creature can't be in simultaneous intentional states, one of which has the intentional object *that P* and the other of which has the intentional object *that not-P*. All that follows is that, if a creature is simultaneously in two such states, then *it can't be that both of them are states of belief.* (Maybe P is something the creature believes, and not-P is something it would prefer.) Similarly, if a creature is in two intentional states both of which have the object that P, then it can't be that one of these states is a desire and the other a belief. And so forth.

As far as we can tell, nothing in mental representation theory conflicts with this. Mental representation theory requires that rationality constraints like "not both P and not-P as propositional objects" are associated with the conditions for belief and not with the conditions for content per se. Well, there must be *some* constraints on the attribution of each type of propositional attitude *over and above* those that derive from constraints on content attribution; otherwise all the attitudes would be the same.

We're almost done. But before we conclude this discussion, we want to pick up a thread that was left dangling in the Preface. We remarked there that a rather surprising number of philosophers with whom we've discussed these matters take the view that semantic holism really doesn't require *any* arguments; that it is, in fact, just *obviously* true. We find it hard to accept this claim at face value. As remarked above, it only became obvious that semantic holism is obvious quite recently; it wasn't obvious to Plato, Aristotle, Descartes, Locke, Berkeley, Mill, Russell, the early Wittgenstein, or many other philosophers whose intuitions about what is obvious we are inclined to respect. Anyhow, we are now in a position to offer a diagnosis.

We've seen that, if the failure of the a/s distinction is once granted, a key issue about holism is whether semantic properties are intrinsically anatomic (that is, whether punctate minds and languages are possible even in principle). Now many philosophers take it as just self-evident that belief is anatomic. The reason they do is that they take it as just self-evident that beliefs have to be "systematic"; that nothing would count as Jones believing that aRb unless Jones were the kind of creature that can entertain the belief that bRa; that nothing could count as Jones believing that $P \to Q$ unless Jones were the kind of creature that could entertain the belief that $Q \to P$, that $P \to P$, and so forth. (See, for example, the discussion of the "generality constraint" in Evans, *Varieties of Reference*, pp. 100–5.) But, of course, if belief is intrinsically systematic, then it is intrinsically anatomic; and if belief is intrinsically anatomic, then a key premise on the way to holism is secured.

Now modal intuitions about these matters are actually a little insecure. (What a surprise!) For every philosopher who claims that it's true a priori that beliefs are systematic, you can find at least one philosopher (and at least six connectionists) who claim that it isn't even true empirically that beliefs are systematic. (For discussion, see the flurry of papers provoked by Fodor and Pylyshyn, "Connectionism and cognitive architecture: a critical analysis"; Fodor and Pylyshyn claimed, in effect, that systematicity of belief is metaphysically contingent but nomologically necessary for higher animals.) We do not propose to wade in this; suffice it to remark that even if one grants as self-evident the modal intuition that belief is anatomic, the most that follows is that *belief* is ipso facto holistic. Barring an argument for the primacy thesis, nothing would follow about the holism of semantic evaluability as such.[12] So you do need an argument for meaning holism, even if you don't need an argument for belief holism.

So, then, to conclude: Lewis's argument that charity is a constituent of belief attribution is just that it follows from our concept of belief that charity is a constituent of belief attribution. The up side of this sort of strategy is that it gives the opponent so little room to maneuver. The down side is the danger that the best you get is a Pyrrhic victory. Suppose it is analytic of *belief* that no creature has any beliefs unless it has mostly true beliefs (or mostly rational beliefs or whatever). Very well, then; if the propositional attitudes we've got are mostly *not* true, it follows that they aren't beliefs. But so what? Barring a defense of the primacy thesis, it doesn't follow that they aren't propositional attitudes. Perhaps what we've got are *shmeliefs*, propositional attitudes exactly like beliefs in their functional roles, their qualitative contents (if any), and their satisfaction conditions except that they are *not* analytically constrained by the principles of charity. To make the case worse, it might be supposed that it is *nomologically* necessary that *shmeliefs* are mostly true (mostly rational or whatever); you might tell some Darwinian story according to which natural selection would prefer creatures with mostly true *shmeliefs* to creatures with mostly false ones.[13] Then, ceteris paribus, the *only* difference between a creature's having beliefs and its having *shmeliefs* would be that, in the latter case, there are logically possible worlds in which what the creature has are mostly false, and in the former case there aren't. It might thus be really *quite* difficult to tell beliefs and *shmeliefs* apart.

Perhaps the reply would be that there just couldn't be such things as *shmeliefs*. But if this reply is more than dogmatic, it requires argument; and, as the discussion in this chapter has emphasized, the argument it requires is precisely a demonstration that charity necessarily constrains *content* attribution as opposed to *belief* attribution. (From this perspective, what Davidson is doing in his "Radical interpretation" is to be viewed as an attempt to provide this argument – though not, according to the discussion in chapter 3, a successful one.) We repeat what we take to be the bottom line: Assume, if you like, that the principles of charity are holistic; assume, if you like, that the principles of charity constrain the attribution of beliefs. Lacking a convincing defense of the primacy thesis, *meaning holism doesn't follow.*

5

D. C. DENNETT:
MEANING HOLISM AND THE NORMATIVITY OF INTENTIONAL ASCRIPTION (AND A LITTLE MORE ABOUT DAVIDSON)

In a short article called "Mid-term examination: compare and contrast" that epitomizes and concludes his book *The Intentional Stance*, D. C. Dennett provides a sketch of what he views as an emerging Interpretivist consensus in the philosophy of mind. The gist is that Brentano's thesis is true (the intentional is irreducible to the physical) and that it follows from the truth of Brentano's thesis that

> strictly speaking, ontologically speaking, there are no such things as beliefs, desires, or other intentional phenomena. But the intentional idioms are "practically indispensable," and we should see what we can do to make sense of their employment in what Quine called an "essentially dramatic" idiom. . . . Not just brute facts, then, but an element of interpretation . . . must be recognized in any use of the intentional vocabulary. ("Mid-term examination," p. 342)[1]

In this context, "making sense of" intentional idiom is *not* explaining why it should be indispensable if there are no beliefs

137

or desires for it to refer to. Nor is it specifying the truth
conditions of intentional ascriptions; Dennett thinks that,
strictly speaking, no intentional ascriptions can be true. Rather,
the project in "Mid-term examination" and his earlier paper
"Intentional systems" is to make clear the sense in which
intentional attribution inevitably involves "an element of
interpretation." The discussion that follows therefore treats
these two papers together.

Our topic is, of course, meaning holism and not Intentional
Realism; but these issues are connected as Dennett construes
them. It turns out that one way of grasping the "element of
interpretation" in intentional ascription is to recognize the
ineliminable role that principles of charity play. And since
Dennett accepts the usual assumption that such principles are
intrinsically holistic, seeing that intentional ascription is interpretive and seeing that it is holistic are seeing two aspects of the
same thing. In this chapter we will briefly survey some of
Dennett's comments about the Realism/Interpretivism issue;
but our main concern will be with the arguments Dennett offers
for an intrinsic connection between charity principles and
content ascription.

According to Dennett, there are two schools of Interpretivism,
two ways in which one might reveal the element of interpretation
in content ascription. These are Projectivism and Normativism:

> Here two chief rivals have seemed to emerge; one or another
> Normative Principle, according to which one should attribute to
> a creature the propositional attitudes it "ought to have" given its
> circumstances, and one or another Projective Principle, according
> to which one should attribute to a creature the propositional
> attitudes one supposed one would have oneself in those
> circumstances. ("Mid-term examination," p. 343)

The Normative principles will be our main concern; they
include such principles of charity as that *most of* the beliefs
ascribed to a creature are true (a fortiori, that most of them are

coherent) and thus imply the holist thesis that there can be content attribution only where there is a *multiplicity* of beliefs. As we're about to see, it's unclear that there is a correspondingly close connection between Projectivism and holism, so our treatment of Projectivism will be comparatively brief.

PROJECTIVISM

Projectivism can be construed as proposing a first approximation to a theory of the logical form of belief sentences (for discussion, see Stich, *From Folk Psychology to Cognitive Science: The Case Against Belief*). Roughly, "Jones believes that it's raining" is equivalent, in Smith's mouth, to "Jones is in the state that would normally cause me (Smith) to say that it's raining."[2] It is notoriously difficult for this sort of account of belief ascription to get the details right (for example, there are difficulties about paraphrasing sentences that contain indexicals in complements to verbs of propositional attitude); but, for present purposes, we can put these relatively technical problems to one side. We want to suggest just two main criticisms of the Projectivist story, and then we'll return to the holism issues.

First, Projectivism seems hopelessly unable to construe sentences that existentially quantify over the contents of propositional attitudes (as opposed to sentences that actually cite their contents). Consider the following kind of case: Smith's three-year-old hears him prattling on about the analytic/synthetic distinction, and it occurs to the child that Smith must have some beliefs about this distinction that he, the child, does not understand and could not express. On the present analysis, this thought – which intuition might plausibly take to be true – is self-contradictory, since it entails both that Smith is in some state that would normally lead the three-year-old to say that "blah, blah, blah, analytic/synthetic, blah, blah, blah" and that there is no such state.

139

Or consider you and your Twin-earth twin *after* you have noticed that what he calls "water" isn't H_2O and hence that the belief he expresses by uttering the form of words "Water is wet" isn't the belief that water is wet. Perhaps you would like to say that there is nevertheless *some or other* belief that your twin uses that formula to express. But how *can* you say this, knowing, as you do, that the belief he expresses isn't one that it's possible for *you* to entertain? (According to the standard story, you can entertain the belief that your twin uses "Water is wet" to express only if you are causally connected to XYZ – which, by assumption, you aren't.)

So you can't coherently believe that there is something that your twin means by what he says when he utters "Water is wet." It would make *no sense* for you to believe this, given the Projectivist analysis of belief ascriptions. Turnabout is fair play, of course; your twin can use the same considerations to exempt himself from thinking that there is anything *you* mean by *your* utterances of "Water is wet." It would be understandable if you were to find this consequence of Projectivism offensive.

These aren't merely technical difficulties. The problem is that if the Projectivist account of the (putative) interpretive element in belief attribution is right, then what *you* can believe depends on what *your interpreter* can say. But if anything is metaphysically independent of anything, surely your repertoire of potential beliefs is independent of anybody else's repertoire of potential speech acts. There is, no doubt, an "element of interpretation" in talk about mountains; where does the mountain end and the valley begin, after all? But only a megalomaniac could suppose that whether there are mountains depends on whether he can say that there are.

The second objection is that Projectivism can't *explain* the putative "element of interpretation" in intentional ascription; on the contrary, Projectivism must *presuppose* it in order to count as a species of Interpretivism.

Consider the following line of inquiry. Why isn't the Projectivist actually a *Realist* about the intentional, albeit a

Realist who disagrees with the usual assumptions about the polyadicity of propositional attitude predicates? That is, why isn't a Projectivist just a Realist who thinks that believing (and the like) is a *four*-place relation (between a creature, its mental state, the propositional object of its mental state, and an interpreter), as opposed to the more conventional view that it's a *three*-place relation (between a creature, its mental state, and the propositional object of its mental state)? Notice that, *so far*, there is no incompatibility between Realism and this view of the polyadicity of intentional ascriptions.[3]

Relativizing intentional ascriptions to an interpreter doesn't, *in and of itself*, impugn their objectivity. For, prima facie, there is a fact of the matter about whether Jones *is* in the sort of state that would normally cause Smith to say that it's raining; and if he is, then, according to the Projectivist analysis, Smith's claim that Jones believes that it's raining is just straightforwardly *true*.[4]

The obvious reply would be that there is no fact of the matter – that it is a question for interpretation – as to whether the state that Jones is in *is* the same state (is a token of the same state type) as the one that normally causes Smith to say that it's raining. (Or, equivalently for these purposes, there is no fact of the matter – it's a question for interpretation – whether what Jones does when he's in that state is to count as saying what Smith does when Smith utters the form of words "It's raining.") This does make Projectivism a species of Interpretivism; but it also gives up on the idea that intentional ascriptions are interpretive *because* they are projective. On the contrary, what we've just seen is that the order of analysis must go the other way around: only when it is given an Interpretivist reading does Projectivism fail to represent attitude ascriptions as fully factual. But then, a fortiori, it can't be that the Projectivist analysis per se accounts for the "element of interpretation" in intentional ascription. From the point of view of our concerns, the relevant moral is that you can't argue from Projectivism to holism via an inference from Projectivism to Interpretivism.

That is, the argument *Projectivism* → *Interpretivism* → *holism* is no good; the first step fails, even if the second is valid.

So much for the discussion of Projectivism. We turn now to the consideration of Normativism, the other form that Interpretivism can take according to "Mid-term examination."

NORMATIVISM

Normativism is the claim that the attitudes that an interpreter attributes to a creature are constrained by the requirement that, in general, the creature should be represented as having the beliefs it ought to have and the desires whose satisfaction would be in its interest. There are, presumably, two sorts of reasons for supposing that Normativism is a species of Interpretivism. For one thing, by definition, Normativists believe that some of the constitutive principles of content attribution is *normative*; and, at least on some views of what normativity amounts to, this would all by itself suffice to make such attributions not fully factual. Second, as we understand Dennett, it is central to his argument for Interpretivism that (at least some of) the normative principles constitutive of content assignment are idealized and heuristic; that they are *not* really satisfied by flesh and blood intentional systems. It is because the conditions for intentional ascription require that we treat fallible creatures *as if* they were fully rational that "an element of interpretation" enters in when intentional states are ascribed.

We propose to question both the argument from Normativism to Interpretivism and the argument that Normative principles are inextricably involved in content attribution. First, however, *which* normative principles? Dennett's view on this doesn't differ in essential ways from the picture of the constraints on interpretation that Davidson and Lewis endorse. There are, however, some differences in detail which we might as well mention, just to keep the record straight.

142

Consider the following principles.

1. The truth principle: Necessarily, intentional ascriptions represent a creature's beliefs as mostly true (by the interpreter's lights).

2. The coherence principle: Necessarily, intentional ascriptions represent a creature's beliefs as mostly coherent (by the interpreter's lights).

3. The closure principle: Necessarily, if a creature is represented as believing P and P entails Q, then the creature must be represented as believing Q.

4. The probity principle: Necessarily, intentional systems mostly desire what it would be good for them to have.

Our reading is that Davidson, Lewis, and Dennett all endorse principles 1 and 2. Dennett also endorses principle 3 as an appropriate idealization governing intentional ascription (see his "Intentional systems," p. 11; "True believers," p. 21; "Making sense of ourselves," pp. 94–5), though it is a principle that we have no reason to believe that either Lewis or Davidson would subscribe to. However, Dennett's argument for principle 3 serves equally well as an argument for principle 2; and the latter is clearly the more plausible option. Similarly, Dennett's argument for principle 1 also serves as an argument for principle 4, a principle that he (like Davidson and Lewis) explicitly endorses. Having said all this, it simplifies the exposition to ignore these distinctions except where they matter. We propose henceforth to do so.

Dennett's Evolutionary Argument for the Truth Principle

What shows that content ascription is required to represent intentional systems as believers (/tellers) of truths? We've seen that Davidson proposes a transcendental argument for this

143

principle and that Lewis holds it to be implicit in our concept of a person. Dennett proposes an evolutionary argument; or, at least, he seems to. Here we must turn to "Intentional systems":

> Suppose we travel to a distant planet and find it inhabited by things moving about its surface, multiplying, decaying, apparently reacting to events in the environment, but otherwise as unlike human beings as you please. Can we make intentional predictions and explanations of their behavior? If we have reason to suppose that a process of natural selection has been in effect, then we can be assured that the population we observe have been selected in virtue of their design: They will respond to at least some of the more common event-types in this environment in ways that are normally appropriate. ("Intentional systems," p. 8)

Dennett later adds that

> there is no point in ascribing beliefs to a system unless the beliefs ascribed are in general appropriate to the environment, and the system responds appropriately to the beliefs. An eccentric expression of this would be: The capacity to believe would have no survival value unless it were the capacity to believe truths. (Ibid., p. 17)

Let's, for the moment, ignore the caveat "eccentric"; we'll come back to it presently. Suppose that the doctrine is simply that, on the one hand, since our cognitive capacities have evolved, they must have been selected and that, on the other hand, only a cognitive system that generally endorses truths would *be* selected, since no other kind of cognitive system would have survival value. So, all this being the case, the truth principle must hold of our beliefs.

Problems with Dennett's Evolutionary Argument for the Truth Principle

The evolutionary assumptions required to run this sort of argument are, in our view, very dubious; that a system is selected does not require that all its subsystems have survival value; some of them may be vestigial.[5] That a disposition to believe mostly truths is ipso facto at a competitive advantage with respect to any and every capacity to believe mostly falsehoods is, in fact, not obvious (for discussion, see Stich, *The Fragmentation of Reason*). However, let's put these issues to one side. For even if the empirical assumptions of the evolutionary argument were impeccable, it doesn't appear to yield either of the conclusions that Dennett wants. What Dennett wants is that Normativism should entail Interpretivism and that principles like principles 1 and 4 should be *necessary* (they should hold of intentional systems as such). It is, to put it mildly, not obvious that either consequence follows from the evolutionary story.

It would look to be a matter of fact whether a creature has an evolutionary history; and it would also look to be a matter of fact whether part of the evolutionary story about the creature is that it is at a competitive advantage in virtue of the character of its cognitive capacities. But if these are matters of fact, and if being selected for one's cognitive capacities is, as Dennett apparently maintains, at least a *sufficient* condition for being mostly a believer of truths,[6] then it would seem to be a matter of fact – and not a matter of interpretation – whether *we* are believers of mostly truths. Epistemologists should be able to settle the issue of skepticism once and for all by consulting the fossil record.

It is, in short, puzzling how Dennett thinks that an appeal to the Darwinian theory – which is, after all, a causal story about the *mechanisms of speciation* – could reveal an "element of interpretation" in content ascription. Interpretivism is, inter alia, the view that, strictly speaking, we don't really have beliefs and desires. But, one supposes, what a creature *doesn't really have* can't help it much in its struggle for survival. It is for exactly this reason that, unlike Dennett, most people who take an evolutionary line on intentionality are correspondingly Realist (not to say reductionist) about content. (See Millikan

145

and Dretske for two examples.) Qua Darwinists, they suppose that there's a matter of fact about what selection history a creature has and about what mechanisms served to mediate its history of selection. So they are required to suppose also that organisms can't be selected for believing truths unless they *do* believe truths.

Dennett himself is apparently sensitive to this sort of point; it's the burden of the caveat "eccentric" in the passage quoted above, which proceeds as follows:

> An eccentric expression of [the evolutionary argument for principle 1] would be: The capacity to believe would have no survival value unless it were a capacity to believe truths. What is eccentric and potentially misleading about this is that it hints at the picture of a species "trying on" a faculty giving rise to beliefs most of which were false, having its inutility demonstrated, and abandoning it. A system might "experiment" by mutation in any number of inefficacious systems, but none of these systems would deserve to be called belief systems presumably because of their defects, their nonrationality, and hence a false belief system is a conceptual impossibility. ("Intentional systems," p. 17)

It's not clear to us what Dennett takes to be the bottom line; but it looks as though it may not be evolution after all that he sees as underwriting the truth principle. Maybe Dennett's position is really the same as Lewis's; namely, that it's just *analytic* that a creature's beliefs are mostly true (a system of mostly false propositional attitudes wouldn't "deserve to be called a belief system"). However, this doesn't really give Dennett the conclusion he wants either, since, as we pointed out when we discussed Lewis (see especially the last several paragraphs of chapter 4), it invites the rejoinder, "Very well, then, it's not beliefs we have after all; what we've actually got is *shmeliefs*. But *shmeliefs* are pretty good; in fact, they're indistinguishable from beliefs except that *shmelief* attribution is not controlled by the truth principle."[7] What Dennett needs to avoid this reply is an argument that *shmeliefs* are conceptually (or metaphysically) impossible; in particular, that a state can't be *intentional* (can't have conditions of semantic evaluation) unless it satisfies the charity principles. This argument is surely *not* provided by the claim that "Beliefs are mostly true" is analytic. At this point the relevant considerations are the ones we examined in the preceding chapter (q.v.).

In some of his recent papers (see especially "Cognitive ethology: hunting for bargains or a wild goose chase?" and "Evolution, error, and intentionality") Dennett offers a rather different line of thought that may be intended to meet this sort of criticism. Apparently the idea is that while, on the one hand, it is indeed the biological function of cognitive mechanisms to fix true beliefs (so a system of false beliefs is an evolutionary impossibility, so the truth principle must be true), yet, on the other hand, ascriptions of biological function themselves involve adopting the intentional stance *towards the evolutionary process* (towards "Mother Nature," as Dennett likes to say) and must therefore exhibit "an element of interpretation" which our ascriptions of intentional states to creatures other than Mother Nature then inherit. Although "attributions of intentional states to us cannot be sustained . . . without appeal to 'what Mother Nature had in mind' " ("Evolution, error, and intentionality," p. 314), it is also true that "Mother Nature doesn't commit herself explicitly and objectively to *any* [sic] functional attributions; all such attributions depend on the mind-set of the intentional stance, in which we assume optimality in order to interpret what we find" (ibid., p. 320). So, apparently, the hermeneutic status of intentional ascriptions (to us) derives from the correspondingly hermeneutic status of ascriptions of biological functions (to mental states), which in turn derives from the hermeneutic status of intentional ascriptions (to Mother Nature). We wouldn't want to insist that this story is circular; but nor would we want to insist that it's not.

In any event, we find it very puzzling. For one thing, there's the point we made above, which does seem to us to be pretty decisive. If there *are* no beliefs and desires, then, a fortiori, there can't be anything that beliefs and desires were selected for, and there can't be any biological (or other) functions that beliefs and desires perform. No doubt interpretation can do a lot – hermeneutics is everywhere these days. Maybe interpretation can somehow determine teleology or selectional history (though with such friends, Darwin hardly needs enemies). But surely interpretation can't bestow a teleology or a selectional history *on things that don't exist*. That there is nothing that the unicorn's horn was selected for *follows from* there not having been any unicorns; there is no place for interpretation to insert a wedge, because there are no unicorns (a fortiori, no unicorn horns) for an interpreter to take a stance towards. It's one thing to claim that what *is* is text; it's a bit much to claim that what isn't is too.

Second, we're not really clear what the doctrine of Interpretivism in biology is supposed to amount to. One would have thought that either evolutionary biology does have entailments of the form "(trait) *t* was selected for performing (function) *f*," or it doesn't. In either case, it's hard to see how our adopting the intentional stance towards evolution (or towards Mother Nature) is supposed to help. It's mysterious, in biology as elsewhere, either how you could make facts out of stances or how stances could make facts disappear.

Perhaps an analogy will clarify the situation. Suppose it's suggested that the *ecological* function of forest cover is to prevent the erosion of topsoil; *that*, according to the suggestion, is what forest cover is *for*. (You can imagine the claim being spelled out by reference to counterfactuals, among which "no forest cover → no topsoil" would presumably be prominent.) Well, either ecology does underwrite a notion of function or it doesn't. If it does, then it's just a matter of fact what forest cover is for; but if it doesn't, we can't improve the situation by adopting the "intentional stance" towards erosion.

No doubt we could tell a fairy tale according to which Father Erosion wants to wash away the topsoil and the Tree Fairy wants to stop him. This might be useful for mnemonic purposes or to amuse small children. But, surely, our telling this story (or not telling it) can't be what determines whether there are ecological functions. If ecology doesn't have consequences of the form "The function of x is f" *independent* of the story about Father Erosion and the Tree Fairy, then there straightforwardly *isn't* anything that forest cover is for; if it does, then there straightforwardly *is* something that forest cover is for. Either way, our decision to adopt the intentional stance towards erosion affects the ontological status of ecological functions *not one whit*. How could it? It is *stance-independent*, after all, that there is no Father Erosion. So adding the story to our ecology can't increase the number of claims that our ecology warrants (a true proposition conjoined with a false one warrants only the inferences that the true proposition does). But if the story about Father Erosion doesn't legitimize interpretivism about functions in ecology, why, exactly, does the story about Mother Nature legitimize interpretivism about functions in biology?[8] See how the gods punish Instrumentalism: refuse to distinguish theories from fables, and soon you can't distinguish fables from theories.

The moral still seems to be that if intentional ascription is to be understood in terms of evolutionary explanation, then it's an empirical rather than a conceptual question whether the truth principle holds. (We of course reserve the right to assert this hypothetical and deny its antecedent.)

Dennett's Argument for the Closure Principle

Preliminary note: If you have an argument that a creature's beliefs are mostly true, then, of course, you have an argument that they are mostly coherent; so the satisfaction of principle 1 entails the satisfaction of principle 2. The satisfaction of principle 1 does *not*, however, entail the satisfaction of principle 3 (the closure principle). Later in this chapter, the distinction between principles 2 and 3 will be important. However, as we remarked above, the argument that Dennett gives for principle

149

3 will do equally well as an argument for principle 2, and we will assume that he intends it to cover both.

Dennett's argument for the closure principle is given in "Intentional systems." It goes like this:

> The assumption that something is an intentional system is the assumption that it is rational; that is, one gets nowhere with the assumption that entity x has beliefs p, q, r . . . unless one also supposes that x believes what follows from p, q, r . . . otherwise there is no way of ruling out the prediction that x will, in the face of its beliefs p, q, r . . . do something utterly stupid, and, if we cannot rule out *that* prediction, we will have acquired no predictive power at all. ("Intentional systems," pp. 10–11)

(Notice that the argument goes through equally well to show that an intentional system that believes P must not also believe not-P; in effect, the coherence principle.) We take this passage to intend a transcendental argument according to which the closure principle is presupposed by the very possibility of intentional predictions. Accordingly, *the argument fails if there is any way to warrant intentional predictions without presupposing closure.*

Problems with Dennett's Argument for the Closure Principle

Much of what needs to be said about Dennett's argument for closure has already been remarked upon in the literature (see Fodor, "Three cheers for propositional attitudes"; Stich, "Dennett on intentional systems"; and Dennett, "Making sense of ourselves"). For example, it seems unclear that anything like *perfect* closure (/coherence) is needed to meet the requirement that *some* predictive power be generated by belief/desire ascriptions.[9] We'd get *some* predictive value out of belief ascription even if it only worked, say, 87 percent of the time that a creature that believes ($P \rightarrow Q$ and P) believes Q. But if

150

getting predictive power from belief/desire psychology doesn't really depend on assuming *flawless* rationality, then perhaps there is, as a matter of fact, enough closure (/coherence) around to make intentional ascription predictive. In which case, intentional ascription would rest upon rationality assumptions that are (not merely heuristic but) *true*. In which case, how would Normativism argue for Interpretivism?

Also, it seems just not to be true that successful prediction "from the intentional stance" always requires that we assume rationality. There are, for example, lots of cases in which we successfully predict someone's behavior on the assumption that he will *not* notice some consequence of his beliefs and desires (the chess player who is reliably a sucker for a knight fork and the like). It may be argued that such predictive successes can operate only "against a background" of presumed rationality; but this needs to be *argued*, and we have, as yet, no hint as to how the argument would go. Clearly, we must have (what Dennett's account doesn't give us) *some* story about how the prediction of counter-rational behavior is even *possible*. Maybe it will turn out that the strategies that underlie predictive successes in these apparently exceptional cases will prove to be perfectly general when they are properly analyzed – hence that assumptions of rationality are never *essential* to intentional prediction. Let's, therefore, actually consider such cases.

Everybody knows that the moon reliably looks larger when it's seen as being on the horizon. It *may* be that this phenomenon has a "cognitive" explanation in terms of (unconscious) judgments, inferences, and the like; but also it may be that it hasn't. The psychologists themselves aren't sure. Clearly, in any event, nobody has detailed knowledge of the presumed underlying inferences, so nobody knows how much closure and coherence they do (or don't) actually exhibit. Yet we confidently predict that we and our friends and relations (and, for that matter, absolute strangers) will be subject to the illusion. And surely this is a prediction "from the intentional stance"; it's ineliminably committed to intentional contexts like "looks to be

. . . . when seen as . . ." How, then, are such predictions possible?

The question answers itself; the phenomenon is that the moon *reliably* looks larger when it's on the horizon. The generalization is lawlike in that it is confirmed by its instances, supports counterfactuals, and so forth. And, given access to a *law* that relates the apparent size of the moon to its apparent position, we don't need to appeal to principles of rationality to predict that if Smith sees the moon as on the horizon, then he will see it as oversized.

Similarly for the guy who is suckered by knight forks. Heaven knows why he keeps falling for them; there's clearly *something* wrong with the way he plans his moves. But we don't have to know *what*'s wrong or *how much* is wrong – in particular, we don't have to know whether, or to what extent, his planning is rational – in order to predict that he'll fall for our traps; all we have to know is that his disposition to get suckered is reliable.

The long and the short of it would seem to be that you can predict behavior from the intentional stance without committing yourself on closure and coherence *so long as there are lawful connections between the subject's behaviors and his intentional states*. We've been illustrating this point by examples of illusions and incapacities, but in fact it's entirely general. If there's a law that makes being in intentional state A nomologically sufficient for being in intentional (and/or behavioral) state B, then, given the knowledge that a creature *is* in state A, you can predict that it will (come to) be in state B, *whether or not the transition from A to B is rational*. The upshot is that the argument that infers charity about rationality from the presuppositions for intentional prediction fails because it *begs the question against there being intentional laws*.[10]

Of course, many philosophers who think that charity about rationality constrains intentional ascription a priori doubt that there *are* intentional laws. We have nothing to say against their doubting this except that they are in need of an argument, and that, whatever this argument is, it mustn't itself depend on assuming that charity is constitutive of intentional ascription (as does, for example, the famous argument that Davidson gives in "Mental events"). In the present context, that assumption would be merely question begging.

Here's another way to put the point. At first thought, it seems perfectly natural to suppose that if rational processes do enter into the intentional etiology of a creature's behavior – if, for example, decision-theoretic calculations bridge the gap between believing P and wanting Q, on the one hand, and performing such and such an action, on the other – then a prediction that runs from premises about the creature's intentional states to conclusions about its behavioral outcomes must postulate that these rational processes transpire. But, on second thought, this surely isn't so. *The Times* shows up on the doorstep every morning; and presumably there is a decision-theoretic story about the newsboy, according to which, his bringing it maximizes his expected utility. But I don't need to postulate the newsboy's decision-theoretic rationality in order to predict the arrival of tomorrow's copy from the intentional stance. All I need is that his intention to deliver the paper is reliable and that, ceteris paribus, people reliably do what they intend to do.[11]

In fact, in this sort of case the argument typically goes the other way around. It's only *because* I have independent evidence that the newsboy reliably brings the paper that I'm prepared to infer that, probably, there is some decision-theoretic calculation according to which it is rational for him to do so; in fact, I've never actually inquired into his motives. *Pace* Dennett, rationality assumptions typically don't enter as presuppositions of intentional predictions, but rather as part of the story we tell when we start to wonder what mental processes could underlie the reliable intentional generalizations by which everyone's experience tells him that behavior is subsumed.

We want to emphasize that we aren't denying that the mental processes that mediate the production of behavior are, in fact, typically rational; or that, if you want to *reconstruct the etiology* of behavior, you must explicate these rational processes.

153

Our point is just that you don't, in general, have to reconstruct the etiology of phenomena in order to predict them.[12] The question "What do you need to assume to get a true theory of the etiology of X's?" and the question "What do you need to assume to get true predictions about X's?" needn't have the same answers. But if this is so, then the possibility of intentional prediction wouldn't have to depend on assuming rationality even if intentional etiological processes actually were fully rational. A fortiori, the possibility of intentional prediction doesn't have to depend on *counterfactual* assumptions of rationality. As long as there are intentional laws and as long as the guy who is doing the predicting has access to the intentional laws that control the behaviors he is trying to predict, people are free to be as crazy as they like, compatible with their behavior being predictable from the intentional stance.

Here's where we take it that things stand. Dennett's argument against Intentional Realism depends on his argument for Interpretivism. His argument for Interpretivism depends on showing that either Normativism or Projectivism (or both) are true; but since Projectivism is hopeless, the argument depends, de facto, on showing that Normativism is true. Dennett's argument for Normativism depends, in turn, on the argument for charity. The argument for charity depends on showing that at least one of the rationality principles is ineliminably involved in content ascription. The argument for the rationality principles is either evolutionary, or it's a transcendental argument about the conditions that have to be satisfied for behavioral prediction from the intentional stance to be possible. But the evolutionary argument yields the wrong conclusion (it makes the relation between interpretation and charity *contingent*), and the transcendental argument begs the question against intentional laws.

So far as we can tell, for all that has been shown, one might as well be an atomistic Intentional Realist.

A LITTLE MORE ABOUT DAVIDSON

We have now, in effect, concluded the discussion that started with chapter 3, where we undertook to survey a family of arguments all of which seek to infer the holism of the intentional from the premise that certain (intrinsically holistic) principles of charity are essentially involved in content attribution. What distinguishes the members of this family is primarily the kind of argument that is offered to support the claim that the involvement of charity in content attribution is indeed essential. We've considered different, though overlapping, proposals by Davidson, Lewis, and Dennett, none of which has proved to be fully convincing. Our view is therefore that, if the case for meaning holism depends on the case for charity, then the case for meaning holism has yet to be made out.

Before we turn to consider other sources of holistic doctrine, however, we want to tidy up one or two loose ends. A question arises about the *independence* of some of the charity principles. This question is of some interest for the holism issues and for the general theory of radical interpretation. And it is of general philosophical interest because, in a surprising way, it ties the issues about interpretation to traditional epistemological issues about skepticism. We propose a brief excursus on this topic; this investigation will serve to recapitulate some of the main ideas of the last three chapters.

Consider, then, the relations between principle 1 (truth) and principle 2 (coherence) on p. 143. Clearly, they aren't independent; you can't have beliefs that are mostly true without having beliefs that are mostly coherent. This means, of course, that if someone has a (for example, transcendental) argument that principle 1 is constitutive of interpretation, he gets it for free that principle 2 is too. In particular, Dennett doesn't need *both* the evolution argument (which is supposed to give him the truth principle) *and* the prediction argument (which is supposed to give him the coherence principle) unless he really is committed to the closure

155

principle. (Principle 3, unlike principle 2, is *not* entailed by principle 1; it's perfectly possible to have beliefs that are all true (a fortiori, mostly true) without their being closed under the consequence relation.)

All this seems perfectly straightforward. What's really surprising is a recent suggestion of Davidson's that principles 1 and 2 are, in a certain sense, *equivalent*; that not only does it hold that if your beliefs are mostly true, then they are mostly coherent, but also that if "many of our beliefs cohere with many others," then "many of our beliefs are true" ("A coherence theory of truth and knowledge," p. 307). This has, as Davidson emphasizes, striking consequences for epistemology; if it is right, then the refutation of skepticism requires only the weak premise of belief coherence.

To understand the argument that is supposed to lead to this conclusion, we must return to the notion of radical interpretation that was under discussion in chapter 3. According to this notion, (1) a "radical interpreter" is defined to be someone who faces the problem of content attribution with only knowledge of the correlation between his informant's local circumstances and the sentences that he holds true in them (together with general principles of warranted deductive and nondemonstrative inference); and (2) it's a metaphysical, necessary truth that any content-bearing state can be interpreted under these epistemological conditions. Suppose, contrary to the discussion in chapter 3, that all this should be granted.

It follows, Davidson says, that "from the interpreter's point of view . . . [there is no] . . . way he can discover the speaker to be largely wrong about the world." The argument is that the interpreter has no alternative but to "interpret . . . sentences held true . . . according to the events and objects in the outside world that cause the sentence to be held true" ("A coherence theory of truth," p. 317). In effect, Davidson holds that the radical interpreter's strategy must be, first, to find out what causes the informant to say what he does and then to identify the truth conditions of the informant's utterances (more or less comprehensively) with their causes.[13] But, Davidson concludes, if the radical interpreter does proceed this way, he can't but accept that, in general, the informant's token-reflexive sentences are true (by the interpreter's lights).

Davidson is on to a very important point, and one that can be detached from the radical interpretation framework and stated quite generally: Insofar as your semantic theory claims that a symbol has the truth conditions it does *because* it has a certain causal history that it does, then your theory will commit you to holding that if a token of that symbol has the right kind of etiology, it must ipso facto be true.[14] If, for example, you run a semantics according to which its tokens being caused (in the right way) by cats being on mats is what makes it the case that *"The cat is on the mat" is true iff the cat is on the mat*, then you must hold that a token of "The cat is on the mat" that *is* caused (in the right way) by a cat's being on a mat is ipso facto true.

However, though this point is of considerable interest for the illumination it sheds on causal theories of content, it does not, so far as we can see, have the epistemological consequences that Davidson claims. For it is unclear that a causal theory must identify the truth conditions of a sentence S with the conditions that *actually* cause S to be tokened. It might be just as good – in fact, it might be even better – to identify the truth conditions of S with what *would* cause it to be tokened *were it the case that* . . .[15] (Notice that none of the *actual* causes of the tokens of a type need satisfy the subjunctive condition.) This is, in fact, the way that causal theories do proceed when they invoke nomological connections – rather than causal histories – as the metaphysical basis of content. What makes "cat" mean *cat*, according to such theories, is *not* that it *is* caused by cats, but only that it's nomologically necessary that it *would* be caused by cats under some or other circumstances that the theory is obliged to specify.[16] (For examples of this sort of theory, see Dretske, *Knowledge and the Flow of Information*; Stampe, "Towards a causal theory of linguistic representation"; and Fodor, "A theory of content"; etc.)

However, this looks to undermine Davidson's anti-skeptical argument. What is required to refute the skeptic is not that there are circumstances such that *if they obtained*, what you believe would be true; skeptics are quite content to concede *that*. What's required, rather, is a demonstration that most of what you believe *is* true in the circumstances that *actually* obtain. The story according to which it is *subjunctive* etiology that determines content is compatible with all your *actual* beliefs (/utterances) being false.

It appears that Davidson needs, not just a transcendental argument for the causal theory of content (see n. 13), but, in particular, a transcendental argument for that version of the causal theory that identifies content with *actual*, as opposed to *subjunctive*, causal history. It may be that Davidson thinks he has such an argument. For, he might say, if it were not the *actual* etiology of token-reflexive sentences that determines their truth conditions, radical interpretation would not be guaranteed to be possible. The point would be that, although it's stipulated that the radical interpreter has access to information about what causes the informant's token-reflexive sentences to be held true in *this* world, it's not obvious that he has access to the etiologies of the informant's utterances in arbitrary other, nomologically possible worlds. And, according to the kind of causal theory we're envisioning, it is these counterfactual causal histories that the truth conditions of the informant's utterances may exhaustively depend on.[17]

This, however, brings us back to the question we raised in chapter 3. Why should it be supposed that radical interpretation is possible; specifically that the radical interpreter's epistemological situation is of any metaphysical interest for semantics? No doubt, supervenience requires that God can know the causal facts on which (by assumption) content depends; but that's alright since, we may assume, God knows not only the actual causal histories of things but everything there is to know about their counterfactual causal histories in all nomologically possible worlds. In short, nothing will do what Davidson wants –

namely, guarantee that the determinants of content are accessible to the radical interpreter – except an argument that content of an expression is determined by the causal history of its tokens in *this* world; and, so far, no such argument is forthcoming.

Suppose, however, that for (and only for) the sake of the argument, we assume that the radical interpreter's epistemological position does have a privileged metaphysical standing. It looks as if all that follows from this is that the sentences the informant holds true must be true *by the interpreter's lights.* Here's how the argument goes. On the assumptions currently operative, the interpreter is not allowed to suppose that "The cat is on the mat" means that the cat is on the mat unless he is prepared to accept that cats are generally on mats in environments in which "The cat is on the mat" tokens are held true by his informant. But, one might suppose, it's always possible that the interpreter should have *mis*identified the causes on which the informant's holding-trues are contingent – in which case, the interpreter might operate on the principle of making the informant's judgments true by the interpreter's lights, and yet, for all we know, the informant might be saying something that is actually false. It looks as if the principle of charity leaves open the possibility of *folie à deux* (which is, of course, just what the skeptic always thought). This is because, although the principle of charity can require the interpreter to make what the informant says come out true-so-far-as-the-interpreter-can-tell, it can't require that the interpreter make what the informant says come out true *tout court.* The latter injunction can't be obeyed for the same sort of reason that the injunction to believe only truths can't be obeyed.

Davidson is quite aware of this problem; he offers a curious argument in reply.

> It cannot be the rule [that what the informant says, though true by the interpreter's lights, is nevertheless false]. For imagine for a moment an interpreter who is omniscient about the world, and about what does and would cause a speaker to assent to any

159

sentence in his (potentially unlimited) repertoire. The omniscient interpreter, using the same method as the fallible interpreter, finds the fallible speaker largely consistent and correct. By his own standards, of course, but since these are objectively correct, the fallible speaker is seen to be largely correct by objective standards. ("A coherence theory of truth," p. 317)

So skepticism is finally refuted.

It seems to us that this line of argument, if seriously pursued, would provide a reductio ad absurdum of the notion that radical interpretation should proceed by the exercise of charity. For the following, surely, is necessarily true: *If an omniscient being interprets my utterances (Ibeliefs) so that they come out true by his lights, then it will misinterpret me whenever I say (Ibelieve) something false.* In consequence, it is precisely the omniscient interpreter who must *not* construe my beliefs as generally true by his lights (unless I am omniscient too – which I'm not). It is true that "the omniscient interpreter, using the same method as the fallible interpreter, finds the fallible speaker largely consistent and correct." But so much the worse for the idea of the omniscient interpreter using the same method as the fallible interpreter. The following, after all, is a truism: To precisely the extent to which a speaker is fallible, it is a *mis*construal to interpret that speaker as "consistent and correct." So, to put it in a nutshell, the omniscient interpreter who employs the method of charity to understand a fallible speaker will perforce arrive at false beliefs about the fallible speaker's false beliefs. Since this outcome is incoherent – the omniscient interpreter *can't* have false beliefs – there must be something wrong with the idea of the omniscient interpreter employing the principle of charity.

As indeed there is; omniscience and charity are incompatible virtues. On pain of misinterpretation, what the omniscient interpreter must do instead of exercising charity is construe my beliefs as true by his lights when my beliefs are true *and as false by his lights when my beliefs are false.* Conversely, the only interpreter who *can* insist on my beliefs coming out true by his lights, consonant with his construing my false beliefs correctly, is one who *isn't* omniscient – one who has, in fact, the very same false beliefs that I do.

The box score: An omniscient interpreter can pursue charity only with respect to an omniscient informant. The notion of omniscience pursuing charity with respect to a fallible informant is incoherent. But it is this latter notion that Davidson's anti-skeptical argument depends on.

That charity with respect to a fallible informant is incompatible with omniscience is, to repeat, a necessary truth; the theory of interpretation must not flout it. But now we are back where we started: the possibility appears to remain wide open that all my beliefs are false, but that they all come out true by the lights of some radical interpreter who happens to believe the same false things that I do. This is, as we remarked above, just the kind of possibility that the skeptic was worried about all along. The skeptic fears that, although my interpreter and I both think that what's causing me to say "The cat is on the mat" is the cat's being on the mat, so that my saying that the cat is on the mat does indeed come out true by both my lights and my interpreter's, still what is *really* causing me to say "The cat is on the mat" is, as it might be, not the cat's being on the mat but my brain's being in a vat. In that case, though what I say is true by my lights and true by my interpreter's lights, it is nevertheless false in the eyes of God. It may be that this skeptical worry is incoherent; it may even be that causal theories of content can show that it is.[18] But not, so far as we can tell, by the route that Davidson proposes. It would be a powerful argument for holism if the premises it independently requires were to provide for a transcendental refutation of skepticism, but they don't.

161

6

NED BLOCK:
Meaning Holism and Conceptual Role Semantics

In the preceding chapters, we surveyed some arguments that seek to infer semantic holism from transcendental constraints on content attribution – specifically, from the premise that content attribution essentially involves appeals to holistic principles of charity. We now consider an argument that doesn't purport to be transcendental. Its tactic is to propose a theory about *what content is* and then to infer from this theory that content must be holistic.

So what we have to consider is an explicitly metaphysical argument for an explicitly metaphysical conclusion: The thesis that *the meaning of an expression is its role in a language/theory* invites the inference that expressions that belong to different languages/theories are ipso facto different in meaning. That is, it invites the doctrine that we've been calling "translation holism." Notice that it is translation holism rather than content holism that is at issue here, unless there is some argument that the meaning of an expression couldn't be its role in a language that contains only that expression.[1]

As in previous chapters, we will develop our discussion from the consideration of a paper that is widely cited in the literature – in this case, Ned Block's "Advertisement for a semantics for psychology." Unlike the authors of the earlier papers, however,

163

Block is arguing not for a specific semantic theory but rather for a whole class of them. Block thinks he can show that *some version of conceptual role theory* (CRT) will meet the warranted conditions of adequacy for a semantics, but he is explicitly not concerned to decide which version of CRT is the best one.[2] Thus, for example, whereas Davidson tells us in some detail what he thinks a truth theory for a natural language would look like, Block goes out of his way not to commit himself about what form a CRT for a natural language should take.[3] This is especially useful for our purposes. Since there is no clear philosophical consensus as to which version of CRT is most promising, there is no CRT theorist whose formulation can be taken as fully representative of the kind.

The structure of this chapter will be as follows. First, we will consider Block's argument that only CRT can satisfy the desiderata that a semantics adequate to the foundations of cognitive science must meet. In the second part we claim that the arguments that Block offers in favor of CRT are not decisive. But though we propose to look closely at these arguments, evaluating CRT is *not* our primary concern. Our main line will be to show that, even if CRT is endorsed, it can offer no support for semantic holism. In particular, we propose the following dilemma for philosophers who want to draw holistic conclusions from CRT: Unless CRT is held in conjunction with an analytic/synthetic distinction, it will fail to meet one of the constraints on semantic theories whose satisfaction Block correctly takes to be essential. However, if CRT *is* conjoined with an analytic/synthetic distinction, then either the inference from CRT to semantic holism fails or the version of CRT that one is left with is preposterous on the face of it. On none of these contingencies do you get a sound argument from CRT to holism.

Setting out this argument will be the main burden of the third part of the chapter.

Block's Defense of CRT

Block enumerates eight desiderata that he says must be satisfied by a semantic theory if it is to provide a notion of content that is appropriate for a naturalistic, computational psychology. And he claims that only some form of CRT can meet all these conditions. In fact, we have no argument with Block's methodology; we accept – anyhow for purposes of argument – that the sort of psychology he has in mind would probably require a semantics that satisfies his eight conditions. We are, however, very inclined to doubt that any version of CRT can do so.

Block's desiderata for a semantic theory are these; it must:

1. Explain the relation between meaning and reference/truth.
2. Explain what makes meaningful expressions meaningful.
3. Explain the relativity of meaning to representational systems.
4. Explain compositionality.
5. Fit in with an account of the relation between meaning and the mind/brain.
6. Illuminate the relation between autonomous and inherited meaning.
7. Explain the connections between knowing, learning, and using an expression, on the one hand, and the meaning of the expression on the other.
8. Explain why different aspects of meaning are relevant in different ways to the determination of reference and to psychological explanation.

Of these points, we propose to discuss only 1, 4, and 5 at any length. (Desiderata 1 and 5 are the pivotal considerations on which Block's defense of CRT turns. Desideratum 4 is of interest because we think we can show that it can't be met by any remotely plausible version of CRT that implies meaning

165

holism.) Since the other desiderata are likely to be satisfied, in one way or another, by any semantic theory that purports to be psychologically motivated, they seem to us to throw no particular light on the status of CRT. Thus, for example, consider desideratum 6: Any "Gricean" in semantics can tell the same story about "inherited" and "autonomous" meaning as Block does; namely, that the meanings of natural language sentences are derivative from the contents of the propositional attitudes that speakers/hearers use them to express. But assuming this Gricean stance would appear to be fully compatible with denying that the contents of the propositional attitudes are themselves derived from their conceptual roles.[4] Similarly for desideratum 7, either it is trivially satisfiable (for example, the relation between meaning and understanding is that to under-stand a term is to know what it means[5]) or it is the demand that semantics be "naturalistic," in which case it doesn't discriminate between CRT and, for example, an informational theory of content (see, among others, Dretske, *Knowledge and the Flow of Information*; Fodor, "A theory of content"). Finally, as Block explains desideratum 8, it is satisfied by any semantic theory that has the resources to draw a narrow content/wide content distinction (including, once again, not just CRT but also informational theories). We leave it as an exercise for the reader to show that desiderata 2 and 3 don't choose between CRT and other theories of content either. Notice, by the way, that desideratum 3 is not an unmixed blessing from the point of view of CRT theorists. It's a problem for CRT how to avoid making meaning *so* relative to representational systems that translational holism is entailed. (We will return to this presently.)

Meaning and Reference (First Desideratum)

Arguments owing to Frege ("On sense and reference") and Putnam ("The meaning of 'meaning' ") are generally taken to show that the relation between meaning and reference is deeply problematic. Frege draws attention to cases where substitutivity fails for extensionally (that is, referentially) equivalent expressions. (In the classic example, even though the expressions "the morning star" and "the evening star" are coreferential, Jones can, without self-contradiction, deny that the morning star is wet while asserting that the evening star is wet.) A standard (though not mandatory – see Salmon, *Frege's Puzzle*; Barwise and Perry, *Situations and Attitudes*; Stalnaker, *Inquiry*, etc.) diagnosis of Frege's examples takes them to show that reference and meaning are independent in at least one direction: identity of reference does not guarantee identity of meaning.[6]

Putnam's "Twin earth" examples (with which we assume the reader is familiar; if not, see "The meaning of 'meaning'") are usually taken to show that meaning and reference are independent in the other direction too; in particular, that difference of reference is compatible with identity of content, assuming that the content of mental states (and, hence, derivatively of linguistic expressions) supervenes on factors that are "in the speaker's head" (for example, on the speaker's neurological structure). Given this supervenience assumption, the Twins in Putnam's example mean the same thing by their tokens of "water," but their utterances of (for example) "That's water" have different truth conditions.

Notice that the symmetry of the Putnam and Frege cases depends on assuming that meaning obeys an "individualistic" principle of supervenience – that is, it depends on assuming a "narrow" notion of mental content, according to which "narrow" content is "in the head." This is where Block's interest in a semantics *for psychology* plays a crucial role in his discussion. Block assumes (very controversially) that Twins must be subsumed by the same intentional psychological explanations, not just by the same neurological or biochemical explanations. He then argues that it is a virtue of CRT that it provides a notion of intentional content that permits this. (See Block's discussion of desideratum 8.) We do not propose to argue the issues about "individualism" here; we're going to grant, for the sake of the present argument, that a semantics adequate to the purposes of intentional explanation should provide for a notion of narrow content. (For a discussion of the connections between "individualism" in semantics and explanation in psychology, see Fodor, "A modal argument for narrow content.") We emphasize, however, that none of our main argument depends on assuming that CRT is offered as an account of *narrow* content. In particular, the things we will have to say about the relation between CRT, holism, and compositionality apply to theories like Harman's (in his article "Wide functionalism"; see also other references cited there) in which it is *wide* content that is analyzed by reference to conceptual role.

Assuming the standard diagnoses, then, the Frege and Putnam examples render the intension/extension relation problematic; they show that "narrow" content doesn't determine reference. We now consider what account of the meaning/ reference relation one gets by accepting the identification of narrow content with conceptual role.

Let's start with the CRT solution of Frege's problem. CRT identifies the meaning of an expression with its inferential role[7] (or, in naturalistic versions of the doctrine, with its causal role).[8] Block assumes that the inferential roles of coextensive expressions can differ; hence that, in principle, CRT has the resources to distinguish the meaning of "the morning star" from the meaning of "the evening star," the meaning of "Cicero" from the meaning of "Tully," and so forth.

However, as Block is fully aware, the presuppositions of this sort of treatment can't simply be taken for granted. Whether the inferential roles of "the morning star" and "the evening star" do differ depends *on how inferential roles are themselves individuated*. If, in particular, the individuation of inferential roles is assumed to be as coarse-grained as the individuation of extensions, then the roles of "the morning star" and "the evening star" are ipso facto *not* different. Suppose, for example, that your notion of inference is built on material equivalence;

then coextensive expressions will have their inferential roles in common. Conversely, if inferential roles are as fine-grained as orthography, then they will distinguish not just "the morning star" and "the evening star," but also "bachelor" and "unmarried man," and we lose the explanation of the (putative) fact that, synonymous expressions, unlike merely coextensive ones, *are* ipso facto intersubstitutable in nonquotational contexts.[9]

Our first point is thus that the appeal to distinctions among inferential roles solves Frege's problem *only given an adequate principle of individuation for inferential roles*. But, of course, no such individuation criterion is in fact available. (Block says that the individuation of inferential roles is *"the* problem" for CRT), and it's not obvious that distinguishing among inferential roles is going to prove any easier than distinguishing among meanings. Indeed, it's not obvious why these problems aren't identical.

Consider now the Putnam examples. We've just seen that the CRT tactic for dealing with Frege's problem is to assume that inferential roles are just fine-grained enough to draw the required distinctions of meaning among coextensive expressions. But notice that what is wanted (and what Block is advertising) is a *simultaneous* treatment of Frege's examples and Putnam's; and prima facie, the two problems pull in opposite directions. According to the usual understanding, Frege's cases require a notion of content that is *more* fine-grained than extensional equivalence – coreferential expressions must somehow be treated as not synonymous – but the Twin cases require a notion of content that is *less* fine-grained than extensional equivalence – (narrowly) synonymous expressions must somehow be treated as extensionally distinct. It's thus hard to see how the same theoretical apparatus could deal with both the Frege and the Putnam examples.

Block's solution is, in effect, to adopt a "two-factor" version of CRT.[10] That is, Block postulates two orthogonal semantic dimensions: CRT proper provides the "aspect" of meaning that copes with Frege's problem, and some independent (perhaps

169

causal) theory of reference provides the aspect of meaning that copes with Putnam's problem (namely, by tying one Twin's use of "water" to water and the other Twin's uses of "water" to XYZ). It seems a little odd, perhaps, to describe this as the solution of the meaning/reference problem by *CRT*. (See Lepore and Loewer, "Dual aspect semantics.") In fact, two semantic theories are being simultaneously invoked, one of which is nothing like a CRT. And the reader should bear in mind that the theory of reference that Block is assuming, like the theory of role individuation, is a blank check. Block is claiming that the meaning/reference problem will be solved by a two-factor theory, neither factor of which is actually available. But so be it.

Suppose, however, that we grant a two-factor architecture for semantics in aid of satisfying desideratum 1. No doubt this gives us enough degrees of freedom to do the job in principle; but there's a price to pay for the extra power that two-factor architectures provide. We now have to face the nasty question: *What keeps the two factors stuck together?* For example, what prevents there being an expression that has an inferential role appropriate to the content *4 is a prime* but the truth conditions appropriate to the content *water is wet*? (We assume that no adequate semantics could allow such an expression. What on earth would it mean? And what would be said by asserting it?) Notice that this is really just the meaning/reference problem reiterated at the level of metatheory. We started out worrying about what the connection is between the meaning of an expression and its reference; what we now have to worry about is what the connection is between a theory that determines the meaning of an expression and a theory that determines its reference. It's not evident that the overall gain has been appreciable.

Block is pretty clearly aware that two-factor theories have this structural problem, but what he has to say about how to solve it is enigmatic. We quote: "I think the conceptual role factor is *primary* in that it determines the nature of the referential factor, but not vice versa" ("Advertisement," p. 643;

emphasis in the original). This might seem surprising in the present context, since the conventional diagnosis of the Twin cases is precisely that conceptual roles *fail* to determine reference. What Block appears to be saying, however, is not that the conceptual role of "water" decides what it refers to, but rather that the conceptual role of names (kind terms, and so forth) is constituted by the fact that their causal relations determine their reference.

> Kripke is convincing [about "Moses"] because we use names such as "Moses" to refer to the person who bears the right causal relations to the use of the name, even if he does not fit the descriptions we associate with the name . . . In short, what theory of reference is true is a fact about how referring terms function in our thought processes. This is an aspect of conceptual role. ("Advertisement," p. 643)

But this doesn't help with the problem at hand. What we need to know is what precludes radical mismatches between intension and extension. Why can't you have a sentence that has an inferential role appropriate to the thought that water is wet, but is true iff 4 is a prime?[11] In this context it does no good to be told what Block appears to be telling us: namely, that T isn't a kind term unless the causal theory of kind terms is true of it. *That consideration doesn't block the possibility that "water" has the extension of a kind term but the logic of a number term.*

In fact, there seems to be a soupçon of use/mention fallacy in the passage from Block that we just quoted. In effect, the present problem is how the sense of an expression is related to its denotation, given the assumption that intensions don't determine extensions. What we're told is just that the expression T falls in the extension of such terms as "name," "kind term," and so forth only if a certain semantic theory is true of T. This tells us how the inferential roles of "name," "kind term," and the like are related to *their* extensions; in fact, it proposes a sort of description theory for such terms. "Name" applies to "Moses," for example, just in case "Moses" has the kinds of

Semantic properties that the causal theory specifies for names.[12] But it doesn't tell us how determining the sense of "Moses" is related to determining its extension; and *that* is the prob—NED BLOCK lem that the two-factor architecture raises.

replace
(publisher's
note)

assuming that charity is constitutive of intentional ascription (as does, for example, the famous argument that Davidson gives in "Mental events"). In the present context, that assumption would be merely question begging.

Our conclusion is not that there couldn't be an acceptable CRT story about the meaning/reference relation; it's just that the idea that (narrow) meanings are conceptual roles doesn't, in and of itself, throw light on the meaning/reference problem.

There's another way to put the sorts of points we've just been making. Let's accept that, in principle, the CRT approach to Frege's problem provides for a sufficiently fine-grained notion of content to distinguish among the meanings of coextensive expressions. But a semantic theory should not only adjudicate issues of *identity* of meaning; it should also provide a canonical form for answering questions about *what* an expression means. (In fact, if it does the latter, it's not entirely obvious that it should also be required to do the former. As Block himself points out, most empirical taxonomies do *not* provide necessary and sufficient conditions for the application of their categories.) So, parallel to the problem of how to align the factors of two-factor semantic theories, there is the problem of how narrow contents – or narrow "aspects" of content – are to be expressed; for example, assuming that the mental states of Twins ipso facto share their contents, what *is* the content that they share? We don't propose to pursue this question at length; suffice it to say that the answer pretty clearly can't be that what one's thought that water is wet has in common with one's Twin's thought that water is wet (that is, with the thought that one's Twin uses the form of words "Water is wet" to express) is that both express the *narrow proposition* that water is wet. After all, the notion of a proposition is ipso facto the notion of something that is truth-valuable. If there is a narrow proposition that water is wet, what are its truth conditions?

We conclude that CRT offers no clear resolution of the meaning/reference problem, contrary to Block's advertisement. Has the Better Business Bureau heard about this?

172

Content and Behavior (Fifth Desideratum)

Block isn't claiming that no semantics other than CRT can meet *any* of his eight desiderata; his claim is that only CRT can meet *all* of them. It is, nevertheless, widely supposed that CRT is suited, in a way that other kinds of semantic theories aren't, to explaining the connection between the contents of mental states and their causal (for example, behavioral) consequences. We want to comment briefly on this issue.

CRT proposes to define states like *believing that P* literally in terms of their (causes and) effects. In consequence, it not only acknowledges a connection between mental states and behavioral outcomes, it actually makes such connections essential features of the propositional attitudes. This is characteristic of theories that provide a "functionalist" account of content.[13] It's important to notice, however, that you don't actually need an *essential* connection between content and behavior in order to appeal to the former in explanations of the latter. All you need is a *reliable* connection; and for that, intentional laws would do.[14]

Block almost notices this point. He says that "wide meaning may be more useful [than narrow meaning] for predicting [behavior] in one respect; to the extent that there are nomological relations between the world and what people think and do, wide meaning will allow prediction about what they think and do without information about how they see things" ("Advertisement," p. 620).[15]

Block's point is that if there are psychological laws that connect behavior to mental states without regard to the intentional content of the states (so that if either of two extensionally equivalent states fall under such a law, both do), then there are ipso facto generalizations that you can state over wide content but not over narrow content. This is correct, but it misses the main point: namely, that there might be psychological laws that are stated *with* respect to intentional contents (for example, laws of the form "Ceteris paribus, if someone believes

173

such and such and desires so and so, then he does this and that"). If there are, then it could be appeals to such intentional laws – rather than to the noncontingent mind/behavior connections that functional definitions of content are supposed to specify – that underwrite psychological explanations. This is essentially the point we made against Dennett (see chapter 5).[16] We conclude that desideratum 5 doesn't argue persuasively for CRT.

THE COMPOSITIONALITY CONSTRAINT

The reader may be wondering what, if anything, the previous discussion had to do with holism. The answer is that our examination of desiderata 1 and 5 was designed to deny to a standard holistic argument one of its essential premises. Arguments for holism are often variants of the following: Assume CRT in the form "The meaning of an expression is its role in a language"; assume that there is no a/s distinction;[17] then infer translation holism in the form "The meaning of an expression is its *entire* role in a language" (see the discussion of "argument A" in chapter 1). Clearly this argument is no better than the reasons for accepting CRT, so what we've been trying to do is to undermine some of those.

In the present section, however, our tactics will be different. We are going to claim that one of Block's desiderata (indeed, one which we think he is entirely right to endorse) can be satisfied only by forms of CRT that are either incompatible with the a/s distinction or patently preposterous on grounds that are independent of the holism issues. So we are claiming, first, that CRT is not well motivated and, second, that no version of CRT that it is possible to take seriously can ground an inference to holism.

Compositionality (Fourth Desideratum)

Compositionality is the idea that "The meaning of a sentence is in some sense a function of the meanings of the words in it (plus the syntax of the sentence)" ("Advertisement," p. 616). This principle is supposed to hold for natural languages like English and also to apply to whatever system of representation a computational psychology may postulate as providing the vehicle of thought. (So, if there is such a thing as Mentalese, then the fourth desideratum requires that it have a combinatorial semantics.)

Block takes the compositionality of thought and language as self-evident.[18] In fact, his account of word meaning appears to presuppose compositionality: "according to CR[T], the semantic values of words and other subsentential elements are a matter of their contributions to the conceptual roles of sentences and supersentential elements" ("Advertisement," p. 667). Recent discussions, both in philosophy and in cognitive science, have occasionally questioned whether the compositionality requirement can really be enforced (see Schiffer, *Remnants of Meaning*; Smolensky, "On the proper treatment of connectionism"), and, of course, this will depend a lot on exactly how the principle of compositionality is formulated. We don't wish to take a stand on the details, but it does seem to us that there are properties of both natural languages and human thought that strongly suggest that some form of compositionality holds for linguistic and mental representation.[19] The most obvious of these is productivity (roughly, that every natural language can express, and every normal mind can entertain, an open-ended set of propositions). (See Frege, "Compound thoughts," p. 390; Chomsky, *Rules and Representations*, pp. 220ff.; Davidson, "Theories of meaning and learnable languages," p. 8.) A related phenomenon is the "systematicity" of thought and language – roughly, the fact that any language (/mind) that can express (/entertain) the proposition P will also be able to express (/entertain) many propositions that are conceptually close to

175

P. (If a mind can entertain the thought that aRb, then it can entertain the thought that bRa; if it can entertain the thought that P → Q, then it can entertain the thought that Q → P; and so forth.[20] For discussion, see Fodor, *Psychosemantics*; Fodor and Pylyshyn, "Connectionism and cognitive architecture.")

Connected with both productivity and systematicity is a further, apparently perfectly universal feature of thoughts and sentences. Their structures are, in the following sense, isomorphic to the structures of the propositions they express: *If a thought/ sentence S expresses the proposition that P, then syntactic constituents of S express the constituents of P.* If, for example, a sentence expresses the proposition that P and Q, then there will be one syntactic constituent of the sentence that expresses the proposition that P and another syntactic constituent that expresses the proposition that Q. If a sentence expresses the proposition that John loves Mary, then there will be a syntactic constituent of the sentence that refers to John, another syntactic constituent of the sentence that refers to Mary, and another syntactic constituent of the sentence that expresses a relation such that, necessarily, that relation holds between x and y iff x loves y. Notice that though all this is patently obvious, none of it is truistic. Idioms and other "holophrastic" constructions are all exceptions, albeit the sorts of exceptions that prove the rule. (See Fodor and McLaughlin, "Connectionism and the problem of systematicity: why Smolensky's solution doesn't work."[21])

Productivity, systematicity, and isomorphism are immediately explicable on the assumption that linguistic and mental representation are compositional, but baffling otherwise. So we propose not merely to grant Block's compositionality constraint, but to insist on it.

However, contrary to what Block suggests, the compositionality constraint is actually an *embarrassment* for CRT. In particular, it invites the following kind of prima facie argument:

Meanings are compositional by general consent.
But inferential roles are *not* compositional.
So meanings can't be inferential roles.

The second step is, of course, the one that's doing the work. But it seems pretty obviously sound. Consider the meaning of the "brown cow"; it depends on the meanings of "brown" and "cow" together with its syntax. (To a first approximation, "brown" means – it connotes the property – *brown*, "cow" means *cow*, and the semantic interpretation of the syntactic structure (adjective+noun)$_n$ is property conjunction. We are aware that there are problems about decoy ducks, rising temperatures, and the like; but the assumption that language is compositional is the assumption that such problems can be solved.) But now, prima facie, the inferential role of "brown cow" depends not only on the inferential role of "brown" and the inferential role of "cow," *but also on what you happen to believe about brown cows*. So, unlike meaning, inferential role is, in the general case, *not* compositional.

Suppose, for example, that you happen to think that brown cows are dangerous; then it's part of the inferential role of "brown cow" for you that it does (or can) figure in inferences of the form "brown cow → dangerous." But, at first blush anyhow, this fact about the inferential role of "brown cow" doesn't seem to derive from facts about the inferential roles of its constituents in the way that, for example, the validity of inferences like "brown cow → brown animal" or "brown cow → not green cow" might plausibly be thought to do. "Brown cow" entails "brown animal" because "cow" entails "animal"; "brown cow" entails "not green cow" because "brown" entails "not green." But it doesn't look as if either "brown" or "cow" entails "dangerous," so, to this extent, it doesn't look as if the inference from "brown cow" to "dangerous" is compositional.

In short, it appears that some, but not all, of the inferential potential of "brown cow" is determined by the respective inferential potentials of "brown" and "cow," the rest being determined by one's "real world" beliefs about brown cows. This should not seem surprising or contentious; it's just a way of saying that "Brown cows are dangerous" (unlike "Brown cows are animals" and "Brown cows are not green") is clearly synthetic.

We intend this as one horn of a dilemma, and we anticipate the following reply: "OK, so if the compositionality of meaning is assumed, meanings can't be identified with inferential roles as such. But this doesn't *really* embarrass CRT, because meanings can still be identified with roles in *analytic* inferences. Thus, on the one hand, the inference 'brown cow → brown animal' is compositional (it's inherited from the inference 'cow → animal'); and, on the other hand, precisely because it *is* compositional, 'brown cow → brown animal' is analytic. Compositional inferences will always be analytic, and analytic inferences will always be compositional; the compositionality of an inference is *the same thing* as its analyticity.

"Look at it this way: If the inference 'brown cow → brown animal' is compositional, then it's warranted by the inferential roles of the expressions 'brown' and 'cow.' That's what it is for an inference to be compositional. But, according to CRT, the inferential roles of 'brown' and 'cow' *are their meanings*. So then, that 'brown cow → brown animal' is warranted follows from the *meanings* of 'brown' and 'cow.' But for an inference to be analytic *just is* for it to be warranted by the meanings of its constituent expressions. So the compositionality of 'brown cow → brown animal' – or, mutatis mutandis, of any other inference – *entails* its analyticity. The same argument also works the other way around. For an inference to be analytic is for it to be warranted by the meanings of its constituents. But, according to CRT, meanings are inferential roles. So, for an inference to be analytic is for its warrant to be determined by the inferential roles of its constituents. But for the warrant of an inference to be determined by the inferential roles of its constituents is for the inference to be compositional. So compositionality entails

178

analyticity and vice versa.[22] So then: meaning is compositional, inferential role isn't, and role in analytic inference is. What all this shows is just that we need a revised version of CRT, one which identifies meaning with role in analytic inference."

The first thing to say about this new suggestion is that the threat of circularity is now very pressing. It is proposed that we reconcile CRT with the compositionality of meaning by identifying the meaning of an expression not with its inferential role *tout court* but with its role in *analytic* inferences. But the difference between analytic inferences and inferences *tout court* is just that the validity of the former is guaranteed *by the meanings* of their constituent expressions. So compositionality, analyticity, and meaning eke out a living by doing one another's wash, and Quine gets to say "I told you so!"

Notice also that the naturalizability of inferential role semantics is jeopardized by the present proposal. A lot of the attraction of identifying meaning with inferential role lies in the thought that the inferential role of an expression (/thought) might in turn be identified with its *causal* role, thereby providing the basis for a solution to Brentano's problem. That causal relations reconstruct inferential relations is a foundational assumption of computational theories of mental processes, so perhaps there is hope here for a unification of semantics with psychology (see Block's discussion of desideratum 5). But, barring proposals for a causal theory of analyticity, this tactic is unavailable to the philosopher who identifies meaning with the role of an expression in analytic inference.[23] The idea that mental processes are computational may provide the basis for a naturalistic account of inference, but it offers no insight at all into the nature of analyticity.

These sorts of considerations suggest that the connection between compositionality and analyticity is quite bad news for CRT. The point we want to stress, however, is that it's much worse news for semantic holists, since there is now no argument *to* holism *from* CRT.

The original argument to holism from CRT depended

179

critically on there *not* being an analytic/synthetic distinction. But now we see that if there is no analytic/synthetic distinction, then CRT fails to satisfy the desideratum of compositionality; and compositionality is a desideratum which, by common consent, a semantic theory is required to meet. Caveats will presently be entered, but a first approximation to the bottom line is this: If you accept the compositionality of meaning, you can't be both a conceptual role semanticist and a holist. A fortiori, you can't *derive* holism from conceptual role semantics.

As far as we can tell, this line of argument is quite robust; in particular, it doesn't depend on detailed assumptions about how a conceptual role semantics construes the notion of conceptual role. There is, for example, an influential paper by Hartry Field in which sameness of conceptual role is analyzed in terms of subjective probability; in effect, the conceptual role of your thought that P is identified with the subjective probability that you assign to P contingent on each of the other thoughts that you can entertain (Field, "Logic, meaning and conceptual role"). So, for example, the conceptual role of your thought that it's raining is determined in part by the subjective probability that you (would) assign to that thought on the assumption that the streets are wet and in part by the subjective probability that you (would) assign to it on the assumption that the sun is shining and in part by the subjective probability that you would assign to it on the assumption that elephants have wings, and so forth.

Our point is that this construal of conceptual roles in terms of subjective probabilities, whatever other virtues it may have, does nothing to help with the compositionality problem. This is because subjective probabilities are not themselves compositional. For example, the subjective probability assigned to the thought that (brown cows are dangerous/P) is *not* a function of the subjective probability one assigns to the thought that (cows are dangerous/P) together with the subjective probability that one assigns to the thought that (brown things are dangerous/P). If this is not obvious, consider a world (or rather a belief world, since the probabilities at issue are supposed to be subjective) in which there are very many things that are cows, almost none of which is dangerous, and very many things that are brown, almost none of which is dangerous, and a very small number of brown cows, almost all of which are very, very fierce. On these assumptions, the probability that something that is brown is dangerous is small, and the probability that something that is a cow is dangerous is small, but the probability that a brown cow is dangerous is as big as you please.

Where we've arrived is this: The only sort of CRT that provides for compositionality is one which identifies the meaning of an expression with its role in analytic inferences. But the standard argument from CRT to holism runs via the assumption that there is no a/s distinction. So compositionality rules out the standard argument from CRT to holism.

So are we claiming that, given compositionality, holism is literally *incompatible* with CRT? Not quite. For although CRTs can't have the compositionality of an inference without its analyticity, there is a way to reconcile analyticity with holism – namely, by accepting a semantics that represents *every* inference as analytic (see n. 17). For example, you might hold that the inferential role of "brown cow" does, after all, derive compositionally from the inferential roles of its constituents; for example, you might take "cow → x such that, if brown, then dangerous" to be part of the inferential role of "cow" (hence part of the meaning of "cow").[24] On this assumption, "brown cow" *does* imply "dangerous" in virtue of the inferential roles of its constituents, together with its syntactic structure, just as the compositionality of inference requires.

The trouble is that, as we've seen, if "brown cow → dangerous" is *compositional*, it follows that it is also *analytic*. For, on the one hand, an inference is compositional iff its validity is determined by the *inferential roles* that its constituents contribute; and, on the other hand, an inference is analytic iff its validity is determined by the *semantic values* of its constituents; but, on the third hand (as it were), CRT says that the meaning of a constituent is *the same thing* as the inferential role it

181

contributes to the expressions that contain it. So, to repeat, the cost of representing an inference as compositional is that you then have to represent it as analytic. But since meanings are compositional in the general case (that is, barring idioms, metaphors, and such), the cost of a semantic theory that identifies meanings with inferential roles is that inferences come out analytic in the general case and, a fortiori, necessary in the general case. But, surely, this is preposterous. An acceptable semantics must be able to make sense of contingent inferences.

The moral is that, although you *can* reconcile CRT with compositionality by taking the (counter-intuitive) line that all inferences are compositional, and although a semantics that says that all inferences are compositional is compatible with holism, this still does not save the argument from CRT to holism. For the idea that all inferences are compositional is the idea that all inferences are analytic, and the idea that all inferences are analytic, though it, too, is compatible with holism, is, on independent grounds, perfectly mad.[25]

Although the present line of argument doesn't depend on this point, it's worth remarking that there is also an epistemological cost for making inference compositional in the general case; in effect, you have to give up the Quine/Duhem thesis. This is another of the respects in which it turns out that there is considerable tension between the assumptions required for semantic holism and those required for epistemic holism (see chapter 2). The argument is this: Notice that what is compositionally determined is ipso facto *locally* determined. For example, the idea that spelling is compositional is the idea that the lexical analysis of an expression is fully determined locally,[26] namely, by the sequence of letters that it contains; the idea that syntax is compositional is the idea that the structural description of an expression is fully determined locally, namely, by the sequence of lexical items that it contains. And so forth. By contrast, the point of confirmation holism – specifically, of the Q/D thesis – is that what inferences are rational is *not* determined *locally* (for example, by the meanings of its

182

constituent terms) but *globally* (namely, by features of one's whole science). What underlies the intuition that inferential roles are *not* compositional is thus precisely what underlies Quine's rejection of analyticity: a recognition of the holistic, nonlocal character of empirical inference.

To summarize: There are, as his critics have often remarked, two ways of reading Quine's claim that there is no a/s distinction: either that the distinction is *incoherent* or that the distinction is coherent but *the class of analyticities is empty.* We've argued that, given the compositionality of meaning, neither of these readings of Quine's rejection of the a/s distinction is compatible with CRT. For, to repeat, if meaning is inferential role, then meaning is compositional for all and only the analytic inferences. Since you can't have semantics without compositionality and you can't have compositionality without analyticity, it follows that you can't have CRT without analyticity. A fortiori, you can't have CRT without an a/s distinction, contrary to a main assumption of the argument from CRT to holism. But this doesn't make CRT and holism *incompatible,* since, of course, holism could be true even if the main argument for it is unsound. In particular, you can reconcile CRT with holism if you embrace an option which Quine, quite sensibly, didn't even bother to consider: namely, that the a/s distinction is coherent and it's the class of *synthetic* inferences that is empty; that is, that *all* inferences are analytic. On this option you get compositionality *and* holism, but at the price of a semantics that is incapable of being taken seriously. The pertinent conclusion is surely that only a version of CRT that embraces an a/s distinction and is *non*holistic – that is, one which recognizes synthetic inferences – can hope for a plausible account of compositionality.

So, then, if Quine is right about the a/s distinction, then CRT is incompatible with compositionality, and hence false. And if Quine is wrong about the a/s distinction, and there are some analytic inferences and some synthetic ones, then CRT is compatible with compositionality, but there is no sound argument from CRT to holism. For our present purposes, it doesn't matter which of these you prefer.

What would Block say about all this? Well, Block isn't a holist, of course, and he does accept an a/s distinction. In fact, his motive for accepting an a/s distinction presumably *is* to avoid holism by providing an adequately coarse-grained principle for individuating inferential roles. So Block could say this: "If the a/s distinction is independently motivated by the compositionality requirement, so much the better for the a/s distinction." Thus, as far as we can see, Block can live with everything we've said about there being an internal connection between analyticity and compositionality. However, you might wonder whether he can also live with Quine's arguments in "Two dogmas," since they are widely supposed to show that an a/s distinction can't be sustained. And of course, this is part and parcel of what Block calls *the* problem for CRT – namely, the lack of a principled criterion for individuating inferential roles.

Block doesn't say much about how he thinks this problem should be solved. But, like many CRT theorists, he expresses the hope that the arguments in "Two dogmas" don't preclude a denatured sort of a/s distinction, perhaps one that is somehow "graded" or contextually relativized.[27] Similar hopes have been voiced by Bilgrami, Devitt, Dummett, and others.

We have two points to make about this. The first is that our primary concern isn't to undermine CRT but to show that no remotely tenable form of CRT could imply holism. Given the compositionality of meaning, the following is an inconsistent triad: *CRT, holism,* and *no a/s distinction* (reading "no a/s distinction" as false in, inter alia, the case where all inferences are analytic). You can sort philosophers by which of these three they are prepared to give up; all the philosophers we've just listed are prepared to give up *holism* and *no a/s distinction*. That's OK with us.

The second is that the intrinsic connection between analyticity and compositionality that we've been examining makes it look less likely than ever that you *can* save CRT by appealing to a denatured form of a/s distinction – not even if you're prepared to live with the fact that if CRT *is* saved this way, then it can't be used as a premise in an argument for holism. For example, according to Block, analyticity is graded; the basic semantic notion is therefore *similarity* of meaning, not *identity* of meaning. But, as we've been noticing, *for inferences, analyticity and compositionality are the same thing.* So, if your semantic theory reconstructs meaning as analytic inference and if you have a graded notion of analyticity, *then you have to live with a graded notion of compositionality* as well. But what would a graded notion of compositionality be like? And, in particular, would such a notion be able to do what a theory of compositionality is required to do: namely, account for systematicity, isomorphism, and productivity?

Wouldn't a graded notion of compositionality entail, at best, that a finite acquaintance with a language is adequate to *sort of understand* expressions not previously encountered? Or that if a language is capable of expressing the proposition that aRb, then it is *sort of* capable of expressing the proposition that bRa? Or that if the sentence S expresses the proposition P, then the constituents of S *sort of* express the constituents of P? But is there any sense to be made of such claims as, for example, that ("John loves Mary" sort of expresses the proposition that John loves Mary) only if "John" sort of refers to John? These are deep waters; we do not envy Block and other CRT theorists for having to wade in them.[28]

Since we are inclined to think that Quine is right about the a/s distinction,[29] we are inclined to think that the moral of the discussion in this chapter is that conceptual role semantics is untenable; since inferential roles aren't compositional and meanings are, meanings can't be inferential roles. If this is right, it is a powerful result; quite a lot of the philosophy of language and philosophy of mind since the 1940s has taken it for granted that some version of CRT must be true. And, combining conceptual role semantics with the denial of the a/s distinction is perhaps the received position in cognitive science. The idea is

185

that, on the one hand, concepts (/meanings and the like) are stereotypes; they're something like bundles of probable or typical traits. But, on the other hand, none of the traits belonging to such a bundle is *definitional*, so the a/s distinction fails. We take it that this option is closed when one notices the connection between compositionality and analyticity. If meaning is compositional, then either meaning isn't inferential role or it is role in *analytic* inference. It's precisely *because* the bundles of inferences that constitute stereotypes aren't analytic (and hence aren't compositional) that meanings can't be stereotypes. (The stereotypical brown cow can be dangerous even though the property *dangerous* doesn't belong to the *brown* stereotype or the *cow* stereotype. Indeed, the stereotypical *brown* cow can be dangerous even if the stereotypical *cow* is a pussycat.) So, either the meanings of "brown" and "cow" are their roles in *analytic* inferences – in which case, meanings aren't stereotypes – or they aren't their roles in inferences at all – in which case meanings still aren't stereotypes. In either case, it looks very much as if meanings aren't stereotypes.

If, as we suspect, Quine is right about the a/s distinction, then the moral of our discussion is that CRT is false. It may be, however, that our inclination to think that Quine is right about the a/s distinction is ill-advised. In that case, the moral of the discussion is just that there is no sound inference from CRT to holism. For our purposes in this book, we would settle for either.

7

PAUL CHURCHLAND:
State Space Semantics
(and A Brief Conclusion)

For those who take it that atomism is a dead issue in the theory of meaning, there would appear to be only three remaining options. These are:

1. Buy into semantic holism and learn to live with the consequences. *Probably* these will include doing without propositional attitude psychology for any serious scientific purposes, however much beliefs and desires might hang on as a sort of *façon de parler* in commonsense psychological explanation.
2. Resuscitate the analytic/synthetic distinction and identify the meaning of a symbol with the analytic relations it enters into.
3. Buy into an attenuated form of semantic holism in which the notion of *identity* of meaning is replaced by some graded notion of *similarity* of meaning. Intentional generalizations will then be viewed as subsuming individuals in virtue of the *similarity of their mental states*; translation and paraphrase will be viewed as preserving *similarity of content*, etc.

The consequences of option 1 would seem to be horrendous: either behaviorism or materialistic eliminativism in the philosophy of mind and massive unemployment in cognitive science

187

(the Churchlands advocate the second and possibly the third). The prospects for option 2 are viewed with pretty general skepticism, at least in the philosophical community. If, therefore, one feels no sense of an impending crisis in the foundations of semantics, perhaps that's because something like option 3 is so widely supposed to be plausible.

As we said in chapter 1, we think the prospects for constructing a "robust" notion of similarity of meaning – one that is adequate to the purposes of semantics and cognitive science – are really pretty remote. If this prognosis isn't widely shared, that may be because the friends of semantic similarity have generally been careful not to say what they take the relation of semantic similarity to consist in, so that option 3 has had the status less of a substantive proposal than of a pious hope. Recently, however, Paul Churchland has proposed a sketch of the sort of similarity theory that is required, a notion of mental (or, anyhow, neural) representation that "embodies . . . *metrical* relations . . . and thus embodies the representation of *similarity* relations between distinct items thus represented" ("Some reductive strategies in cognitive neurobiology," p. 102; barring notice to the contrary, emphases are Churchland's throughout).

Since Churchland's attitude towards the intentional/semantic generally tends to be eliminativist, it's unclear just what properties of contentful states his "state space" representations are supposed to preserve. Suffice it that, when he's in "highly speculative" mode, he contemplates, for example, the possibility of

a way of representing "anglophone linguistic hyperspace" so that all grammatical sentences turn out to reside on a proprietary hypersurface within that hyperspace, with the logical relations between them reflected as spatial relations of some kind . . . [This would hold out] the possibility of an alternative to, or potential reduction of, the familiar Chomskyan picture. ("Some reductive strategies," p. 109)

188

This entails that state spaces can represent grammars and such. And like much else that he says, it certainly sounds as though Churchland has in mind a kind of representation that specifies the *contents* of neural states,[1] in which case he is into intentionality up to his neck. In any event, we propose to read him that way and ask how much of the intuitive notion of content similarity state space representation allows us to reconstruct.

In the first part of this chapter we will outline and discuss Churchland's proposal. We hope to convince you that, for all that's on offer so far, the problem of semantic similarity appears no less intractable than the problem of analyticity; and, indeed, that the two problems appear to be intractable for much the same reasons. We then conclude the chapter, and the book, with a brief review of the options that are left to a philosopher/cognitive scientist who has convinced himself that none of options 1–3 will do.

STATE SPACE REPRESENTATION

"The basic idea . . . is that the brain represents various aspects of reality by a *position* in a suitable *state space*; and the brain performs computations on such representations by means of general *coordinate transformations* from one state space to another" ("Some reductive strategies," pp. 78–9). For our present purpose, which is semantics rather than the theory of mental processes, only Churchland's account of neural representation need concern us. We commence by trying to make clear how Churchland's state space proposal connects with the more familiar "network" picture of semantics. The former is, we suggest, profitably viewed as an attempt to generalize the latter and to free it from its specifically empiricist assumptions.

Suppose we start with a roughly Quinean picture of the structure of theories (/languages/belief systems). According to this picture, there are two sorts of ways in which the

189

(nonlogical) symbols belonging to a theory get semantically interpreted. The semantics of the "observation vocabulary" is fixed by conditioning (or other causal) relations between its expressions and observable properties of the distal or proximal environment. The semantics of the rest of the vocabulary is fixed by a network of inferential or (in case the semantics is intended to be naturalistic) causal/associative relations to one another and to the observation terms. The semantic theory of a language thus represents its vocabulary as nodes in a network, the paths of which correspond to semantically relevant relations among the vocabulary items. Observation terms are at the "periphery" of the network, nonobservational vocabulary is further in. We take it that this geography is familiar.

Recall how the problem of content identity arises on this "network" picture. If the paths to a node are collectively constitutive of the identity of the node (as presumably they will be if no a/s distinction is assumed), then only identical networks can token nodes of the same type. Identity of networks is thus a sufficient condition for identity of content, but this sufficient condition isn't robust; it will never be satisfied in practice. The long and the short of it is that a network semantics offers no robust account of content identity if it is denied access to an a/s distinction. (For a more extensive discussion of the holism of network theories and of its relation to the a/s distinction, see chapter 1.) But maybe a network semantics can nevertheless be made to offer a robust notion of content *similarity*? The present proposal is to make content *similarity* do the work that content *identity* did in semantic theories that endorsed the a/s distinction (in effect, by interpreting the *distances* between nodes as well as their connectivity).

How, then, might a robust metric of content similarity be constructed, one which is defined for nodes belonging to networks that are (perhaps arbitrarily) different from each other? An immediate problem is that, according to the usual understanding, the only fixed points in a network are the nodes that correspond to observation vocabulary. It's only these

190

peripheral nodes that can be identified nonholistically, without specifying the rest of the network that contains them. (We're supposing that we know what it is for two arbitrarily different theories to both have a node that expresses an observable property like *red*; it's for both to have vocabulary items that are appropriately connected (for example, conditioned) to redness.) It thus appears that if we are to define a similarity relation over terms in the nonobservation vocabulary, it will have to be by reference to their (direct or indirect) relations to observation terms.

But this picture might well strike one as intolerably empiricistic. It just doesn't seem to be true that the dimensions of content along which words (/concepts) can be similar are reducible to the various ways in which they can be connected to observables. There is plausibly something semantically relevant that everything subsumed by the concept *uncle* has in common with everything subsumed by the concept *aunt*; but a couple of hundred years of unsuccessful empiricism suggests that what they have in common is not expressible by reference to the *observable* properties of aunts and uncles. Similarly, mutatis mutandis, for the similarity between the things subsumed by the concept *ice* and the things subsumed by the concept *steam*; or between the things subsumed by the concept *the President of the US* and the things subsumed by the concept *Cleopatra*. And so on, endlessly.

Churchland's state space story is best understood in this context. At least since *Scientific Realism and the Plasticity of Mind* (1979), he has been attracted to network semantics and inclined to think that a good semantics must make similarity, rather than identity of content, its basic theoretical notion. But he is also suspicious of the sort of empiricism which reduces all semantically relevant relations eventually to relations to observation vocabulary.

The semantic identity of a term derives from its specific place in the embedding network of the semantically important sentences of the language as a whole. Accordingly, if we wish to speak of sameness of meaning *across* languages, then we must learn to

191

speak of terms occupying *analogous places* in the relevantly *similar networks* provided by the respective sets of semantically important sentences of the two languages at issue. (*Scientific Realism*, p. 61)[2]

However,

the aims of translation should include no fundamental interest whatever in preserving observationality. . . . Languages, and the networks of beliefs that they embody, have an identity that transcends and can remain constant over variations in the particular sensory conduits to which they happen to be tied, and in the particular locations within the language where the sensory connections happen to be made. Accordingly, any conception of translation that ties its adequacy to the preservation of "net empirical content" as conceived by Quine will lead to nothing but confusion. (Ibid., pp. 65–6)

For Churchland, the question is thus how to free the network picture of semantics from its empiricist assumptions and somehow to generate a robust notion of content similarity in the course of doing so. We read "Some reductive strategies" as a failed attempt to do this, and we'll argue that a recidivist empiricism is in fact its bottom line.

Churchland's current proposal may now be summarized: A "Quinean" network semantics of the sort we have been discussing can be thought of as describing a space whose dimensions correspond to observable properties and in which each expression of the object language is assigned a position in the space. To say that the concept *dog* is semantically connected to the properties of barking and tail wagging is thus equivalent to saying that it occupies a position in semantic space that is (partially) identified by its value along the barkingness and tail-waggingness dimensions. Since the empiricism of the standard network proposal resides in the requirement that all the dimensions of the semantic space in which the concepts are located must correspond to *observable* properties, all you have to do to get rid of the empiricism is to abolish this requirement. What's left are semantic state spaces of arbitrary dimensions, each dimension corresponding to a parameter in terms of which the semantic theory taxonomizes object language expressions and in which similarity of content among the object language expressions is represented by propinquity relations among regions of the space.[3]

Let's now see how Churchland proposes to develop a theory of the semantics of mental representation that accords with this conception. Rather surprisingly, Churchland's analysis starts, not with the paradigms of intentionality (propositional attitudes and concepts), but with sensations. The more or less explicit suggestion is that if we had a treatment that provided an illuminating semantic account for sensations, it might generalize to mental representation at large. Let us, therefore, consider how the state space story is supposed to apply to sensations, bearing in mind that it is Churchland's account of mental representation, rather than his theory of qualitative content, that is our primary concern.

The qualitative character of our sensations is commonly held to pose an especially intractable problem for any neurobiological reduction of mental states . . . and it is indeed hard to see much room for deductive purchase in the subjectively discriminable but "objectively uncharacterizable" qualia present to consciousness. . . . Even so, a determined attempt to find order rather than mystery in this area uncovers a significant amount of expressible information. . . . Consider . . . the abstract three-dimensional "color cube" proposed by Edwin Land, within which every one of the many hundreds of humanly discriminable colors occupies a unique position or small volume . . . Each axis represents the eye/brain's reconstruction of the *objective* reflectance of the seen object at one of the three wavelengths to which our cones are selectively responsive. Two colours are closely similar just in case their state-space positions within this cube are close to one another. And two colors are dissimilar just in case their state-space positions are distant. We can even speak of the

193

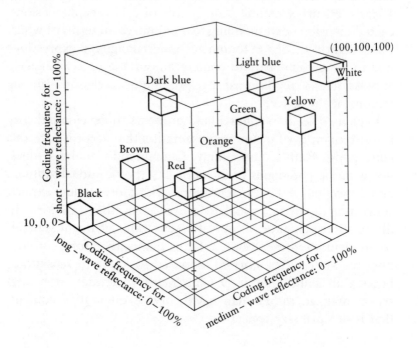

degree of the similarity, and of the dimensions along which it is reckoned. ("Some reductive strategies," pp. 102–3)

We emphasize that Churchland views this as an account of the qualitative content of color sensations, not just of the nervous system's capacity to discriminate among colors.[4]

In particular, it suggests an effective means of expressing the inexpressible. The "ineffable" pink of one's current visual sensation may be richly and precisely expressible as a "95 Hz/ 80 Hz/ 80 Hz chord" in the relevant triune cortical system. . . . This more penetrating conceptual framework might even displace the common-sense framework as the vehicle of intersubjective description and spontaneous introspection. (Ibid., p. 106)

194

How plausible is this story for the representation of the qualitative content of sensations? And how close does it get us to a robust notion of content similarity in general? We'll say just a word or two about the first question, saving most of our attention for the second.

There is, notoriously, a problem of qualitative content that philosophers of mind worry about. It's closely connected with problems about qualia inversion. For example, it seems conceptually possible that the sensation you have when you see things that are grass-colored is "just like" the sensation that I have when I see fire engines. If this inversion is systematic, then perhaps there is *nothing* – in particular, there is no behavioral consequence of our capacity to respond selectively to colors – that would tell this case apart from the normal one in which grass-colored things look the same to you as they do to me. The possibility of inverted qualia thus appears to show that behaviorism is false, and an extension of the same considerations suggests that it may show that functionalism is false too. (For discussion, see Block and Fodor, "What psychological states are not"; Shoemaker, "Functionalism and qualia.")

You might suppose that a theory of the qualitative content of sensations ought to resolve this problem. After all, it's supposed to be precisely qualitative content that gets inverted in inversion examples and precisely the notion of identity of qualitative content that the examples render equivocal. Churchland's account of qualitative content is, however, of no help at all with these issues. The reason is that if qualia inversion makes any sense at all, it seems conceptually possible that you and I should share the state space pictured in the figure, but that the labels on your cube should be inverted with respect to the labels on mine. Notice that the reason why this seems to be conceptually possible is that the dimensions of this state space specify *physical properties of visual stimuli rather than parameters of qualitative content per se.* Since the relation between the property of being a 95 Hz/ 80 Hz/ 80 Hz chord and being a sensation of ineffable pink would appear to be thoroughly contingent (or, at an any event, thoroughly nonsemantic), it would seem to be conceptually possible that something should have the first property but not the second. This just *is* the qualia inversion problem; there appears to be no property of a sensation *except* its qualitative content upon which its qualitative content is guaranteed to supervene. (In particular, there appears to be no behavioral or functional or neurological property upon which it is guaranteed to supervene.) So if you were worried about the qualia problem before you read Churchland, what you should do is keep worrying.

To put this same point in an old-fashioned way, the dimensions of Churchland's state space appear to specify qualia by reference to properties they have *non*essentially, and any such specification begs the inversion problem. (Or, if you think that it is "metaphysically necessary" that color sensations have the psychophysical properties they do, then our point is that this necessity is not engendered by any *semantic* connection between sensation concepts and psychophysical concepts.) You could, in consequence, know perfectly well that a certain sensation corresponds to a certain "chord in the relevant triune cortical system" and have *no idea at all* of "what it's like" to have a sensation of that kind or, indeed, that there *is* anything that it is like.

The problem so far is that the dimensions in terms of which Churchland proposes to taxonomize qualia don't specify their content. Rather, they appear to taxonomize qualia according to the psychophysically sufficient conditions for having them. But it might be thought that this is a defect of the example, not a defect of state space semantics as such. Why not stick to the state space notion of mental representation but add the proviso that the dimensions of the semantic space must really *be* semantic; they must taxonomize content-bearing states *by their contents*. Perhaps concepts (like *aunt, uncle, steam, ice, the President of the US, Cleopatra*, and the like) can be identified with positions in a state space of semantically relevant dimensions, so that similarities among these concepts could be identified with propinquities in the state space. (*The President of the US* is close to *Cleopatra* on the *politician* dimension, but maybe less close on the dimension *nubile.*) This, as opposed to the vicissitudes of Churchland's treatment of qualia, is the issue we are really interested in; it's the proposal that promises a robust theory of content similarity to replace the robust theory of content identity that was lost when the a/s distinction went down.

In fact, however, we now propose to argue that this suggestion is without substance. The same problems that traditionally arose for theories of content identity also arise for this theory of content similarity, so the appearance of progress is simply an illusion. To begin with the crucial point, the state space story about content similarity actually *presupposes* a solution to (and therefore begs) the question of content identity.

PROBLEMS OF STATE SPACE SEMANTICS

The Individuation of Dimensions

What Churchland has on offer is the idea that two concepts are similar insofar as they occupy (relatively) similar positions *in the same state space.* The question thus presents itself: *When are S_1 and S_2 the same state space? When, for example, is your semantic space a token of the same semantic space state type as mine?* Well, clearly a necessary condition for the identity of state spaces is the identity of their dimensions – specifically, the identity of their *semantic* dimensions, since the current proposal is that concepts be located by reference to a space of *semantically relevant properties.* We are thus faced with the question of when x and y are the same semantic dimensions (for example, when positions along x and y both express degrees of being a politician or of nubility). But this is surely just the old semantic identity problem back again. If we don't know what it is for two words both to mean *nubile*, then we also don't know – and for the same reasons – what it is for two spaces both to have a *nubility* dimension. Perhaps it will be replied that semantic similarity doesn't, after all, require concepts to be propinquitous in the *very same* state space; perhaps occupying corresponding positions in *similar* state spaces will do. That a regress has now appeared is, we trust, entirely obvious.

It's worth getting clear on what has gone wrong. The old (empiricist) version of network semantics had a story about the identification of the dimensions by reference to which it did its taxonomizing; they were to express observable properties, and an externalist (for example, causal) theory of some kind was to explicate the relation between observable properties and terms in the observation vocabulary. In particular, that relation was assumed to be specifiable independent of the interpretation of the rest of the vocabulary. However, as we've seen, Churchland's proposal comes down to the idea that the dimensions of semantic state space *don't* generally correspond to observable properties; they can correspond to *whatever* properties the brain may represent. This avoids empiricism alright, but it begs the question of how identity of state spaces is itself to be determined. On the one hand, we are assuming that dimensions of semantic state spaces can express whatever properties you like. On the other hand, we *don't have and can't assume* any identity criterion for dimensions that express other than observable properties. And, on the last hand, *to take such a criterion for granted would just be to beg the semantic identity problem*.

To repeat, we have a robust notion of semantic similarity only if we have a criterion for the identity of state spaces. We have a criterion for the identity of state spaces only if we have a criterion for identity of dimensions of state spaces. And we have a (nonempiricist) criterion for the identity of dimensions of state spaces only if we have a criterion of "property expressed by a dimension of a state space" that works for arbitrary properties, not just for observable properties. But a criterion for "property

198

expressed" that works for arbitrary properties *just is* a criterion for identity of meaning. So Churchland's proposal for a robust theory of content similarity fails to avoid the problem of robust content identity – and, of course, fails to solve it.

In chapter 1 we offered it as a plausible methodological principle that you *can't have* a robust notion of content similarity (one that applies across languages, across minds, or across theories) unless you have a correspondingly robust notion of content identity. Churchland's space state semantics provides a graphic illustration of how this principle applies. His explication of an interpersonal notion of content *similarity* as proximity in semantic state space *presupposes* an interpersonal notion of identity for the semantic spaces themselves, a notion that Churchland leaves entirely without explication. In consequence, if you're worried about how concepts can be robust – perhaps because you're worried that there isn't an a/s distinction – then Churchland's state space semantics provides no illumination at all.

We're claiming, in effect, that Churchland has confused himself by taking the *labels* on the semantic dimensions for granted. The label on a dimension says *how positions along the dimension are to be interpreted*; for example, it says that they're to be interpreted as expressing degrees of F-ness. To label a dimension as the F-ness dimension is thus to invite the question "In virtue of what do the values of this dimension express degrees of F-ness rather than, say, degrees of G-ness?" (equivalently, for these purposes, "What makes it the case that a dimension in your state space expresses the same property F as some dimension in my state space does?") Patently, a semantic theory mustn't beg this sort of question, on pain of assuming the very concepts it is supposed to explicate.

Cognitive scientists are forever getting themselves into trouble in this way; it's a fallacy that is particularly endemic among connectionists. Connectionists draw diagrams in which the label on a node tells you what the intentional interpretation of the excitation of the node is supposed to be. But no theory is offered to explain why a node gets the label it does; it's just semantics by stipulation.

Churchland makes exactly this mistake, only it's the dimension labels rather than the node labels that he stipulates. This, however, is actually a distinction without a difference, since stipulating a semantic interpretation for the dimensions *just is* stipulating semantic interpretations for points (regions, and the like) in the space they define. This fact is obscured in the figure because the labels that are provided for points in that semantic space (namely, the color labels "brown," "dark blue," and so on) are not actually the ones implied by the labels on the axes. The labelling of the axes implies that points in the space are ordered triples corresponding to values of short-, medium-, and long-wave reflectances. By contrast, the color labels represent not the semantics of the state space but Land's empirical proposal about how the qualitative character of sensations varies as a function of psychophysical properties of light.

This slight tension in Churchland's notation turns out, upon reflection, to be the tip of a substantial iceberg. It's worth a digression to make the issues clear.[5] Consider the following question: How does Churchland decide what gets represented by *dimensions* of state spaces and what gets represented by *regions* in the state spaces that the dimensions define? What decides, for example, that "brown" and "dark blue" correspond to regions rather than dimensions? There is, after all, nothing obviously wrong with taxonomizing bananas according to their degree of brownness or oceans according to their degree of dark blueness, and there are presumably lots of cases where one's concept of an X includes information about the color of X's – blondes, for example.

One principled way of making this decision might be to stipulate that the dimensions of state spaces express always and only psychophysical (or possibly neurological) parameters; indeed, this may well be what Churchland has in mind. If so, however, what he is offering isn't a semantics at all. For a semantics taxonomizes mental states by their contents, not by their causes. Churchland may be assuming that if a stimulus has such and such psychophysical properties, then if the brain responds to the stimulus, the brain *thereby* represents the stimulus *as having those psychophysical properties*. But the brain represents red things as red, not as reflecting light of such and such a wavelength; and it represents aunts as aunts, not as possessing whatever psychophysical properties we employ for purposes of aunt detection (assuming, indeed, that there *are* such properties). Psychophysics would be a lot easier were this not so; we could do it by introspection.

Churchland's state spaces thus vacillate between being psychophysical spaces and being semantic spaces. Correspondingly – and this point really is essential – *proximity in state space* means quite different things on the two interpretations of Churchland's theory. According to the semantic reading, proximity expresses the similarity of the content of mental states; according to the psychophysical reading, it expresses the similarity under physical description of the (proximal) stimuli that elicit the states. Apparently, Churchland hasn't decided which sort of similarity he has in mind; so there's a crucial respect in which he hasn't decided what his space state theory is a theory *of*.

That Churchland really has confused the semantic with the psychophysical enterprise is suggested by revealing hesitations like his suggestion that state spaces offer "*an alternative to, or potential reduction of*, the familiar Chomskian picture" (our emphasis). One or the other, perhaps, but surely not both. An *alternative* to the Chomskian picture would be a new story about what a native speaker knows about his language – that is, a new story about *the intentional content* of the native speaker's knowledge of his language. Qua "alternative" it would, by definition, be *in competition* with Chomsky's picture. A "reduction," by contrast, would presumably be a story about the neural format in which what the native speaker knows about his language is coded in his brain.[6] By definition, a reduction is *not* in competition with the theory that it reduces.

The semantic theory and the reductive theory are in quite different lines of work, and nothing can do both jobs. Churchland really will have to make up his mind as to which kind of theory state space theory is supposed to be.[7]

The Analytic/Synthetic Distinction

As you might expect, all the other standard worries about content identity now come trooping back in. Consider the a/s distinction itself. It's analytic (let's say) that dogs are animals; it's not analytic (let's say) that they typically have wet noses. Consequently, to change to Churchland's notation, the space in which the concept *dog* is resident must have a dimension corresponding to the property of being an animal, but it needn't have a dimension corresponding to the property of typically having a wet nose. (In fact, it had *better not* have such a dimension if the location of an item in the space is to predict its behavior in modal inferences.) This is to say that it is constitutive of the concept *dog* that it subsumes only animals, but not constitutive that it subsumes only things whose noses are typically wet. Problem: If you are convinced that there is no principled way of drawing an a/s distinction, what principle will you appeal to in order to distinguish the dimensions that *are* relevant to defining semantic spaces from the dimensions that aren't? You can have the problem of individuating meanings as the analytic/synthetic problem (see chapter 2) or as the problem of saying what makes something a bona fide conceptual role (see chapter 6) or as the problem of saying what makes something a bona fide dimension of semantic state space (as per Churchland). The point is that it's the same problem whichever way you choose to have it; in particular, it doesn't go away when you start to think of semantic relations among concepts as "metric."[8]

Collateral Information

If it is to turn out that your concept *dog* occupies much the same region in your semantic space that my concept *dog* occupies in mine, then it had better be that your semantic space has whatever dimensions mine has; as we've seen, this raises the question of how the dimensions of semantic state space are to be identified/individuated, which would seem to be the content identity problem all over again. Well, suppose that the problem of individuating dimensions is somehow solved; it's still not guaranteed that your *dog* concept and my *dog* concept will turn out to be similar. The problem is that I know a lot of things about dogs that you don't (and, of course, vice versa). For example, I know that I once had a dog named Spot and that my grandmother is allergic to Dalmatians and that there aren't any dogs in the room in which I'm writing this. But you wouldn't have known any of those things about dogs if I hadn't just told you. Nor is there any particular reason why the various beliefs about dogs that we fail to share must in general be token-reflexive. If you're a dog buff and I'm not, you have very many standing beliefs about dogs that I don't have and don't have any desire to acquire.

The point is that if a semantics recognizes dimensions of state space corresponding to all the properties of dogs about which our beliefs differ, then even assuming that your state space has exactly the same dimensions as mine, the location of the *dog* concepts in our respective spaces is likely to turn out to be quite significantly different.[9] This should all be sounding like old news; it's just the worry, familiar from attempts to construct a notion of content *identity*, that a lot of what anybody knows about dogs counts as idiosyncratic; it's "collateral information," the sort of thing that Frege says belongs to psychology rather than semantics. If we are to have a notion of meanings as shared, public property, a robust notion of meaning, we must somehow abstract from this idiosyncratic variation.[10] This holds just as much for similarity of meaning as it does for identity of meaning. Or, if it doesn't, an argument is needed to show *why* it doesn't. We're not aware that there's any such argument around.

If, in short, *all* dimensions – all the properties in respect of which the contents of concepts can be classified – count in determining positions in state space, then even if everybody's state space has exactly the same dimensions as everybody else's, the collateral information problem makes it quite unlikely that anybody's concepts will turn out similar to anybody else's. One way out would be to assume that the dimensions of state space are *weighted*, that agreement along some dimensions counts more for conceptual similarity than agreement along other dimensions. In traditional theories of content identity, this weighting of dimensions was accomplished precisely by appealing to the a/s distinction: it matters that your concepts have the same values as mine *on dimensions that correspond to properties that feature in the analysis of the concepts*; with respect to the other dimensions, the concepts are allowed to vary idiosyncratically. Once again, nothing changes when the topic changes to content similarity. Our concepts are similar if they have similar locations along certain dimensions, regardless of whether they have similar locations along other dimensions. The collateral information problem is to find a principled way of deciding which dimensions count a lot, which ones count a little, and which ones don't count at all. And nobody has the slightest idea of how to do this without invoking an a/s distinction.

We hope the moral will now be clear; we spare the reader further exposition. What Churchland has is a dilemma: it may be that he isn't intending to require that the dimensions of his state space correspond to properties of the contents of the mental states (objects, events) that they taxonomize. In that case, he isn't doing semantics at all. He's doing, as it might be, psychophysics, and we have no quarrel with anything he says except that he is not really entitled to describe what he has on offer as a theory about how "the brain *represents* various

204

aspects of reality by a position in a suitable state space" (our emphasis). If, on the other hand, Churchland *is* taking the talk about neural *representation* seriously, his move to state spaces leaves all the old problems about content identity still to be solved. We think that probably, given these options, Churchland would prefer the first. He is, as we remarked above, very much inclined to be an eliminativist about intentional/semantic properties when metaphysical push comes to shove. (We've seen throughout this book how many semantic holists end up that way.) An eliminativist doesn't need a notion of semantic similarity, however, any more than he needs a notion of semantic identity. An eliminativist doesn't want to reconstruct semantic discourse; he wants to change the topic.

But couldn't Churchland somehow contrive to have it both ways? Couldn't he somehow work it out that state spaces do semantics and psychophysics *at the same time?* Sure he could. What he has to do is just assume the "empiricist principle" that all our concepts are functions (possibly Boolean functions, but more likely *statistical* functions) of our psychophysical concepts.[11] As far as we can tell, this is what connectionists, Churchland included, actually do assume (though, understandably, they aren't eager to put it that way).[12] The reason that assuming the empiricist principle is helpful in this context is that it provides a robust identity criterion for semantic spaces. If all concepts are ultimately sensory concepts, then every concept is a location in a semantic space whose dimensions express sensory properties. So two organisms share a semantic space if they have their sensory transducers in common.[13] The reason why assuming the empiricist principle is nevertheless to be avoided, however, is that it isn't true. Most concepts are *not* Boolean or statistical functions of psychophysical or sensory concepts, and most concept learning is not either Boolean or statistical inference. A fortiori, one's concepts and theories are not to be identified with points in a space whose dimensions express sensory or psychophysical properties or constructs thereof. You might have thought that this would have been the one thing that philosophers would have learned from 200 years or so of epistemological bad weather. But no: the smoke clears, and the landscape is revealed as having hardly changed at all.

That Churchland's account of content similarity is question begging doesn't, of course, constitute a *proof* that a robust notion of content similarity can't compensate holistic semantics for its lack of a robust notion of content identity. Somebody might come up with a robust notion of content similarity that's not question begging by early tomorrow afternoon (though one would be well advised not to hold one's breath). But what's not a proof may nevertheless serve as an object lesson. The current situation is that nobody has any idea of what content similarity is, just as nobody has any idea of what content identity is – and, as we remarked at the outset, for much the same reasons.

GENERAL CONCLUSION

It looks as though, if semantic properties are typically anatomic and there is no a/s distinction, then meaning holism is true. On the other hand, if the arguments in this book are right, then there is no very pressing reason to suppose that semantic properties are typically anatomic. But, on the third hand, if the reason why there are no pressing reasons to suppose that semantic properties are typically anatomic is that, as a matter of fact, semantic properties are typically punctate, then conceptual role semantics won't work and we desperately need an atomistic theory of meaning to replace it. Whichever point of view you take, the present position in meaning theory would seem to be quite unstable; something's gotta give.

What happens next? There are, it would seem, lots of possibilities. For example, neither meaning atomism nor meaning holism has actually been refuted; all that has happened is that the first hasn't performed very well and the second hasn't been convincingly motivated. One line of research would be to try to rule one or the other in or out by conclusive – preferably a priori – argument. For example, the Davidson/Dennett strategy of showing that interpretation is intrinsically holistic because it depends upon intrinsically holistic principles of charity could be vindicated by a convincing argument that charity is indeed holistic and a prerequisite to interpretation. We argued in chapters 3 and 5 that, so far, the case hasn't been made for either claim; but for all we've shown, somebody might do that by early tomorrow afternoon too. Or somebody might make a convincing case for the primacy of belief thesis; this would vindicate holism on the assumption that belief is itself holistic, and as we saw in chapter 4, that assumption is perfectly plausible.

Conceptual role semantics hasn't been refuted either, though we think we have shown that its dependence on the a/s distinction is ineliminable. But then, as we saw at the end of chapter 2, neither has the a/s distinction been refuted; the most that Quine showed about the a/s distinction in "Two dogmas" is that if there *is* a notion of content identity, it can't be reconstructed in terms of *epistemic* categories like unrevisability or a prioricity. So it's still wide open that some kind of semantic molecularism might work; perhaps even a semantics according to which some, but not all, of the properties of its inferential role are constitutive of a concept's identity. All that's needed in order to resuscitate this sort of semantics in the face of Quine's rejection of the a/s distinction is for somebody to invent a nonepistemic notion of conceptual role. And finally, we suppose, nihilism about semantics might actually turn out to be true even if, as recent discussion has suggested, there are transcendental reasons why its doing so would be literally unthinkable.

Contrary to widely received philosophical opinion, there are, as far as we can tell, practically *no* closed options in semantics; the arguments that were reputed to close them are, in our view, comprehensively flawed. In that respect this book hasn't made any headway either, of course. But our ambitions were modest from the outset: there was getting to be a lot of dust behind the door, so we thought we'd better sweep up.

NOTES

1. By which we intend "not atomistic" rather than "of or pertaining to anatomy."
2. We will, throughout, use the authorial "I" and the authorial "we" interchangeably, as ease of exposition dictates. "He" and "his" are often used without implication of gender.
3. We'll generally save "meaning holism" or "semantic holism" for the broader, and less precise, doctrine that meaning is somehow holistic. So meaning holism is true if (but perhaps not only if) either content holism or translation holism is true. The main reason for bothering to distinguish content holism from translation holism is that a meaning holist might admit the possibility of punctate languages, minds, and the like as a sort of metaphysical curiosity but still deny that a punctate language could express anything that can be expressed in English, the idea being that in *non*punctate languages (like English) the meanings of sentences are constituted by their relations to one another. Content holism thus precludes possibilities that translation holism leaves open. We will call the doctrine that asserts translation holism but allows punctate languages "semi-holism" when it's important to distinguish it from other holistic options.

   For many purposes, however, the various kinds of meaning holism tend to stand or fall on much the same considerations; we will, therefore, often run them together.
4. This way of putting things depends on allowing the notion of a language itself to be construed relatively narrowly – as a set of sentences, say, rather than a life-style. Anthropological holism is, in part, the idea that

this narrow reading of "language" is hopelessly artificial and that, in the long run, there is no real distinction between what is linguistic behavior and what isn't or, ultimately, between languages and whole cultures. That may be right. If it is, then a lot of linguists have been wasting their time barking up phrase-structure trees. We remark in passing, however, that it is possible to imagine a view that is holist in the broad, anthropological sense but nevertheless leaves open the possibility of punctate languages. For example: symbols get their meanings from the way they are embedded in Forms of Life, but there's no internal connection between being so embedded and being part of a symbol *system* (for example, being part of a language with a compositional syntax and semantics). The "primitive languages" that Wittgenstein imagines in the early paragraphs of the *Philosophical Investigations* are, perhaps, meant to be holistic in the broad but not the narrow sense.

·5. Where Frege·himself stands is a little unclear. On the one hand, it's a famous Fregean view that words have meaning only as constituents of (hence, presumably, only in virtue of their use in) sentences, and this view looks to be inherently anatomic; but, on the other hand, Frege certainly thought that the semantics of sentences is compositionally determined by the semantics of the words they contain (plus their syntax), and this suggests that lexical semantics must in some sense be prior to sentence semantics. Whether, and in exactly what way, these doctrines can be reconciled is a notorious crux in Frege interpretation.

6. This sort of issue isn't made to go away by taking the objects of theoretical interest to be idiolects rather than languages (as, indeed, many linguists are inclined to do, even at the cost of denying that the basic function of natural languages is to mediate communication between its speakers; see Chomsky, Halle, and others). For there is still the problem of communication between *time slices of an idiolect*; if holism is true and idiolects are the minimal units of meaning, how could I have incrementally learned the idiolect that I now speak?

Davidson suggests that "we cannot accurately describe the first steps towards the conquest [of a language] as learning part of the language; rather it is a matter of partly learning" ("Theories of meaning and learnable language," p. 7). That is, it is possible for a child to *partially learn a language* without learning *part of the language*. This is not, however, a suggestion we claim to fully understand.

7. We only say it *might* turn out this way. We're currently running the discussion on the assumption that there is an argument from the premise that semantic properties are *anatomic* to the conclusion that they are *holistic*. But precisely which holistic consequence follows from the assumption that a semantic property is anatomic depends, of course, on

exactly how this argument is supposed to go. We will return to this question presently.

8. The argument that properties like R* are holistic often assumes that *meaning* is holistic and that meaning determines reference. Whether reference holism can be defended without this assumption is a question of great philosophical interest, but not one that we will consider in this book.

9. It wouldn't follow from R*'s being holistic that theories are incommensurable unless their ontologies are *identical*. There might be some sense of "similar" in which theories are commensurable if their ontologies are similar enough. (We'll discuss this sort of possibility presently.) Nor would it follow that if T_2 and T_3 are both commensurable with T_1, then there are things that T_2 and T_3 can both refer to. The ontological requirements for commensurability might permit that T_2 is commensurable with T_1 because they can both refer to a's, b's, and c's and T_3 is commensurable with T_1 because they can both refer to d's, e's, and f's; that is, having expressions that refer to a, b, and c and having expressions that refer to d, e, and f are both sufficient for sharing the ontology of T_1, though neither is necessary. (This sort of possibility was pointed out to us, in a slightly different context, by Paul Boghossian, Barry Loewer, and Tim Maudlin; see below.)

   In either case, the urgent issue for Scientific Realism is whether there is, short of identity, a *principled* answer to the question "Which sorts of overlaps between ontologies are sufficient for empirical commensurability?" In the terminology of Kuhn's *The Structure of Scientific Revolutions*, this is approximately the question as to whether it's principled when different theories belong to the same paradigm.

10. Paul Churchland appears to hold, largely on the ground that properties like R* are holistic, that only the final, literally true physics will be able to refer to *anything at all*. Churchland seems to take this view to be good news for Realism, but it's not clear to us why he does. On his account, the only science that has an ontology – a fortiori, the only science for whose ontology reality can be claimed – is not one that any human scientist is ever likely to profess.

11. We make a point of *not* using shopworn examples like "If you believe $(P \rightarrow Q)$ and P, then you believe Q." These sorts of generalization presuppose a notion of *identity and difference* of belief content rather than a notion of belief content *per se*.

12. This is a bullet that is frequently bitten. For example, Field holds that the meaning of a sentence is determined by its "referential meaning" together with its "conceptual role" ("Logic, meaning and conceptual role," p. 390). As he recognizes, the conceptual role part implies semantic holism. (Field

211

shares the usual doubts about the a/s distinction.) Field accepts the
consequence that his semantics is therefore

> compatible with a great deal of pessimism about the clarity of the
> notion of inter-speaker synonymy. . . . My own inclination is not to
> try to provide such an account but to learn to live without the
> concept of inter-speaker synonymy, and all other concepts in terms
> of which inter-speaker synonymy could be defined. (The place that
> such concepts appear to be needed is in belief–desire psychology. I
> believe that any such psychology formulated in terms of such
> concepts can be reformulated so as not to employ them and that
> there are independent grounds for preferring the reformulated theory.
> (Ibid., pp. 398–9)

Field doesn't, however, say how this reformulation is to be achieved.

In a quite different context, but a rather similar spirit, Roy Harris
remarks that "It is arguable that if translation is taken as demanding
linguistic equivalence between texts, then the Saussurean [structuralist]
position must be that translation is impossible" (in Saussure, *Course in
General Linguistics*, p. xiii). Harris does not take this to be a reductio ad
absurdum of the Saussurean position.

13. A generalization is "robust" to the extent that the individuals that fall
under it are otherwise heterogeneous in lots of ways; correspondingly, a
definition is robust if it is satisfied under lots of otherwise heterogeneous
conditions, and so forth.

14. This is the received account of Davidson's view, but Davidson's view
may be more nuanced than the received account supposes. Davidson
clearly holds that there can't be *exceptionless,* or *"homonomic,"*
intentional laws; but it wouldn't *seem* to follow from this that intentional
laws can't support counterfactuals, back singulary causal truths, and so
on. After all, the (presumably) heteronomic character of geological laws
doesn't prevent them from doing so. What Davidson takes the bottom
line on these topics to be is not something we're at all sure about. See
Lycan, "Psychological laws"; Rosenberg, "Davidson's unintended attack
on psychology"; Dennett, "Mid-term examination: compare and contrast."

15. It's sometimes pushed pretty hard that the holistic and systematic
character of the semantic (/intentional) isolates hermeneutical investigations from modes of criticism that are pertinent elsewhere. Sometimes it's
pushed to the verge of mysticism:

> The logic of difference is a non-self-identical logic, one that eludes all
> the normative constraints which govern classical reason. If language

is marked by the absence of "positive terms" – if meaning is differential through and through – then any theory which attempts to conceptualize language will find itself up against this ultimate limit to its own explanatory powers. (Norris, *Derrida*, p. 91)

16. For example, here's Gilbert Harman in *Thought*:

> Two people can be said to mean exactly the same thing by their words if [sic; "only if"?] the identity-translation works perfectly to preserve dispositions to accept sentences under analysis and actual usage. To the extent that the identity-translation does not work perfectly, people do not mean *exactly* the same thing by their words; but if the identity-translation is better than alternatives we will say that they mean the same thing by their words. Here we mean by *the same, roughly the same* rather than *exactly the same*. . . . The only sort of sameness of meaning we know is similarity in meaning, not exact sameness of meaning. This is where the defender of the analytic-synthetic distinction has gone wrong; he confuses a similarity relation with an equivalence relationship. (pp. 109–10)

17. Twin worries (à la Putnam, "The meaning of 'meaning' ") are not the issue here; choose any physical state of affairs, relational or otherwise, on which you are prepared to believe that belief systems supervene.
18. Notice that this is much the same problem as has led so many philosophers to despair of the project of constructing a robust notion of content *identity* by appealing to some suitably abstract notion of identity of inferential role. Some inferences (traditionally the analytic ones) count, and some inferences (traditionally the synthetic ones) don't count, and there appears to be no principled way of saying which are which. This problem *does not disappear* if you replace "count"/"don't count" with "count much"/"don't count much."
19. Nor, of course, would the more sanguine conclusions that are often drawn from meaning holism – as, for example, that the assumptions of commonsense Intentional Realism are immune to challenge from the physical sciences. See above.
20. Others deny the a/s distinction, accept that holistic consequences are entailed, and argue that the right moral to draw is that there really aren't any intentional properties. Quine takes this line in certain of his moods, and so do Dennett and Stich in certain of theirs; the Churchlands take it all the time.
21. This is one reason for being skeptical as to whether Quine's "Two dogmas of empiricism" contains an argument for semantic holism along

213

the lines of A, though it is widely interpreted as doing so. See the next chapter.

22. The relevant consideration is this: If A is a proposition that you have to believe to believe P, then presumably P → A must be analytic. (If nobody could believe that something is a dog unless he believed that that thing is an animal, then the belief that if something is a dog, then it's an animal is a semantic truth.) According to the present assumptions, however, there is *no* proposition that you must believe in order to be able to believe P. (Either believing A or believing B is sufficient, but neither believing A nor believing B is necessary.)

23. More precisely, it closes the book against the possibility of atomism about *belief*. This is a distinction we dwell on in chapter 4, q.v.

24. It's worth emphasizing, in the current atmosphere of near universal holistic consensus, that until very recently, and for a very long while, the philosophical consensus for semantic atomism seemed equally secure. We commend this historical reflection to philosophers who say that no argument for semantic holism is required because it is self-evidently true, or that the anatomism of semantic properties is intuitively obvious.

25. The variations on this theme in the secondary literature on semiotics are endless. Here are examples, chosen practically at random:

> It is a cardinal precept of modern (structural) linguistics that signs don't have meaning in and of themselves, but by virtue of their occupying a distinctive place within the systematic network of contrasts and differences which make up any given language. (Norris, *Derrida*, p. 15)

> For it is a major precept of modern structural linguistics that meaning is not a relation of identity (sic!) between signifier and signified but a relation of differences, the signifying contrasts and relationships that exist at every level of language. (Ibid., p. 85)

> The choice is thus between a linguistic atomism that grounds meaning in a language/world ("sign"/"signifier") relation (though not, one might have thought, an *identity* relation) and a linguistic holism which grounds meaning in the relation between a symbol and its role in a language; and "modern structural linguistics" teaches us to prefer the second option.
> This is, of course, a wildly tendentious account of what linguistics teaches us about meaning. Consider how badly it comports with model theoretic, or situational, approaches to the semantics of natural languages, all of which assume that language/world relations (like "satisfaction," "extension," and "denotation") are what the theory of meaning is about.

(In particular, they assume that it's about how the syntactically complex expressions in a language inherit these language/world relations from their syntactically simpler constituents.)

26. Philosophical interest in resemblance theories of meaning much pre-dates the British empiricists, of course. See Plato, *Cratylus*, and Aristotle, *De Interpretatione*.

27. For a brief discussion of why resemblance theories don't work, see Fodor, *The Language of Thought*, ch. 4. For the classic discussion of why conditioning theories don't work, see Chomsky, "Review of B. F. Skinner's *Verbal Behavior*."

28. For a discussion of some recent attempts to construct an atomistic theory of content, see Fodor "A theory of content."

NOTES TO CHAPTER 2

1. We will follow what we understand to be Quine's usage, according to which *reductionism* is a species of *verificationism*. (What precisely the distinction between the two amounts to will be discussed below.) Readers who are accustomed to use "reductionism" to name a type of *ontological* theory should bear in mind that Quine's usage is eccentric.

2. An ontological – specifically, an anti-Realist – construal of the pragmatism in the last pages of "Two dogmas" certainly seems natural. But, on a close reading, it is less than fully apparent that that's what Quine actually intended. For example, though Quine says that gods and physical objects are both just "cultural posits," the explicit claim is only that they are comparable "*epistemologically*" (our emphasis). The ontological moral – if, indeed, there is supposed to be one – is pretty carefully not drawn.

3. Another version of the Q/D thesis says that "the unit of confirmation is the whole theory"; and this *doesn't* follow from these Realist considerations. But we doubt that Quine actually holds the Q/D thesis in this latter form. Glymour remarks that "[even] without analytic truth we need not . . . defy history and good sense by insisting that evidence must bear on all of a theory (let alone on all of science) or none of it or that we must accept or reject our theories as a single piece" (Glymour, *Theory and Evidence*, p. 152). Glymour's point is that, given recalcitrant data, we can pick and choose which bit of theory to give up; we don't have to give it all up. Glymour is surely right about this; but it's far from clear to us that Quine intends to deny it. Quine's claim isn't that if you get recalcitrant data,

everything has to go; it's that *what goes and what stays is rationally up for grabs*. Specifically, what goes and what stays can't be decided a priori by appeal to semantics.

4. The reference to Frege is, however, labile. In the original *Philosophical Review* version of "Two dogmas," the reference is to Russell; in the first edition of *From a Logical Point of View*, the reference is to Frege; and in later editions of *From a Logical Point of View*, the reference is to Bentham. For our present purposes, any of the three will do.

5. Since Quine exegesis is always dangerous territory, perhaps we'd best quote some philosophers who read the text in this way. Here is Putnam: "Quine's argument for meaning holism in 'Two dogmas of empiricism' is set out against the meaning theories of the positivists . . . Quine argues that . . . individual sentences are meaningful in the sense of making a systematic contribution to the functioning of the whole language" ("Meaning holism," p. 405). Similar views are expressed in Putnam, "The analytic and the synthetic," to which Quine refers approvingly in *Word and Object*, p. 57.

Consider also the following from Gibson (*The Philosophy of W. V. Quine: An Expository Essay*) (a source which Quine commends for its "full understanding" of his work).

Let's call Quine's version of Peirce's thesis (P):

P: The meaning of a sentence turns purely on what would count as evidence for its truth.

(P) is a form of verificationism. It is the thesis that equates the concepts of meaning and evidence. . . . Let us call Quine's version of Duhem's thesis (D).

D: Single theoretical sentences do not always or usually have a separable fund of *evidence* to call their own; they have their funds of evidence only when connected to larger blocks of theory.

Now, if (P) is regarded as a statement of the equivalence of the concepts of meaning and evidence, then (D) could as well be read as:

(D') Single theoretical sentences do not always or usually have a (separable) *meaning* to call their own; they have their meanings only when connected to larger blocks of theory. (pp. 80–1)

For other philosophers who more or less explicitly hold (or hold that Quine holds, or both) that verificationism together with the Q/D thesis entails semantic holism, see P. S. Churchland, *Neurophilosophy: Toward an Unified Theory of the Mind/Brain*, pp. 265–7; P. M. Churchland,

Matter and Consciousness: A Contemporary Introduction to the Philo-sophy of Mind, ch. 3; Gilbert Harman, "Meaning and semantics," pp. 11–12.

6. "Quine's theory, as presented at the end of 'Two Dogmas,' is verificationist, since it has entirely to do with the effect which experience has on what we hold to be true, as opposed to the truth of what we say independently of whether we have reason for it" (Dummett, *Frege*, p. 592).

Notice, by the way, that the identification of meaning with means of confirmation needn't be viewed as a metaphysical *reduction* of either to the other. The morning star doesn't *reduce* to the evening star; it just is it.

7. See also Quine, "Epistemology naturalized":

If we recognize with Peirce that the meaning of a sentence turns purely on what would count as evidence for its truth . . . then the indeterminacy of theoretical sentences is the natural conclusion. . . . Should the unwelcomeness of the conclusion persuade us to abandon the verificationist theory of meaning? Certainly not. The sort of meaning that is basic to translation, and to the learning of one's own language, is necessarily empirical meaning and nothing more. . . . Surely one has no choice but to be an empiricist so far as one's theory of linguistic meaning is concerned. (pp. 80–1)

Not only *is* Quine a verificationist; he thinks there aren't any other options.

We're stressing this because many philosophers apparently read "Two dogmas" as *rejecting* verificationism. This is because they fail to notice a distinction that it is centrally important to keep in mind. As we've seen, what is rejected in "Two dogmas" is not *verificationism* but what Quine calls "reductionism": namely, the theory that there is, for each statement, a corresponding range of confirming conditions determinable a priori. Reductionism is inherently localist with regard to confirmation; whereas verificationism, as such, is neutral on whether confirmation is holistic. The former is explicitly attacked in "Two dogmas," but there's every reason to suppose that rejecting verificationism is an option Quine would never have considered.

8. See, for example, Loar:

The confirmation or verification of a sentence is, for Quine, undetachable from its potential evidential connections with virtually any other sentence. Within the positivist tradition, in which meaning and evidential responsiveness are identified, that epistemological theory naturally leads to a holistic conception of meaning. . . . It is quite in . . . [this] . . . spirit to take each sentence to have a kind of meaning, identified not with its own empirical meaning, but with the totality of its evidential connections to other sentences and perceptual stimuli. ("Conceptual role and truth conditions," p. 273)

See also Fodor, *Psychosemantics: The Problem of Meaning in the Philosophy of Mind*, ch. 3.

9. The point isn't just that you can always imagine a state of affairs such that, *if it obtained*, then the truth of, as it might be, "Grass is green" would bear on the truth of, as it might be, "Mars has rings." Since *potential* confirmation relations, in this sense, presumably hold between *any* contingent statements, it's unclear how a plausible version of Peirce's thesis could reconstruct semantic relations in terms of them. The point is rather that the level of confirmation of a theory (and hence, derivatively, of each of its entailments) depends in part on such considerations as simplicity, conservatism, and the like, which, because they are global, are simultaneously sensitive to *all* the theory's commitments.

10. Conversely, as Dummett has remarked, Quine likes an ecumenical story according to which the connectives *mean different things* in classical and intuitionistic logic. But, again, barring some trans-theoretic notion of statement identity, it's unclear how you decide *which* connectives it is that the two kinds of logic assign different meanings to. (The thought that there are perhaps *no* theorems that classicists and intuitionists can both accept without equivocation seems, to put it mildly, unintuitive.)

11. Because of this problem, Quine's post–"Two dogmas" writings seem increasingly inclined to treat observation statements as exceptions to the Q/D thesis; that is, as having their confirmation conditions *locally* determined. See, for example: "The observation sentence, situated at the sensory periphery of the body scientific, is the minimal verifiable aggregate; it has an empirical content all its own and wears it on its sleeve" ("Epistemology naturalized," p. 89). Heaven only knows how this is supposed to square with the version of the Q/D thesis according to which *any* sentence may be rationally abandoned given sufficient pressure from global simplicity, coherence, conservatism, and the like. In any event, the exception in favor of observation sentences shows, all by itself, that Quine can't unreservedly suppose that the argument from the Q/D thesis and Peirce's thesis to semantic holism is sound. (For some of Quine's recent views on this issue, see his "Reply to Hilary Putnam.")

12. Among those who reject the Q/D thesis are Dummett, "What is a theory of meaning?"; Glymour, *Theory and Evidence*; Grunbaum, "The falsifiability of theories: total or partial? A contemporary evaluation of

the Duhem–Quine thesis." Among those who reject verificationism are all the informational semanticists and all the semantic eliminativists (including, from time to time, Quine).

13. It's a vexed question, and one we do not wish to enter into, which (if any) of these options Quine himself intends. (A footnote in his most recent book (*Pursuit of Truth*, p. 78) suggests that it is probably the third.) In any event, the argument we're running is not primarily intended to be *ad hominem*; we claim not just that there is no reading of "statement" that Quine could accept, consistent with his accepting verificationism and Q/D, but that there is no reading of "statement" that makes the putative argument for holism coherent.

We remark in passing that, in the many conversations about these matters that we've had with colleagues, we've been told repeatedly that only one of these options could conceivably have been Quine's intention – indeed, that there's only one worth discussing. Our interlocutors, however, have been divided about equally as to *which* one. In the circumstances, we thought we'd better discuss all three.

14. This is what Grunbaum calls the "trivial" reading of the Q/D thesis ("The falsifiability of theories").

15. The issue is not, of course, whether it's possible to have a "syntactic" treatment of inductive logic. The question such a treatment would answer is not whether it's *statements* that enter into confirmation relations; it's whether, when they do so, it's in virtue of their *form*.

16. We're grateful to Georges Rey for suggesting another way of reading Quine's use of "statement" which construes statements as formulas but which nevertheless makes a kind of semantic holism come out true. According to this reading, (1) "statement" means *formula*; (2) Peirce's thesis identifies the meaning of a statement (not with its *means* of confirmation but) with its empirical content – namely, with the set of observation sentences that (dis)confirm it (an observation sentence is a formula that is confirmed by/conditioned to proximal stimulations); (3) the Q/D thesis holds as usual. Since meaning is identified with observational consequences and since, according to the Q/D thesis, observational consequences are things that only *total theories* can have, the upshot is that (excepting observation sentences) no formula has a meaning outside a total theory.

This would be a pretty wild sort of semantics. For example, since the meaning of every sentence is the observational consequences of the total theory in which it is embedded, it follows that every sentence in a theory has the same meaning as every other sentence in that theory. Immediate consequences are that no theory can entail a contingent hypothetical, that if a disjunctive statement is true (/false), then both its disjuncts are true

(/false), and so forth. Further, every statement in a theory translates every statement in any empirically equivalent theory (and there are *no* translation relations among statements in theories that aren't empirically equivalent). Perhaps a Quinean might be prepared to accept all this, with the remark "So much the worse for people who insist on having a semantics for sentences." However, there remains what seems to us a crucial difficulty: namely, that the Q/D thesis is trivialized. All that you need to hold onto, in order to hold onto a statement under theory change, is its pronunciation.

17. If you read "concept" the way psychologists usually do, so that concepts are mental particulars, then the first premise of the argument begs the question that's at issue.

18. This is, by the way, the motivation for Jerry Katz's stipulation that if an implication relation among concepts is *semantic* (as opposed to merely *necessary*), then the implied concept must be literally a *constituent* of the implying concept. (See, for example, Katz, *Semantic Theory*.) The effect of this stipulation is to enforce the principle that if one concept analytically implies another, you can't *entertain* (acquire/grasp) the first concept without entertaining (and so on) the second.

In consequence, Katz can hold that it is literally incoherent to ascribe to Jones the belief that some cats purr while denying that Jones believes that some animals do. (We stand neutral as to whether it is well advised of Katz to hold this; whether, for example, it's a view that can be squared with Mates's examples. We also stand neutral on (what appears to be) Katz's assumption that you can't grasp a concept unless you grasp its internal structure.)

19. This bears emphasis because, in later writings, Quine does appear to contemplate a trans-linguistic (trans-theoretic) notion of statement identity (albeit one that is relativized to a choice of "analytic hypotheses"). Whatever other merits this maneuver may have, it doesn't help with the problem of reconciling Peirce's thesis with the Q/D thesis.

20. It doesn't matter, for the discussion that follows, how you construe "conditions of semantic evaluability." For example, they might be satisfaction conditions. Or it might be in Quine's spirit to identify a statement with an ordered pair of a formula and a complex of community-wide speech dispositions of the sort that can be exhibited in publicly observable responses to publicly observable stimuli. In effect, a statement is then a formula together with an inductively certifiable causal regularity in the utterances of the formula. This sort of construal would fit with many of the things that Quine says about translation.

21. More precisely, since every statement must bear to some extent on the level of confirmation of every other (because of simplicity considerations

220

and the like; see n. 9), what's being said to be an a posteriori issue is *how much* the truth of statement A matters to the truth of statement B.

22. We are grateful to Georges Rey for comments that prompted the two previous paragraphs.

23. This same assumption is implicit in Quine's notorious tendency to identify *languages* with *theories*. One would have thought that, whereas theories are collections of things that have truth values (say, propositions), languages are collections of things that have meanings (say, formulas). But propositions don't *have* meanings because they *are* meanings. So how could theories and languages be the same things? (For some of Quine's views on this issue, see his "Reply to Chomsky.")

24. Since this diagnosis patently begs the question against Quine's skepticism about propositions, we want to emphasize that our case that there is something wrong with the "Two dogmas" argument for semantic holism is internal and does *not* rest on whether we're right about the diagnosis.

25. For example, one might think that the way out of Putnam's Twin worries is to take a "two-factor" view of content, with the "narrow" or "conceptual role" factor being, in effect, verificationist. Quite a lot of people have suggested something of this sort (for example, Block, Field, Loar, Lycan, McGinn, and Putnam). See chapter 6.

26. It's well to notice that even if there is this *ontological* dependence of the syntactic properties of words on the syntactic properties of sentences, no corresponding *epistemological* dependence would follow. In particular, it wouldn't follow that you can't know what syntactic role W has in S unless you know the syntactic structural description of S. It's important that this doesn't follow, because it seems clear that the compositionality of the semantics of a language typically depends on the fact that the syntactic structural description of a sentence is a function of the syntactic structural descriptions of its lexical constituents. It presumably follows that the syntactic analysis of the lexical items must be recoverable ("up to ambiguity") without the prior recovery of the syntax of the sentence. All the grammars and parsing theories we've come across take it for granted that this is so.

The compositionality of syntax is, of course, compatible with there being syntactically ambiguous lexical items. Syntactic compositionality requires only that the entire *range* of possible syntactic analyses of a lexical item be epistemically accessible in each context in which the item occurs. This is what linguists mean when they say that the lexicon of a language specifies the syntactic analysis of words "up to ambiguity."

27. It's a rather nice question whether Russell's treatment of "the F that is G" defines "the" with respect to the semantic or the syntactic properties of its context. What one says about this depends a lot on what one thinks

221

logical syntax is, a topic that we do not propose to broach here. Suffice it to say that the view that logical syntax really is *syntax* strikes us as perfectly respectable.

28. So, for example, we won't discuss "molecularist" theories of meaning (like Dummett's) which rely on the a/s distinction in order to steer between atomism and holism. See chapter 1.

29. Nihilism, and *not* semantic holism, is the view that most people take Quine to hold; and perhaps he does. He says in *Theories and Things*: "Meaning, like thought and belief, is a worthy object of philosophical and scientific clarification and analysis, and like them it is ill suited as an instrument of philosophical and scientific clarification and analysis" (p. 185). Our point is just that he wouldn't be justified in drawing nihilistic conclusions on the basis of the sorts of arguments that are on offer in "Two dogmas" *even if* those arguments are sound against the a/s distinction as Quine construes it.

30. He did argue, plausibly in our view, that you can't reconstruct analyticity by appeal to a prioricity; that is, that if there *are* analytic truths, we don't know them a priori. But this epistemological prohibition needn't imply a prohibition against semantics. Notice that although the kind of Skinnerian theory just sketched can ground a notion of analyticity, it isn't at all committed to the claim that there can be a priori knowledge of the analyticities it grounds.

   We are grateful to Paul Boghossian for emphasizing the difference between denying that there is an a/s distinction and denying that there is an a/s distinction grounded in an epistemological property (e.g., aprioricity); and also for emphasizing that *any* meaning Realist is sure to endorse *some* notion of content identity. Unlike us, however, Boghossian denies that the arguments in "Two dogmas" undermine an epistemological a/s distinction.

NOTES TO CHAPTER 3

1. It's easy enough to run the arguments in the opposite direction and deduce charity from holism. That is, to assume the kind of semantics in which the meaning of a predicate is constituted anatomistically, by its role in an inferential network, and then deduce that some of the inferences in which the predicate is implicated – namely, the semantically constitutive ones – must be sound. This is the tactic pursued by Vermazen. Given the assumption that "a predicate gets its meaning by its place in a network of predications corresponding to the user's network of beliefs" ("General beliefs and the principles of charity," p. 114), it's going to follow that "no matter whether we translate the speaker's sentences about individuals charitably, each time we use one of our predicates in translating such a

sentence, we are attributing to him one part of the central network of our own system of beliefs" (ibid., p. 116). Which is to say that we are so translating that many of the informant's general beliefs come out true by our standards.

This argument that network semantics entails charity towards general beliefs is, of course, of no interest for our present purposes, since it starts out by begging the question against the view that the semantic properties of predicates are punctate.

2. It's not actually clear that this second consideration is very forceful. True, a radical interpreter (unlike a bilingual one) is ipso facto unable to intuit translation relations between the native language and his home language. But it doesn't follow that it "pre-empts the point of radical interpretation" to assume that he can have *evidence* that certain of the native's sentences translate certain sentences of his own; that would depend on whether the *evidence* for translation must inevitably be couched in semantic terms, not on whether the *success criterion* for translation is couched in these terms. So, pending further argument, there's no obvious reason why accepting Tarski's view of success (adopting Convention T) would beg the question about radical interpretation. Similar remarks would hold, mutatis mutandis, if success were defined by an adequacy condition which requires the right-hand side of a T-sentence to be synonymous with, to mean the same as, and so forth, the quoted object language formula on the left.

We're inclined to think that if there is a serious reason for not equating success with material adequacy, it must be the Quinean objection that unexplicated semantic notions like *translation* are not at the disposal of a philosophical account of meaning. Let's suppose this is accepted for the sake of argument. Then "successful truth theory" cannot be elucidated in terms of "materially adequate truth theory."

3. How many of the intuitive semantic relations *is* Davidson requiring a T-theory to "reconstruct"? Equivalently, to what extent is his semantics revisionist? It seems clear that the minimum he wants of the correct truth theory is that it should display whatever information is required to "interpret" the speaker's utterances. That will do for our purposes.

4. The issue *isn't* underdetermination. Even if there are many equally correct but nonequivalent meaning theories, we surely can't allow that a semantics for English should assign all the true sentences to 2+2=4 and all the false ones to 2+2=5. But that would be consonant with construing success as extensional adequacy.

5. It's always open to someone to say that, contrary to appearances, child 2's language "really does" have compositional structure, since, by assumption, child 2 can say both that this is snow and that snow is white. But this move is question begging in the present context. If compositional-

ity is to resolve the extensionality problem, we need to be able to determine whether object language sentences are structurally related *independent of* determining whether they are semantically related. Another way to put this observation is as follows: having a compositional language is not just a matter of having a language that can express related propositions. It's a matter of having a language in which there are formal similarities among sentences when there are semantic similarities among the propositions they express.

6. Children actually do go through a "holophrastic" stage in the course of normal language acquisition. Could there be a transcendental argument showing that the utterances they produce at this stage have no truth conditions? But, in fact, the child's holophrastic utterances are quite often *interpretable*. (See Bloom, *Language Development: Form and Function in Emerging Grammars.*)

7. It might be supposed that the way out is to appeal to the plausible methodological principle that the *simplest* axioms consonant with the data are always to be preferred. However, the present sorts of considerations make it equivocal what the data *are*. When the informant utters "This is snow," is he saying that this is snow or that this is snow and LT?

8. We're construing "token-reflexive" broadly to include, for example, tense and any other feature that can function to relativize truth values to contexts of utterance. See Davidson, "The structure and content of truth": "The interpretation of common predicates and names depends heavily on indexical elements in speech, such as demonstratives and tense, since it is these that most directly allow predicates and singular terms to be connected to objects and events in the world" (p. 320).

9. It's important to bear in mind that there are extensionality problems and logical truth problems about the token-reflexive sentences themselves. There is, for example, the problem of distinguishing between "That's snow" and "That's A," where "A" is some atomic predicate coextensive but not synonymous with "snow." For *that* problem the compositionality arguments provide no solution, as we pointed out above.

10. It is often suggested to us that this conclusion would be acceptable to Davidson, since semi-holism (that is, the doctrine that translation holism is true but content holism is false; see chapter 1) is all that his anti-reductionism requires. Since it is, after all, meaning theory and not reductionism or the autonomy of the intentional that is primarily under discussion in the papers we're considering here, it's not entirely clear what implications Davidson would wish to draw from the kind of holism that these arguments purport to establish. But it's worth noticing that semi-holism isn't strong enough to support an a priori argument against the possibility of psychophysical laws (see, especially, his "Mental events").

For, if punctate minds are possible, then holism is not a "constitutive principle" of intentional ascription. If that is so, it would appear that any argument that the intentional can't reduce to the physical which turns on the assumption that holism is constitutive of the intentional must fail.

11. The reader should bear in mind that "radical interpretation" is a term of art and hence subject to explication.

12. Viewed simply as a piece of epistemology, RI theory as developed by Davidson (and radical translation theory as developed by Quine) appears to assume a species of empiricist foundationalism that one might well be unprepared to grant: namely, that an empirical theory can be substantively constrained by the requirement that it be discoverable by an investigator whose epistemic condition is specifiable a priori. This kind of epistemology almost always has an ontological agenda. If someone claims that the truth about X's *must* be discoverable from a certain epistemological position (short, anyhow, of omniscience), you can be pretty sure that he is an anti-Realist about X's.

    Prima facie, the epistemological assumptions of RI theory flout the Quine/Duhem thesis. Q/D asserts that what counts as evidence for an empirical theory is always to be determined a posteriori (see chapter 2). How RI theory and the Q/D thesis might be reconciled is thus unclear to us. This appears to be another of the cases in which confirmation holism and semantic holism turn out not to be comfortable bedfellows.

13. In Quine's case, radical translation theory is a first step in an attempt to show that the notion of linguistic meaning is not scientifically useful and that there is a great deal of "scope . . . for empirically unconditioned variation in one's conceptual scheme" (Quine, *Word and Object*, p. 26). Davidson draws the contrary conclusion: Radical interpretation is a basis for denying that there is sense to the claim that different individuals or cultures operate with different conceptual schemes. In fact, quite a lot of Davidson's philosophy of language, philosophy of mind, metaphysics, and epistemology (in particular, his anti-skepticism arguments) depends on the assumption that radical interpretation is possible.

14. We're not proposing to raise the question of whether it's reasonable to construe children and other language learners as *constructing a theory* of the language they are learning. Davidson (and Quine) think that there is a "harmless" way of understanding the theory-construction account of language learning; our intention is to understand it in this harmless way, whatever that might be.

15. Strictly speaking, the view must be that what the radical interpreter qua radical interpreter has access to is the evidence that observing the informant could make available to the linguist or the child (this constitutes the contingent constraints on the selection of a T-theory) plus

general principles of nondemonstrative inference (that is, whatever methodological principles mediate the construction of empirical theories when intentional states and processes are *not* at issue) plus whatever "constitutive" principles (of charity, for example) can be justified by transcendental arguments that reflect upon the conditions of intentional ascription as such. The status of these transcendental principles will loom large later in the discussion. For now, we want to consider whether the behavioral data that are available to the child or the linguist are reasonably held to exhaust the *contingent* information available to an interpreter.

We remark in passing that talk of the child as possessing "principles of nondemonstrative inference," like talk of the child "constructing truth theories," should perhaps be taken with a grain of salt. What the child requires is a mechanism for inductively generalizing his observational data. Quine's "innate quality spaces" (see *Word and Object*, pp. 80–90) are intended to do this sort of work without offending empiricist scruples.

16. Innateness isn't the only possibility. Lots of psychologists think that learning a first language requires the previous acquisition of all sorts of conceptual and social capacities; see, for example, Piaget, *The Language and Thought of the Child*; Bruner, *Child's Talk: Learning to Use Language*.

17. See Lightfoot:

> It is clear that the P[rimary] L[inguistic] D[ata] which trigger the growth of a child's grammar do not include much of what linguists use to choose between hypotheses. To this extent the child is not a "little linguist" constructing her grammar in the way that linguists construct their hypotheses. For example, the PLD do not include well organized paradigms nor comparable data from other languages. Nor do the PLD include rich information about what does not occur, that is, negative data. ("The child's trigger experience: degree-0 learnability," p. 323)

Arguably the child and the linguist aren't in the epistemic situation of the radical interpreter, or in one another's epistemic situation either.

18. See the parallel point in Hume: It's enough that children and animals take the principle of causation seriously; they don't need to have justified true beliefs about it. (In fact, Hume's view appears to be that *un*justified *false* beliefs about causation are what serve them best.) Hume says that children don't have to solve the problem of induction in order to learn to avoid open flames. We say, in a similar spirit, that children don't have to solve the problem of radical interpretation in order to learn English.

Hume is worth quoting:

> When a child has felt the sensation of pain from touching the flame of a candle, he will be careful not to put his hand near any candle; but

will expect a similar effect from a cause, which is similar in its sensible qualities and appearance. If you assert, therefore, that the understanding of the child is led into this conclusion by any process of argument or ratiocination, I may justly require you to produce that argument; nor have you any pretext to refuse so equitable a demand. You cannot say, that the argument is abstruse, and may possibly escape your search and enquiry; since you confess, that it is obvious to the capacity of a mere infant. (*An Inquiry Concerning Human Understanding*, Essay IV, "Skeptical doubts concerning the operations of the understanding, part 2")

19. However, Wittgenstein doesn't actually use the phrase "Nothing is hidden" to express this thesis. See *Philosophical Investigations*, para. 92.
20. Thus Davidson: "As a matter of principle . . . meaning, and by its connection with meaning, belief also, are open to public determination. . . . What a fully informed interpreter could learn about what a speaker means is all there is to learn; the same goes for what the speaker believes" (Davidson, "A coherence theory of truth and knowledge," p. 315). It is clear from the context that Davidson thinks it's *because* meaning is open to public determination that what a fully informed interpreter could learn is all there is to learn. The relevant questions are: "What argument sustains this inference?" and "What's the force of 'fully informed'?"

See also Davidson's "The structure and content of truth":

We *should* demand . . . that the evidence for the [interpretation] theory be in principle publicly accessible. . . . The requirement that the evidence be publicly accessible is not due to an atavistic yearning for behavioristic or verificationist foundations, but to the fact that what is to be explained is a social phenomenon. Mental phenomena in general may or may not be private, but the correct interpretation of one person's speech by another must *in principle* be possible. A speaker's intention that her words be understood in a certain way may of course remain opaque to the most skilled and knowledgeable listener, but what has to do with correct interpretation, meaning and truth conditions is necessarily based on available evidence. As Wittgenstein, not to mention Dewey, Mead, Quine and many others have insisted, language is intrinsically social. This does not entail that truth and meaning can be *defined* in terms of observable behavior, or that it is "nothing but" observable behavior; but it does imply that meaning is entirely determined by observable behavior, even readily observable behavior. That meanings are decipherable is not a matter of luck; public availability is a constitutive aspect of language. (p. 314)

The reader should note for later reference (see chapter 5) Davidson's tacit assumption that the constraints on natural languages ipso facto hold for semantic interpretability at large (namely, that they are conditions for "correct interpretation, meaning and truth conditions" as such). We will want to challenge the inference that if language is "intrinsically social," then intentionality must be too. See, also, Davidson's "The inscrutability of reference," p. 235.

21. Dummett provides a variant of the argument which makes clear how closely the child/linguist construal of radical interpretation is related to the "Nothing is hidden" construal. According to Dummett, language is constrained by the principle that "there must be an observable difference between the behavior or capacities of someone who is said to have [knowledge of the language and someone who] is said to lack it" ("The philosophical basis of intuitionistic logic," p. 217). We take this to be a version of the "Nothing is hidden" thesis. But the argument that leads Dummett to this depends on the consideration that "our proficiency in making use of the statements and expressions of the language is all that others have from which to judge whether or not we have acquired a grasp of their meanings." We take this to be a claim that languages aren't learnable unless they are teachable; and that they aren't teachable unless nothing relevant is hidden from the teacher. (Strictly speaking, Dummett makes this claim for the language of mathematical theories; but it is clear that he thinks the point is general.) This line of argument, if it were successful, would indeed show more than that nothing is hidden from someone in God's epistemic position; it would also show that nothing is hidden from someone in the teacher's epistemic position. However, that natural languages can be learned does not entail that they can be taught, and the assumption that they can be taught is substantive and tendentious (as Chomsky has often pointed out). Moreover, what follows from that assumption depends on what the epistemic situation of the learner is supposed to be (nothing interesting follows from the assumption that English can be taught to someone who knows English). So we're back where we started: Dummett's version of the "Nothing is hidden" thesis depends on unargued assumptions about the epistemic position from which natural languages are actually learned.

22. At least since "Belief and the basis of meaning," and more obviously in his most recent papers, Davidson takes the basic evidence for interpretation to be not "holding true under such and such circumstances," but rather, "information about what episodes and situations in the world cause an agent to *prefer that one rather than another sentence be true*" ("The structure and content of truth," p. 314; our emphasis). As far as we can tell, this change doesn't affect the line of argument we will be pursuing.

23. The caveat is that you get GHT-sentences that are evidenced by SHT-sentences only for object language formulas that contain token-reflexives; the reader who followed the discussion of compositionality will have anticipated this point. So, while every GHT-sentence for which there is this kind of evidence may license a corresponding T-sentence (see immediately below), there will be many (typically infinitely many) T-sentences entailed by the accepted meaning theory that are not so licensed.

24. Davidson apparently still holds this. "T-sentences . . . have the form and function of natural laws; they are universally quantified biconditionals, and as such are understood to apply counterfactually and to be confirmed by their instances" ("The structure and content of truth," p. 313). In a note (n. 57) inserted here, Davidson remarks: "This goes some way to answer a frequent criticism of theories of truth as theories of meaning. For example, given the (unusual) case of two unstructured predicates with the same extension, a theory of truth may make a distinction if there are circumstances which never arise but under which the truth conditions would be different" (ibid.).

25. By which we mean the principle that it is "arbitrary" how languages pair truth conditions with morpho-syntactic forms. Davidson thinks that it's not helpful to describe languages as systems of conventions (see "Communication and convention"), but that's not what's at issue here.

26. Perhaps it goes without saying that L couldn't really be a law because it isn't literally true that English speakers hold "It's raining" true iff it's raining in their vicinity. (Consider *unconscious* English speakers.) For the same reason, GE (see above, p. 83) can't be a law either. We're proposing to ignore this sort of worry for the present purposes, but it will be crucial when we turn to the role of principles of charity.

27. R doesn't even have to be nonintentionally specifiable. Davidson denies the radical interpreter "detailed knowledge" of the informant's intentional states. But we don't see why the interpreter shouldn't be allowed to *quantify over* intentional states, and that's all that expressing L requires.

28. This is a special case of a quite general point; as we remarked above, there is considerable tension between Davidson's idea that interpretation requires establishing *nomological* generalizations and his idea that if "nothing is hidden," it follows that radical interpretation must be possible. L is a law iff [(S holds true "It's raining") in every nomologically possible world where S bears R to ⟨"It's raining," it's raining⟩]. Now, whether S *does* bear R to ⟨"It's raining," it's raining⟩ is something that God knows on the assumption that God knows all the intensional (with an "s") facts. But there is no reason to suppose that it's something that radical interpreters know qua radical interpreters, since, surely, radical

229

interpreters aren't intensionally omniscient. If, in short, "It's raining" meaning *it's raining* supervenes on L's being a law, then, on the one hand, nothing is hidden, but, on the other hand, it's still on the cards that radical interpretation isn't possible.

Notice that this has implications for the question of whether the possibility of a language containing "standing" sentences (for example, "Rain is wet") depends on its containing token-reflexive sentences ("This is rain," "This is wet"). Suppose that Kurt holds true "Rain is wet" in every nomologically possible world in which rain is wet, and he bears R to ("Rain is wet," rain is wet). That might be enough to secure that Kurt means *rain is wet* by "Rain is wet" even if, in some of these worlds, Kurt speaks a language in which "rain" and "wet" don't occur in sentences with token-reflexives.

29. Compositionality might do the job here, since "H_2O" is plausibly a description. But the possibility of biconditional laws connecting properties all of which have unstructured names in some language or other can't be ruled out a priori.

30. As far as we can tell, translation holism isn't at issue in this argument.

31. In fact, finding out that Karl holds "Es schneit" true when it's raining wouldn't really count against T. "Es regnet" and "Es schneit" might be synonyms. The right way to vary the quoted formula in applications of the method of differences would be to look at other expressions in which "regnet" occurs. (It tends to confirm the hypothesis that *"Es regnet" means that it's raining* that "Es regnet und es schneit" is held true iff it's raining and snowing. This is just the appeal to compositionality discussed above.)

32. It might be objected that this is ruled out because the notion of a *law* is itself holistic; there *couldn't be* just one of them. But the objection is misguided even if its assumptions are correct. From the fact that there couldn't be just one law, it doesn't follow that there couldn't be just one *semantic* law (all the rest being laws about the nonintentional).

33. There are, notoriously, lots of ways that a principle of charity might be formulated and lots of principles which, though not exactly equivalent to charity principles, might be supposed to do the work that charity principles do in interpretation theory. For example, Grandy suggests a principle that appears to be weaker than charity: "a pragmatic constraint on translation, the condition that the imputed pattern of relations between beliefs, desires, and the world, be as similar to our own as possible" (Grandy, "Reference, meaning and belief," p. 443). As far as we can tell, these sorts of differences between formulations of the charity principle don't affect the considerations raised in the text, either in this chapter or in the next two.

34. The idea that there is a direct route from the constitutive role of charity in interpretation to the holism of content is endorsed by many philosophers other than Davidson. For example: "What our words mean depends on *everything* we believe, on *all* the assumptions we are making. This is a consequence of the fact that we take another to mean the same by his words as we do only if this does not lead to the conclusion that certain of his beliefs are radically different from our own" (Harman, *Thought*, p. 14).

35. What we have conceded is something of the form $(A \to B) \to C$. In particular, if a T-sentence about E is warrantedly inferable from a GHT-sentence about E, then, ceteris paribus, E is true on the sort of occasions when the GHT-sentence says that it's held true. But, of course, it doesn't follow from $(A \to B) \to C$ that C is required as a premise (or as a presupposition) of the inference from A to B. For example, suppose *if something is a cat, then it is an animal* (corresponding to $A \to B$). Then it is entailed that *if Greycat is a cat, then Greycat is an animal* (this whole conditional corresponds to C). It does not, however, follow from there being this entailment that *if Greycat is a cat, then Greycat is an animal* is a premise of, or is presupposed by, the argument from *something is a cat* to *that thing is an animal*. Exactly analogously, it doesn't follow from what we conceded in the text that POC is a premise (or a presupposition) of the inference from GHT-sentences to T-sentences.

36. The reader will have it in mind that if T-sentences are inferred from sentences like L, GHT-sentences don't have to be laws, but L-sentences do. We are putting this aside for present purposes, however; the governing principle is that *whatever* generalizations license T-sentences must support counterfactuals.

37. And, of course, ceteris paribus, the overall simplicity and coherence of the meaning theory is maximized by accepting the T-sentence. But it can't be the appeal to overall simplicity and coherence that makes interpretation theory holistic; if it were, then every empirical theory would be holistic. In that case, the "constitutive principles" of intentional and physical explanation wouldn't be different after all, and Davidson loses his transcendental argument against psychophysical reduction.

38. That is, with those conditions under which it's counterfactual-supporting that its tokens are held true; that is, with those conditions articulated by the nomologically necessary GHT-sentence that the SHT-sentences support.

39. Suppose an *un*hedged POC were employed in interpretation. Then, because of what has come to be called the "disjunction problem" (see Fodor, "A theory of content"), the consequence would be that the favored truth theory for L would invariably misinterpret the sentences of L. (The

231

same point applies to GHT-sentences that aren't hedged by ceteris paribus clauses.)

In fact, this consideration is another reason for doubting that POC is actually doing any work in solving the extensionality problem. Suppose English speakers sometimes hold "It's raining" true when it's raining and that sometimes they hold it true when they are walking under a leaking air conditioner. The intuitively correct story is that the former hold-trues are true and the latter are false. But there is a candidate T-theory that says that "It's raining" is true iff either it's raining nearby or there's a leaking air conditioner overhead. Notice that this candidate is compatible with all the SHTs and that an unhedged POC actually prefers it to the intuitively correct one, since it makes *all* the (relevant) hold-trues true.

The disjunction problem shows that there is simply no way of saying whether POC yields a solution to the problem of extensionality until you know what the hedges are.

40. In fact, Davidson must have ceteris paribus clauses in both places. Even if GHT-sentences support counterfactuals, they couldn't be strictly true universal generalizations; see n. 26 above.

41. In effect, this is the assumption that Davidson calls "semantic innocence"; see his "On saying that," p. 104.

42. We have argued that appeals to compositionality are neither necessary nor sufficient to solve the extensionality problem; not the first because of the possibility of languages in which all the symbols are unstructured, and not the second because compositionality doesn't help with distinguishing nomologically coextensive predicates. But we do agree that languages that have syntactically structured expressions will have a compositional semantics in all the interesting cases. Not only do we concede this, we propose to insist on it. See chapter 6.

43. The reader is invited to try to find cases in which POC would help the radical interpreter and in which appealing to POC would *not* violate the stipulated epistemological constraints on radical interpretation. What is required is an iterable expression that is as opaque as "believes that" but is nonintentional (with a "t"). We can't find one. And even if we could, we can't believe that a language is interpretable only if it contains one.

44. We're not endorsing *either* a principle of charity *or* a principle of humanity. To repeat: most token-reflexive sentences come out true both on the story that says that charity/humanity is constitutive of translation *and* on the story that says that the nomological necessity of a GHT- (or L-) sentence is metaphysically sufficient for the truth of the corresponding T-sentence.

45. Compare Hacking: "Davidson revives meaning by proposing a theory of translation located in a theory of truth. Meaning will never be mentioned;

we get along fine with sentences and their truth conditions. . . . Davidson resuscitates meaning by administering the kiss of death" (Hacking, *Why does Language Matter to Philosophy*, p. 179).

NOTES TO CHAPTER 4

1. The interpretation is, however, still "radical" in that the interpreter is assumed to know no contingent *intentional or semantic* descriptions of the informant. We return to this point below.
2. This passage makes it sound as though Lewis's question is: According to what principles do intentional facts supervene on physical facts? But in his actual practice, the "physical facts" that Lewis appeals to are primarily behaviors under physical descriptions; and they come in not as a supervenience base for intentional states (Lewis is no behaviorist), but rather as providing the data against which the empirical adequacy of intentional ascriptions is to be assessed. So far as we can tell, the question that Lewis actually tries to answer in his "Radical interpretation" is something like: By reference to what constraints on interpretation do behavioral data, physicalistically described, choose among intentional theories? To the extent to which he views such constraints as constitutive of our concept of the intentional, Lewis takes this question to be metaphysical rather than epistemological.
3. You could say, if you like, that *best* fit determines a *direction* of fit; what we want of a law is the *maximum* of simplicity and power. (But also, what we want of the criminal is the maximum of being the perpetrator.)
4. Perhaps it is analytic that if people don't like being F'd, then, ceteris paribus, they try to avoid situations in which they believe that they are likely to be F'd. But this doesn't predict pin avoidance unless you add the *contingent* intentional premise that people don't like getting stuck by pins.
5. Compare Wallace: "In our actual practice of interpreting and learning about other people, both the evidence and the evidenced make, to borrow Wittgenstein's language, a medley, mixing physical concepts and mental concepts up together in a single report" (Wallace, "Translation theories and linear B," p. 233). Wallace's paper is excellent at conveying the profound differences between the stipulated epistemological situation of radical interpreters and the actual epistemological situation in which translation, decipherment, and the like are carried out.
6. Or would necessarily quantify over, if your model of functional definition is the Ramsey sentence; see Lewis, "How to define theoretical terms."
7. That one might wish to opt out of the whole game of defining things is a

move that is not seriously considered. Why should one suppose that "believes that P" has a *definition* when, apparently, nothing else does? Psychology (commonsense or otherwise) requires a vocabulary the reference of whose terms is fixed to intentional states. Why does it follow that its intentional vocabulary has to be *definable*, functionally or otherwise?

Notice, in particular, that this is a different question from whether, as Intentional Realists generally suppose, intentional vocabulary has to be susceptible of naturalistic reduction. Not all reductions depend on definitions; for example, the reduction of water to H_2O doesn't.

8. Lewis quotes with approval Davidson's remark that we "will try for a theory that finds [the informant] consistent" ("Radical interpretation," p. 112). So, presumably, he subscribes to at least the first conjunct.

9. This does not, of course, say that you can't want that A unless you believe that A; only that you can't want that A unless you believe (can believe) something or other. The claim is that you couldn't have a creature whose mental life consists entirely of wanting.

10. Unless there is some independent argument that the things that an organism does count as its *behavior* only if beliefs enter into their etiology. It would be fun to try to construct such an argument, if only in order to tease behaviorists. But, offhand, we don't see how it would go.

11. Hume supposes that a wan idea and a forceful one can both resemble the same thing and hence both be about the same thing. This assumption is by no means untendentious. But we needn't worry about that, since we're not endorsing resemblance theories of content or force and vivacity theories of belief.

12. Perhaps some philosophers have the intuition that systematicity is a precondition not just for being a belief but for having satisfaction conditions at all. Philosophers who have this intuition are welcome to it. But we doubt that the decision as to whether what a tribe talks is a language waits upon the determination that what it talks is systematic. Compare the "primitive languages" that Wittgenstein discusses in the early paragraphs of *Philosophical Investigations*; though they are thoroughly unsystematic, Wittgenstein thinks that one or the other of them could be "the *whole* language of A and B; even the whole language of a tribe" (para. 6; emphasis original).

13. See the discussion of Dennett's evolutionary arguments for principles of charity in chapter 5.

NOTES TO CHAPTER 5

1. Among those Dennett lists as *not* party to the putative emerging consensus are Anscombe, Burge, Chisholm, Fodor, Geach, Kripke, and Searle. He might have added Barwise and Perry, Dretske, McGinn, Millikan, Stalnaker, and many others. We are reminded of Peter de Vries's joke about the woman who was stark naked except for her clothes.

2. Qua species of Interpretivism, Projectivism is not a reductionist program; remember that Interpretivists accept Brentano's thesis. So there is no principled objection to a construal of "believes that" that makes essential use of semantic notions like "says that." One can imagine a reductionist (hence, of course, not Dennett) embracing an analysis in which "uttering" replaces "saying that." So, "Jones believes that it's raining" in Smith's mouth comes out equivalent to something like "Jones is in the state that would normally cause me (Smith) to utter 'It's raining.' " The points we're about to make generally hold for both kinds of Projectivist analysis, as far as we can tell.

3. Nor would such a view seem to be inherently committed to holism. For a kind of atomistic Intentional Realism that takes a similarly eccentric view of the polyadicity of attitudes, see Fodor, "Substitution arguments and the individuation of beliefs."

4. One might argue that this sort of relativization of intentional ascriptions would nevertheless make them unfit for purposes of scientific explanation. But, prima facie, that would be a different claim from Interpretivism; the latter would follow only on the tendentious assumption that the facts that can figure in scientific explanation are the only facts there are. It is instructive, in this respect, to compare Dennett's treatment of Projectivism with Stich's (in *From Folk Psychology to Cognitive Science: The Case Against Belief*). The conclusions Stich derives from the Projectivist account of attitude attribution are scrupulously methodological, *not* ontological.

5. Beware the fallacy *post hoc; ergo, propter hoc*. Pace Dennett, it just isn't true that if we find a creature that has a selectional history and an intentional structure, we can assume straight off that its intentional structure was designed by its selectional history. Consider: "Sheep are stupid; sheep are selected; so sheep are selected for their stupidity." (For discussion of this sort of case, see Gould and Lewontyn, "The spandrels of San Marco and the Panglossian paradigm: A critique of the adaptionist programme.") To make his argument for charity even begin to run, Dennett would have to restrict it to intentional systems whose selection

235

depended on the truth of their beliefs. We know of no argument that people are such creatures.

6. We're not sure whether Dennett considers it also to be a *necessary* condition. If he does, then we are presumably at risk that a Kuhnian revolution in macrobiology will show that none of us has a mind.

7. There was a time when even a respectable philosopher might have sought to establish that we have beliefs (and not *shmeliefs*) by appeal to a paradigm case argument. But not, we trust, any more.

8. One way to answer this question is to bite the bullet and go Instrumentalist about Darwinism. In "Intentional systems in cognitive ethology: the 'Panglossian paradigm' defended," Dennett says that "adaptationism and mentalism (intentional system theory) are not *theories* in one traditional sense. They are stances or strategies that serve to organize data, explain interrelations and generate questions to ask Nature. Were they theories in the 'classical' mold, the objection that they are question begging or irrefutable would be fatal" (p. 265). So far as we can make out, Dennett's argument for these surprising claims is just that vacuous, ad hoc, or question-begging adaptationist (/mentalist) explanations can always be devised if the data prove recalcitrant. By that standard, however, *no* theories count as being "in the 'classical' mold," physical theories included. That a theory permits of ad hoc defense can't be enough to make it just a stance, since, if it did, all theories would be just stances.

9. The most that predictivity could conceivably require is that if an agent believes P and P → Q and believes that Q is relevant to the success of his plans, then the agent believes Q. This is clearly still far too strong to be realistic; but at least it's weaker than the closure principle.

10. Notice, in passing, that Brentano's thesis does not imply that there are no intentional laws; Brentano tells us only that if there are intentional laws, then they must be irreducible.

11. If there are intentional laws, they are surely ceteris paribus laws; special science laws generally are. For a recent discussion, see Schiffer, *Remnants of Meaning*, and Fodor, "Stephen Schiffer's dark night of the soul: a review of *Remnants of Meaning*."

12. We take this to be *patently* true. Sailors reliably predict that the wind will blow southwest in fair weather in the summer on the Atlantic coast of the US. Few of them have any idea as to why it works that way. (We used to know, but we've forgotten.)

13. It's not entirely clear what shows that the radical interpreter *must* proceed in this fashion. Davidson says that "causality plays an indispensable role in determining the content of what we say and believe. This is a fact we can be led to recognize by taking up . . . the interpreter's point of view"

("A coherence theory of truth," p. 317). But we're not told what the argument is by which we come to recognize this. Lots of philosophers have held that causal relations to the world are constitutive of semantic properties, but their arguments turn on detailed intuitions about cases – for example, on the need to distinguish between the mental states of Twins. It looks as if Davidson thinks that he has a *transcendental* argument for a causal theory of meaning; that is, that it follows simply from constraints on the possibility of radical interpretation. It's very unclear what this argument could be.

It's worth noting that Quine does *not* have this problem of explaining why what causally prompts assent to a type of utterance must be what determines its truth conditions. For, as Davidson correctly notes, what prompts assent for Quine is, in the first instance, "sensory criteria, *something [Quine] thinks . . . can be treated also as evidence*" ("A coherence theory of truth," p. 317; our emphasis). And since Quine is a verificationist, he takes it that evidence relations are ipso facto constitutive of semantic relations. What Quine pays for this convenience is that he has no semantic argument against skepticism (as, indeed, Davidson insightfully remarks; "A coherence theory of truth," p. 313).

14. This is a special case of a general principle that we discussed in chapter 3, q.v.

15. For example, consider Davidson's discussion of the "Swampman":

> Suppose lightning strikes a dead tree in a swamp; I am standing near by. My body is reduced to its elements, while entirely by coincidence (and out of different molecules) the tree is turned into my physical replica. My replica, The Swampman . . . seems to recognize my friends, and appears to return their greetings in English. It moves into my house and seems to write articles on radical interpretation. No one can tell the difference. . . . But there is a difference. My replica can't recognize my friends; it can't re-cognize anything, since it never cognized anything in the first place. It can't know my friends' names (though of course it seems to), it can't remember my house. It can't mean what I do by the word "house" for example, since the sound "house" it makes was not learned in a context that would give it the right meaning – or any meaning at all. Indeed, I don't see how my replica can be said to mean anything by the sounds it makes, nor to have any thoughts. ("Knowing one's own mind," pp. 443–4)

If these consequences strike you as threatening a reductio ad absurdum of Davidson's sort of externalism, you might wish to consider construing intentionality in terms of subjunctive rather than actual causal history.

16. Or perhaps there isn't this obligation after all; perhaps it's enough for a

semantics to say " 'cat' means *cat* if there is a nomological connection between the property of being a cat and the property of being a cause of 'cat' tokens," without saying what actual and counterfactual causal patterns must hold in order for such nomological connections to obtain. It's arguable that we *usually* can't say what counterfactuals our law statements require to be true (except, maybe, for the most basic laws).

17. The exegetical situation is, in fact, a little unclear. Davidson's account of radical interpretation arguably permits him to endorse a subjunctive version of a causal theory of truth conditions. For, it will be remembered, the radical interpreter is presumed to extrapolate from observations of sentences held true under such and such circumstances to *laws* about the circumstances under which token-reflexive-sentences are held true. These laws, together with their theoretical interconnections, support counterfactuals; and there is no reason to deny that they might support the very counterfactuals upon which content supervenes. So the argument might go. (Indeed, Davidson says as much in his recent "The structure and content of truth.")

We think it's not obvious that this will work; it's one thing to say that Davidson's story allows content to depend on counterfactuals; it's another to claim that it would guarantee that the radical interpreter has access to the counterfactuals that content supervenes on. (Remember that no argument has yet been given that the radical interpretation of a natural language is actually possible.) In any event, if Davidson does assume this, he again loses his anti-skeptical argument, since it is then an open possibility, compatible with radical interpretation, that none of the causal relations on which the content of an utterance type depends should *actually* be exhibited by any of its tokens.

18. See, for example, the discussion by Putnam, *Reason, Truth and History*, ch. 1.

NOTES TO CHAPTER 6

1. As the reader may remember from chapter 1, the essential claim of "content holism" is that semantic properties, including *belonging to the language L*, are holistic; that is, that if anything has them, then lots of things must have them.

2. At one or other point in his article, Block cites Churchland, Johnson-Laird, Loar, Lycan, McGinn, Miller, Putnam, Schiffer, and Woods as recent proponents of variants of CRT, among which his discussion is intended to be largely neutral.

3. Block thinks that the desiderata for a semantic theory that he enumerates

preclude versions of CRT that have been proposed by Harman (in the tradition of Sellars) and by Field. Block's objection to Field's theory is that conceptual roles are "not quite causal" ("Advertisement for a semantics for psychology," p. 630) if they are construed as subjective probabilities, and thus cannot satisfy his desideratum 5 (see below). Block's objection to Harman/Sellars is that satisfying desideratum 1 requires drawing a distinction between "broad" and "narrow" content, and hence requires a "two-factor" semantics. We won't discuss these in-house disagreements among CRT theorists; the worries we will raise in the third part of this chapter apply to Harman and Field.

4. Schiffer (*Meaning*) and Searle (*Speech Acts*) do, in fact, propose Gricean theories that are not versions of CRT.

5. Even Frege, whose lack of interest in the psychology of semantics is notorious, has a theory about the relation between meaning and understanding; namely, that to understand a term is to "grasp the concept" that the term expresses.

6. This way of reading the moral of Frege's examples is in jeopardy of the Mates cases, since it assumes that *identity* of meaning *does* guarantee substitutivity *salva veritate* in nonquotational contexts. We do not propose to pursue these issues.

7. There is thus a considerable spiritual affinity between CRT theories of meaning in philosophy and the structuralist semiotics that has sometimes been influential in linguistics. According to the latter, languages are to be viewed as "systems of differences"; the basic idea is that the semantic force (or "value") of an utterance is determined by its position in the space of possibilities that one's language offers. Saussure, for example, apparently held this sort of view both for linguistic and for mental representation: "A [linguistic] unit is a segment of a spoken sequence which corresponds to a certain concept. Both are purely differential in nature" (Saussure, *Course in General Linguistics*, p. 119).

It's worth noticing that, unlike many other varieties of functional role semantics, "contrast" theories of meaning suggest not only translational holism but also content holism; in particular, they entail that semantic properties can't be punctate. For philosophical theories that explicitly embrace a "contrast" approach to meaning, see Ziff, *Semantic Analysis*; Ryle, "The theory of meaning." For illustrations of the role it has played in the structuralist tradition, see Eco, *Semiotics and the Philosophy of Language*.

8. We want to emphasize that, at this stage, we're using notions like *infererence* and *inferential role* as blank checks. So deductive inferences, inductive inferences, plausible inferences, prudential inferences, mere associations, and Heaven knows what else, are included pro tem. A lot of

what follows will be about problems that arise when a CRT theorist tries to say exactly which inferences are constitutive of the meanings of the terms that enter into them.

9. Once again, we're ignoring Mates's examples. If you are convinced that *no* two expressions are substitutable in all nonquotational contexts (as, indeed, the Mates examples rather suggest), then Frege's problem does not require a *semantic* solution; any notation that distinguishes among linguistically distinct expressions will do, and desideratum 1 is trivially satisfiable.

10. See also Loar, *Mind and Meaning*; Lycan, *Logical Form*; McGinn, "The structure of content"; and so forth.

11. Perhaps Block would allow there to be such a sentence; it might figure in the world view of someone who has a *very* misguided theory of prime numbers. But if Block does allow this, then it's hard to see how CRT is going to contribute to satisfying desideratum 7. From the assumption that someone believes that 4 is a prime (that is, from the fact that his belief is true iff 4 is a prime), *nothing* will follow about how he understands or uses the corresponding expression or about what inferences he is prepared to draw. This is the kind of point that Block himself likes to make against "externalist" theories of content.

12. Could someone who is a causal theorist about, as it might be, kind terms avoid the conclusion that the causal theory is false of the relation between expressions like "kind term" and their extensions? Yes, if – unlike Block – he denied that his semantic theory has metaphysical status. That is, he could argue that the causal theory of kind terms picks out the extension of "kind term," but not by reference to an essential property of kind terms. If a causal theory does say that the *essence* of being a kind term is bearing a certain causal relation to (members of) a kind, then a causal theory of the semantics of "kind term" is true iff a description theory of the semantics of "kind term" is true, a situation that might reasonably be viewed as paradoxical.

13. As has often been noted, this is the respect in which functionalism continues the tradition of logical behaviorism. See next note.

14. A functionalist semantics implies intrinsic connections between propositional attitudes and behavioral outcomes, and, of course, philosophers have sometimes had epistemological motivations for postulating such connections. Ryle and Wittgenstein, for example, tried to exploit "criterial" relations between mental states and behaviors to refute skepticism about other minds. The cost of this strategy is that the generalizations about behavioral consequences that *define* a mental state are ipso facto noncontingent – hence Ryle's doubts about the existence of psychological *laws*.

Notice that if you are both a functionalist *and a holist* about mental states, then you hold that *all* the generalizations that connect them to behavior are noncontingent. This is certainly a price that Block would be unwilling to pay. Nor does he think he has to pay it; since he accepts an a/s distinction, he assumes that he can have his functionalism *without* holism. More on this below.

15. Remember, in reading this passage, that for Block, narrow meaning is the kind (or aspect) of meaning that CRT defines, and wide meaning is the kind (or aspect) of meaning that is defined by symbol/world causal connections. In effect, these correspond, respectively, to sense and reference.

16. In fact, Dennett must himself be assuming some sort of CRT semantics for the attitudes, since, on the one hand, he thinks that principles of rationality constrain their inferential roles and, on the other hand, he takes the constraints that rationality imposes to be constitutive of the intentional states which satisfy them.

17. As we'll presently have cause to stress, this isn't quite the same as assuming that there are no analyticities, since it's compatible with *this* argument for holism that *all* propositions should be analytic. What would undermine the argument for holism is there being *synthetic* propositions. For a synthetic proposition is one you can deny without equivocation, hence one whose truth is *not* constitutive of the meanings of its constituents. If "Dogs bark" is analytic, then CRT presumably entails that you couldn't have a language that can express the concept *dog* but not the concept *bark*. But if it's synthetic, there is clearly no such prohibition.

18. Block is, of course, a "two-factor" theorist for whom inferential roles constitute only one of the factors; so, he could say that it's a "fallacy of subtraction" (see his discussion in "Advertisement," *c.* p. 626) to suppose that since *meaning* is compositional, it's inferential role "aspect" has to be compositional too. But though the architecture of Block's position permits him to make this move, it's pretty clear that he wouldn't want to make it. As we're about to see, the point of assuming compositionality is primarily to explain the productivity of linguistic (/cognitive) capacities. The productivity of English answers the question of how it is possible for an English speaker to grasp the senses of new expressions on the basis of a finite acquaintance with his language. Correspondingly, in the case of Mentalese, the point of assuming compositionality is to explain how an infinite inferential capacity could be determined by a finitely specifiable arrangement of neurons. So, the compositionality of inferential roles is required to explain the productivity of inferential capacities. And if, as Block implies, sense is to be identified with inferential role, the

compositionality of inferential roles is also required to explain the productivity of senses.

Nothing Block says remotely suggests that he would disagree with this. But, as we will see below, the notion that inferential roles are compositional can't be sustained.

19. It may be that the compositionality of language is derived from the compositionality of thought, or vice versa. On this question too we propose to remain neutral. But we do take it for granted that whatever system of representation exhibits *underived* intentionality must be compositional.

20. We remark (since the issue often comes up) that pairs like "John calculated the answer" and "The answer calculated John" are *not* exceptions to the systematicity of English. Systematicity requires that, in general, if a language can express the proposition P and if the proposition P is semantically close to the proposition Q, then the language can also express Q. If, however, there *is no* such proposition as Q, it is no objection to its systematicity that a language can't express it. We are inclined to think that there is no such proposition as that the answer calculated John, hence that the present examples do not constitute an objection to the systematicity of English. We do not wish to dogmatize, however. If there *is* such a proposition as that the answer calculated John, then English *can* express it; indeed the form of words "The answer calculated John" does so. English is thus systematic on either assumption.

21. In a characteristically illuminating passage, Frege notices both the phenomenon of productivity and the phenomenon of isomorphism and the connection between them:

> It is astonishing what language can do. With a few syllables it can express an incalculable number of thoughts, so that even a thought grasped by a human being for the very first time can be put into a form of words which will be understood by someone to whom the thought is entirely new. This would be impossible, were we not able to distinguish parts in the thought corresponding to the parts of a sentence, so that the structure of the sentence serves as an image of the structure of the thought. . . .
>
> If, then, we look upon thoughts as composed of simple parts, and take these, in turn, to correspond to the simple parts of sentences, we can understand how a few parts of sentences can go to make up a great multitude of sentences, to which, in turn, there correspond a great multitude of thoughts. ("Compound thoughts," pp. 390–1)

Our statement of the isomorphism principle is intentionally left pretty vague; deep issues arise when more precision is attempted. Suppose, for example, that you hold that (in a null discourse) the sentence "It's raining" expresses the proposition that it's raining here. Then either you must say that "It's raining" has more constituents than appear on its surface or that the isomorphism principle can be violated by pragmatically carried information. For present purposes, we propose not to broach these sorts of issues.

22. The point that compositionality and analyticity are intrinsically connected is, in fact, perfectly general and quite independent of the assumption that meanings are inferential roles. For example, it's hard to see how you could hold the view that "brown cow" is compositional and *not* hold the view that "brown cow → brown" and "brown cow → cow" are valid in virtue of the syntax of "brown cow" together with the meanings of the constituent expressions. Quine's examples of dubious analyticities generally concern the putative semantic connections among items of the nonlogical vocabulary ("cow → animal" and the like.) So far as we have discovered, he doesn't discuss the kind of analyticity that appears to arise from the compositional structure of the language as such. It would be interesting to know what he would say about it.

23. There are causal theories of meaning around; see, for example, Skinner, *Verbal Behavior*; Dretske, *Knowledge and the Flow of Information*; and Fodor, "A theory of content," among others. And, like any account of meaning, each of these implies a corresponding notion of analyticity (see chapter 2). But all these theories are externalist and atomist and thus offer no comfort either to CRT or to holism.

24. Alternatively, you might take it that part of the inferential role of "brown" is "x such that, if cow, then dangerous." We leave it to the reader to decide which of these options is less implausible.

25. Block insists, of course, that inferential roles must be individuated "abstractly"; so it is open to him to just *stipulate* that only those of its inferences that are compositionally inherited count as constitutive of the inferential role of a complex expression. This saves compositionality and avoids making all inferences analytic, but only at the cost of trivializing CRT. For the question of what the inferential role of a complex expression is would then be as obscure as – indeed, would not be distinct from – the question of what the expression means. The identification of meaning with inferential role is substantive only if we have some independent grasp of the former.

The bottom line is that inferential roles really aren't compositional and meanings really are. There are various shells that Block could try hiding this pea under, but none of them looks like much of a fit.

243

26. Fully determined only "up to ambiguity," of course. This, however, is the kind of caveat that proves the rule; for an item to be ambiguous *just is* for its identity not to be determined locally (that is, for its identity to be determined "by context," if at all). This applies, by the way, even to idioms and metaphors, since they are ambiguous between their literal and their idiomatic/metaphoric readings.

27. Block says:

> My guess is that a scientific conception of meaning should do away with the crude dichotomy of same/different meaning in favor of a multidimensional gradient of similarity of meaning. After all, substitution of a continuum for a dichotomy is how Bayesian decision theory avoids a host of difficulties – for example, the paradox of the preface – by moving from crude pigeon holes of *believes/doesn't believe* to degrees of belief. ("Advertisement," p. 624)

This analogy strikes us as unfortunate; the Bayesian move to degrees of belief depends precisely on assuming a notion of propositional *identity*; what typically distinguishes Bayesian believers is the degree to which they believe *that* P. It's not clear that you could make sense of Bayesian decision theory on the assumption that there are degrees not just of belief but also *of propositional identity*. See the discussion of "content similarity" in chapter 1.

28. There is, however, no end to the bullets that some folks are prepared to bite. Here are Bechtel and Abrahamsen setting out what they take to be a mainstream connectionist view: "Language is not exactly [sic] compositional, recursive, productive, systematic, or coherent . . . therefore one would not want a model that *exactly* [sic] exhibits these properties" (*Connectionism and the Mind*, p. 227). Note the lurking equivocation between "The model doesn't represent languages as *exactly* compositional" and "The model doesn't *exactly* represent languages as compositional." That the first is a desideratum, everybody grants; all languages have idioms, for example. That the second is a desideratum doesn't begin to follow.

29. You may be wondering how we can agree with Quine about there being no a/s distinction *and* hold that compositionality entails analyticity *and* hold that languages are compositional. There is, in fact, no paradox. Compositionality licenses *structurally* governed analyticities of the "brown cow → brown" variety. But the analyticities Quine is worried

about are *lexically* governed ones of the "cow → animal" variety (see n. 22). You're only required to acknowledge the latter if you accept CRT and thus hold that the behavior of "cow" in inferences like "cow → animal" is constitutive of its content. (As Quine says, "logic chases truth up the tree of grammar," in *Philosophy of Logic*, p. 35.)

NOTES TO CHAPTER 7

1. Thus, in "On the nature of theories: a neurocomputational perspective," where a version of state space semantics is presented in an explicitly connectionist framework, Churchland says that

   we are confronting a possible conception of knowledge or under-standing that owes nothing to the sentential categories of current common sense. An individual's overall theory-of-the-world, we might venture, is not a large collection or a long list of stored symbolic items. Rather, it is a specific point in that individual's synaptic weight space. (p. 177)

   For an even more explicit example of the claims that Churchland is prepared to make for the generality of state space semantics, see the passage quoted in n. 12 below.
2. It is often less than clear whether the nodes in a semantic network are supposed to correspond to *terms* or *sentences* or both. Fortunately, it doesn't matter much for present purposes.
3. Thinking about semantics this way is an old idea in cognitive psychology, though not one that has proved particularly fruitful. For close analogs to Churchland's state spaces, see the semantic theory set out in Osgood, Suci, and Tannenbaum, *The Measurement of Meaning*. Decline in enthusiasm for semantic spaces in cognitive psychology was part and parcel of a general disillusionment with the use of factor analysis as a research tool and with statistical models of mental processes. Here, as elsewhere, "cognitive neuroscience" recapitulates cognitive psychology, usually about 25 years too late.
4. By contrast, Land was proposing a psychophysics for color sensations, together with a neurological theory about what color sensations *are* (namely, an identification of specified types of color sensations with specified types of brain states). What he was surely not offering, however, was a *semantic* analysis, either of our color concepts or of the qualitative content of color sensations. For this reason, none of the objections that

we'll be developing against Churchland's state space semantics is relevant to the truth – or falsity – of Land's theory of color vision.

5. The following several paragraphs concern problems that appear to be specific to Churchland's theorizing rather than to similarity-based semantics as such. In particular, they appear to stem from Churchland's tendency to vacillate between wanting to eliminate the semantic/intentional and wanting to reduce it to the neural. Readers not concerned with the idiosyncracies of Churchland's views should skip to the next subsection.

6. Though it doesn't matter to the points at issue, we're taking it for granted that the grammar case must be different from the sensation case in at least the following respect: a reduction of grammatical theory would have to be *neurological* rather than *psychophysical*. It may be that the property of *being a certain color* reduces to some psychophysical property of light. But it surely isn't going to turn out that *being a sentence token of a certain syntactic type* reduces to a psychophysical property of utterances. Maybe, however, it reduces, in some complicated way, to some property of the speakers of a language that is neurologically specifiable.

7. It's just possible that what Churchland really has in mind is the truly Wagnerian hypothesis that similarity of intentional content and similarity of neural realization always go together, so that if what you believe when you believe P is rather like what you believe when you believe Q, then the brain state that corresponds to believing the one is rather like the brain state that corresponds to believing the other *under the neurological descriptions of the brain states*. This would be, quite univocally, not a hypothesis about semantics but about mind/brain reduction. And perhaps it goes without saying, there isn't the slightest reason in the world to suppose that it's true.

8. A way out that Churchland would surely find congenial would be to take concepts as stereotypes; on that account the distinction between empirical and constitutive inference is statistical rather than semantic, since the distinction between stereotypical properties and others is itself statistical. (The stereotypical properties for F-ness are, roughly, the ones that people are most prepared to infer that F's have.) The stereotype account of concepts has, notoriously, problems of its own; but we don't propose to press them here. Suffice it to say that, assuming that concepts are stereotypes, whatever other virtues this may have, does not help avoid the problem of how the dimensions of state spaces are individuated. This is because a robust notion of similarity of stereotypes presupposes a robust notion of identity for the stereotypical features. To say that the stereotypical dog has a wet nose is to take the identity of the property of *having a wet nose* and of the mental representation that expresses that property for granted.

If this problem doesn't worry stereotype theorists nearly as much as it should, it is because most of them, deep down, suppose that the stereotypical features are sensory/psychophysical. They thereby tacitly endorse the empiricism which we have seen Churchland struggle unsuccessfully to avoid.

9. This way of putting it is, however, misleadingly concessive; the notion *dog*-concept – and, mutatis mutandis, the notion concept-sufficiently-similar-to-a-*dog*-concept – is what the semantic theory is trying to characterize; so, on pain of circularity, the theory mustn't take these notions for granted. Thus far, the only notion of *dog* concept the theory has access to is: concept that occupies a certain specified region in a semantic space.

It is, as usual, essential that the labels in state space diagrams not merely be stipulated (that is, treated as free parameters). See above.

10. And, by the way, not just from actual idiosyncratic variation but also from potential idiosyncratic variation. There are presumably indefinitely many ways in which your beliefs about dogs could be different from mine without disturbing the fundamental similarity of our *dog* concepts. A principled theory of concept similarity would have to specify somehow the *possible* regions in state space that a *dog* concept can occupy.

11. Strictly speaking, of course, the classical empiricist held that all our concepts are functions of our *sensory* concepts. We've seen that Churchland's treatment of qualia depends on fudging the distinction between being sensory and being psychophysical. But the present charge (namely, of recidivist empiricism) doesn't depend on his having done so.

12. Here, for example, is Churchland doing his level best to make a virtue of this necessity. Anyone who wants to understand what epistemological assumptions underlie the connectionist version of state space semantics should pay especially close attention to the passage that starts "it may be that."

> The activation-vector spaces that a matured brain has generated, and the prototypes they embody, can encompass far more than the simple sensory types such as phonemes, colors, smells, tastes, faces, and so forth. Given high-dimensional spaces, which the brain has in abundance, those spaces and the prototypes they embody can encompass categories of great complexity, generality, and abstraction . . . such as harmonic oscillator, projectile, traveling wave, Samba, twelve-bar blues, democratic election, six-course dinner . . . [etc.] It may be that the input dimensions that feed into such abstract spaces will themselves often [sic!] have to be the expression of some earlier level of processing, but that is no problem. The networks

247

under discussion are hierarchically arranged to do precisely this as a matter of course. In principle, then, it is no harder for such a system to represent types of *processes, procedures,* and *techniques* than to represent the "simple" sensory qualities. From the point of view of the brain, these are just more high-dimensional vectors. ("On the nature of theories," p. 191)

Take home exercise: What is there in this understanding of the relation between "abstract" and sensory concepts that Hume would not have endorsed?

13. It would *not*, of course, follow that organisms that have the same sensory transducers must have the same or similar concepts. That would depend on whether their concepts occupy the same or similar *positions* in the semantic space.

REFERENCES

Aristotle, *De Interpretatione*, in *The Works of Aristotle*, vol. 1, ed. W. D. Ross, Oxford University Press, Oxford, 1928.

Barwise, J. and Perry, J., *Situations and Attitudes*, MIT Press, Cambridge, Mass., 1981.

Bechtel, W. and Abrahamsen, A., *Connectionism and the Mind*, Basil Blackwell, Oxford, 1991.

Block, N., "Advertisement for a semantics for psychology," in *Midwest Studies in Philosophy*, Vol. 10: *Studies in the Philosophy of Mind*, ed. P. French, T. Uehling and H. Wettstein, University of Minnesota Press, Minneapolis, 1986, pp. 615–78.

Block, N. and Fodor, J. A., "What psychological states are not," *Philosophical Review*, 81 (1972), pp. 159–81.

Bloom, L., *Language Development: Form and Function in Emerging Grammars*, MIT Press, Cambridge, Mass., 1970.

Bruner, J., *Child's Talk: Learning to Use Language*, Norton, New York, 1983.

Chomsky, N., "Review of B. F. Skinner's *Verbal Behavior*," *Language*, 35 (1959), pp. 26–58.

Chomsky, N., *Rules and Representations*, Columbia University Press, New York, 1980.

Churchland, P. M., *A Neurocomputational Perspective: The Nature of Mind and the Structure of Science*, MIT Press, Cambridge, Mass., 1991.

Churchland, P. M., *Matter and Consciousness: A Contemporary Introduction to the Philosophy of Mind*, MIT Press, Cambridge, Mass., 1984.

Churchland, P. M., "On the nature of theories: a neurocomputational perspective," in *A Neurocomputational Perspective*, pp. 153–96.

Churchland, P. M., "Perceptual plasticity and theoretical neutrality: a reply to Jerry Fodor," in *A Neurocomputational Perspective*, pp. 255–80.

Churchland, P. M., *Scientific Realism and the Plasticity of Mind*, Cambridge University Press, Cambridge, 1979.

Churchland, P. M., "Some reductive strategies in cognitive neurobiology," in *A Neurocomputational Perspective*, pp. 77–110.

Churchland, P. S., *Neurophilosophy: Toward an Unified Theory of the Mind/Brain*, MIT Press, Cambridge, Mass., 1986.

Davidson, D., "A coherence theory of truth and knowledge," in *Truth and Interpretation*, ed. E. Lepore, pp. 307–19.

Davidson, D., "Belief and the basis of meaning," in *Inquiries into Truth and Interpretation*, pp. 141–54.

Davidson, D., "Communication and convention," in *Inquiries into Truth and Interpretation*, pp. 265–80.

Davidson, D., *Essays on Actions and Events*, Clarendon Press, Oxford, 1980.

Davidson, D., *Inquiries into Truth and Interpretation*, Clarendon Press, Oxford, 1984.

Davidson, D., "Knowing one's own mind," in *Proceedings and Addresses of the American Philosophical Association*, 1987, pp. 441–58.

Davidson, D., "Mental events," in *Essays on Actions and Events*, pp. 207–28.

Davidson, D., "On saying that," in *Inquiries into Truth and Interpretation*, pp. 93–108.

Davidson, D., "Psychology as philosophy," in *Essays on Actions and Events*, pp. 229–44.

Davidson, D., "Radical interpretation," in *Inquiries into Truth and Interpretation*, pp. 125–39.

Davidson, D., "Rational animals," in *Actions and Events*, ed. E. Lepore and B. McLaughlin, Basil Blackwell, Oxford, 1985, pp. 473–81.

Davidson, D., "Reality without reference," in *Inquiries into Truth and Interpretation*, pp. 215–26.

Davidson, D., "Reply to Foster," in *Inquiries into Truth and Interpretation*, pp. 171–9.

Davidson, D., "Semantics for natural languages," in *Inquiries into Truth and Interpretation*, pp. 55–64.

Davidson, D., "The inscrutability of reference," in *Inquiries into Truth and Interpretation*, pp. 227–42.

Davidson, D., "The material mind," in *Essays on Actions and Events*, pp. 245–59.

Davidson, D., "Theories of meaning and learnable languages," in *Inquiries into Truth and Interpretation*, pp. 3–16.

Davidson, D., "The structure and content of truth," *Journal of Philosophy*, 87 (1990), pp. 279–328.

Davidson, D., "Thought and talk," in *Inquiries into Truth and Interpretation*, 155–70.

Davidson, D., "Truth and meaning," in *Inquiries into Truth and Interpretation*, pp. 17–36.

Dennett, D. C., *Brainstorms*, MIT Press, Cambridge, Mass., 1981.

Dennett, D. C., "Evolution, error, and intensionality," in *The Intentional Stance*, pp. 287–322.

Dennett, D. C., "Intentional systems," in *Brainstorms*, pp. 3–22.

Dennett, D. C., "Intentional systems in cognitive ethology: the 'Panglossian paradigm' defended," in *The Intentional Stance*, pp. 237–86.

Dennett, D. C., "Making sense of ourselves," in *The Intentional Stance*, pp. 83–116.

Dennett, D. C., "Mid-term examination: compare and contrast," in *The Intentional Stance*, pp. 339–50.

Dennett, D. C., *The Intentional Stance*, MIT Press, Cambridge, Mass., 1987.

Dennett, D. C., "True believers," in *The Intentional Stance*, pp. 13–42.

Dennett, D. C., "Cognitive ethology: hunting for bargains or a wild goose chase?" in *The Explanation of Goal-seeking Behaviour*, ed. D. McFarland, Oxford University Press, Oxford, forthcoming.

Devitt, M., "Meaning holism," MS.

Dretske, F., *Knowledge and the Flow of Information*, MIT Press, Cambridge, Mass., 1981.

Dummett, M., *Frege: Philosophy of Language*, Harper & Row, New York, 1973.

Dummett, M., "The philosophical basis of intuitionistic logic," in *Truth and Other Enigmas*, Harvard University Press, Cambridge, Mass., 1978, pp. 215–47.

Dummett, M., "What is a theory of meaning? (1)," in *Mind and Language*, ed. S. Guttenplan, Oxford University Press, Oxford, 1975, pp. 97–138.

Dummett, M., "What is a theory of meaning? (2)," in *Truth and Meaning*, ed. G. Evans and J. McDowell, pp. 67–137.

Eco, U., *Semiotics and the Philosophy of Language*, University of Indiana Press, Bloomington, 1983.

Evans, G., *Varieties of Reference*, ed. J. McDowell, Oxford University Press, Oxford, 1982.

Evans, G. and McDowell, J. (eds), *Truth and Meaning: Essays in Semantics*, Clarendon Press, Oxford, 1976.

Field, H., "Logic, meaning and conceptual role," *Journal of Philosophy*, 74 (1977), pp. 379–408.

Fodor, J. A., "A modal argument for narrow content," *Journal of Philosophy*, 88 (1991), pp. 5–26.

251

Fodor, J. A., "A theory of content," in *A Theory of Content and Other Essays*, pp. 51–136.

Fodor, J. A., *A Theory of Content and Other Essays*, MIT Press, Cambridge, Mass., 1991.

Fodor, J. A., *Psychosemantics: The Problem of Meaning in the Philosophy of Mind*, MIT Press, Cambridge, Mass., 1987.

Fodor, J. A., *Representations*, Bradford Books: MIT Press, Cambridge, Mass., 1981.

Fodor, J. A., "Stephen Schiffer's dark night of the soul: a review of *Remnants of Meaning*," in *A Theory of Content and Other Essays*, pp. 177–91.

Fodor, J. A., "Substitution arguments and the individuation of beliefs," in *Meaning and Method: Essays in Honor of Hilary Putnam*, ed. G. Boolos, Cambridge University Press, Cambridge, 1990, pp. 63–78.

Fodor, J. A., *The Language of Thought*, Crowell, New York, 1975.

Fodor, J. A., "Three cheers for propositional attitudes," in *Representations*, pp. 100–23.

Fodor, J. A. and McLaughlin, B., "Connectionism and the problem of systematicity: why Smolensky's solution doesn't work," *Cognition*, 35 (1990), pp. 183–204.

Fodor, J. A. and Pylyshyn, Z., "Connectionism and cognitive architecture: a critical analysis," *Cognition*, 28 (1988), pp. 3–71.

Frege, G., *Collected Papers on Mathematics, Logic and Philosophy*, ed. B. McGuinness, Basil Blackwell, Oxford, 1984.

Frege, G., "Compound thoughts," in *Collected Papers on Mathematics, Logic and Philosophy*, pp. 390–406.

Frege, G., "On sense and reference," in *Collected Papers on Mathematics, Logic and Philosophy*, pp. 157–77.

Frege. G., *The Foundations of Arithmetic*, Basil Blackwell, Oxford, 1980.

Gibson, R. F., *The Philosophy of W. V. Quine: An Expository Essay*, University Press of Florida, Tampa, Fl., 1982.

Glymour, C., *Theory and Evidence*, Princeton University Press, Princeton, 1980.

Gould, S. J., and Lewontyn, R., "The spandrels of San Marco and the Panglossian paradigm: a critique of the adaptationist programme," *Proceedings of the Royal Society*, B05 (1979), pp. 581–98.

Grandy, R., "Reference, meaning and belief," *Journal of Philosophy*, 70 (1973), pp. 439–52.

Grice, H. P., *Studies in the Ways of Words*, Harvard University Press, Cambridge, Mass., 1989.

Grunbaum, A., "The falsifiability of theories: total or partial? A contemporary evaluation of the Duhem–Quine thesis," *Synthese*, 14 (1962), pp. 17–34.

REFERENCES

Hacking, I., *Why does Language Matter to Philosophy?*, Cambridge University Press, Cambridge, 1975.

Hahn, L. E. and Schilpp, P. (eds), *The Philosophy of W. V. Quine*, Open Court, La Salle, Ill., 1986.

Harman, G., "Meaning and semantics," in *Semantics and Philosophy*, ed. M. I. Munitz and P. K. Unger, New York University Press, New York, 1974, pp. 1–16.

Harman, G., *Thought*, Princeton University Press, Princeton, 1973.

Harman, G., "Wide functionalism," in *Cognition and Representation*, ed. S. Schiffer and S. Steele, Westview Press, Boulder, Colo., 1988, pp. 11–20.

Hume, D., *Enquiry Concerning Human Understanding*, Bobbs-Merrill, Indianapolis, 1955.

Katz, J. J., *Semantic Theory*, Harper & Row, New York, 1972.

Katz, J. J., *The Metaphysics of Meaning*, MIT Press, Cambridge, Mass., 1990.

Kripke, S., *Naming and Necessity*, Harvard University Press, Cambridge, Mass., 1972.

Kuhn, T., *The Structure of Scientific Revolutions*, University of Chicago Press, Chicago, 1962.

Lepore, E. (ed.), *New Directions in Semantics*, Academic Press, London, 1987.

Lepore, E. (ed.), *Truth and Interpretation: Perspectives on the Philosophy of Donald Davidson*, Basil Blackwell, Oxford, 1986.

Lepore, E. and Loewer, B., "Dual aspect semantics," in *New Directions in Semantics*, pp. 83–112.

Lepore, E. and Loewer, B., "What Davidson should have said," in *Information, Semantics and Epistemology*, ed. E. Villanueva, Basil Blackwell, Oxford, 1990, pp. 190–9.

Lepore, E. and McLaughlin, B. (eds), *Actions and Events: Perspectives on the Philosophy of Donald Davidson*, Basil Blackwell, Oxford, 1985.

Lewis, D., "A subjectivist's guide to objective chance," in *Philosophical Papers*, vol. 2, pp. 83–132.

Lewis, D., "How to define theoretical terms," in *Philosophical Papers*, vol. 1, pp. 78–96.

Lewis, D., *Philosophical Papers*, Oxford University Press, Oxford, 1983 (vol. 1) and 1986 (vol. 2).

Lewis, D., "Radical interpretation," in *Philosophical Papers*, vol. 1, pp. 108–18.

Lightfoot, D., "The child's trigger experience: degree-0 learnability," *Behavioral and Brain Sciences*, 12 (1989), pp. 321–75.

Loar, B., "Conceptual role and truth conditions," *Notre Dame Journal of Formal Logic*, 23 (1982), pp. 272–83.

253

Loar, B., *Mind and Meaning*, Cambridge University Press, Cambridge, 1981.

Lycan, B., *Logical Form*, MIT Press, Cambridge, Mass., 1984.

Lycan, B., "Psychological laws," *Philosophical Topics*, 12 (1981), pp. 9–38.

Mates, B., "Synonymy," in *Semantics and the Philosophy of Language*, ed. L. Linsky, University of Illinois Press, Urbana, 1962, pp. 111–38.

McGinn, C., "The structure of content," in *Thought and Object: Essays on Intensionality*, ed. A. Woodfield, Oxford University Press, Oxford, 1982, pp. 207–58.

Millikan, R., *Language, Thought and other Biological Categories*, MIT Press, Cambridge, Mass., 1984.

Norris, C., *Derrida*, Harvard University Press, Cambridge, Mass., 1987.

Osgood, C. E., Suci, G. J. and Tannenbaum, P. H., *The Measurement of Meaning*, University of Illinois Press, Urbana, 1967.

Piaget, J., *The Language and Thought of the Child*, Harcourt, Brace and Co., New York, 1926.

Pitcher, G., *Wittgenstein: The Philosophical Investigations*, Anchor Books, New York, 1966.

Plato, *Cratylus*, in *The Collected Dialogues of Plato*, ed. E. Hamilton and H. Cairns, Princeton University Press, Princeton, 1961, pp. 100–23.

Platts, M., *Ways of Meaning. An Introduction to a Philosophy of Language*, Routledge & Kegan Paul, London, 1980.

Platts, M. (ed.), *Reference, Truth and Reality: Essays on the Philosophy of Language*, Routledge & Kegan Paul, London, 1979.

Putnam, H., *Meaning and the Moral Sciences*, Routledge & Kegan Paul, London, 1978.

Putnam, H., "Meaning holism," in *The Philosophy of W. V. Quine*, ed. L. E. Hahn and P. Schilpp, pp. 405–26.

Putnam, H., *Mind, Language and Reality. Philosophical Papers*, vol. 2, Cambridge University Press, Cambridge, 1975.

Putnam, H., "Philosophers and human understanding," in *Realism and Reason*, pp. 184–204.

Putnam, H., *Realism and Reason. Philosophical Papers*, vol. 3, Cambridge University Press, Cambridge, 1983.

Putnam, H., *Reason, Truth and History*, Cambridge University Press, Cambridge, 1981.

Putnam, H., "The analytic and the synthetic," in *Mind, Language and Reality*, pp. 33–69.

Putnam, H., "The meaning of 'meaning'," in *Mind, Language and Reality*, pp. 215–71.

Quine, W. V., "Epistemology naturalized," in *Ontological Relativity and Other Essays*, pp. 69–90.

Quine, W. V., "Ontological relativity," in *Ontological Relativity and Other Essays*, pp. 26–68.

Quine, W. V., *Ontological Relativity and Other Essays*, Columbia University Press, New York, 1969.

Quine, W. V., *Pursuit of Truth*, Harvard University Press, Cambridge, Mass., 1990.

Quine, W. V., "Reply to Chomsky," in *Word and Objections: Essays on the Work of W. V. Quine*, ed. D. Davidson and J. Hintikka, Reidel, Dordrecht, Holland, 1969, pp. 302–11.

Quine, W. V., "Reply to Hilary Putnam," in *The Philosophy of W. V. Quine*, ed. L. E. Hahn and P. Schilpp, pp. 427–32.

Quine, W. V., "Review of Evans and McDowell *Truth and Meaning*," *Journal of Philosophy*, 74 (1977), pp. 225–41.

Quine, W. V., *Theories and Things*, Harvard University Press, Cambridge, Mass., 1981.

Quine, W. V., "Two dogmas of empiricism," in *From a Logical Point of View*, Harvard University Press, Cambridge, Mass., 1953, pp. 20–46.

Quine, W. V., *Word and Object*, MIT Press, Cambridge, Mass., 1960.

Rhees, R., "Can there be a private language?," in *Wittgenstein: The Philosophical Investigations*, ed. G. Pitcher, 1966, pp. 267–85.

Rosenberg, A. "Davidson's unintended attack on psychology," in *Action and Events*, ed. E. Lepore and B. McLaughlin, pp. 399–407.

Russell, B., *The Analysis of Mind*, Allen & Unwin, London, 1971.

Ryle, G., "The theory of meaning," in *British Philosophy in Mid-Century*, ed. C. Mace, Allen & Unwin, London, 1957.

Salmon, N., *Frege's Puzzle*, MIT Press, Cambridge, Mass., 1986.

Saussure, F. de, *Course in General Linguistics*, ed. C. Bally and A. Sechehaye, tr. and annotated by R. Harris, Duckworth, London, 1983.

Schiffer, S., *Meaning*, Oxford, Clarendon Press, 1972.

Schiffer, S., *Remnants of Meaning*, MIT Press, Cambridge, Mass., 1987.

Searle, J., *Speech Acts*, Cambridge University Press, Cambridge, 1969.

Shoemaker, S., "Functionalism and qualia," *Philosophical Studies*, 27 (1975), pp. 291–315.

Skinner, B. F., *Verbal Behavior*, New York, Appleton-Century Crofts Inc., 1957.

Smolensky, P., "On the proper treatment of connectionism," *Behavioral and Brain Sciences*, 11 (1988), pp. 1–23.

Stalnaker, R. C., *Inquiry*, MIT Press, Cambridge, Mass., 1987.

Stampe, D., "Towards a causal theory of linguistic representation," in *Midwest Studies in Philosophy*, vol. 2: *Studies in the Philosophy of Language*, ed. P. French, T. Uehling and H. Wettstein, Minnesota University Press, Minneapolis, 1977, pp. 42–63.

Stich, S., "Dennett on intentional systems," *Philosophical Topics*, 12 (1981), pp. 38–62.

Stich, S., *From Folk Psychology to Cognitive Science: The Case Against Belief*, MIT Press, Cambridge, Mass., 1983.

Stich, S., *The Fragmentation of Reason*, MIT Press, Cambridge, Mass., 1990.

Vermazen, B., "General beliefs and the principle of charity," *Philosophical Studies*, 42 (1982), pp. 111–18.

Wallace, J., "Translation theories and linear B," in *Truth and Interpretation*, ed. E. Lepore, pp. 211–34.

Wittgenstein, L., *Philosophical Investigations*, tr. G. E. M. Anscombe, Basil Blackwell, Oxford, 1968.

Ziff, P., *Semantic Analysis*, Cornell University Press, Ithaca, 1960.

GLOSSARY

This book contains a number of technical terms that are introduced to distinguish among philosophical views. The glossary is meant to help the reader to keep the intended interpretations of these terms in mind, not to provide for their strict definitions.

Anatomic property A property is anatomic just in case if anything has it, then at least one other thing does.

Anthropological holism There is an internal connection between *being a symbol* and playing a role in a system of *non*linguistic conventions, practices, rituals, and performances – an internal connection, as one says, between symbols and Forms of Life.

Brentano's thesis Intentional properties and states are not reducible to physical states or properties.

Centrality of belief All propositional attitude ascription presupposes belief ascription; hence no creature can have any propositional attitudes unless it has some beliefs.

Closure principle Necessarily, if a creature is represented as believing P and P entails Q, then the creature must be represented as believing Q.

Coherence principle Necessarily, intentional ascriptions represent a creature's beliefs as mostly coherent (by the interpreter's lights).

Compositionality A language is compositional iff (idioms aside) the meaning of its syntactically complex expressions is a function of their syntactic structures together with the meanings of their syntactic constituents.

Content holism The metaphysical claim that properties like *having content* are holistic in the sense that no expression in a language can have them unless many other (nonsynonymous) expressions in that language have them too. In effect, the doctrine that there can be no punctate languages.

Empiricist principle All concepts reduce to sensory concepts.

Extensional adequacy A truth theory is *extensionally adequate* iff it entails a T-sentence for each sentence of the object language and all the T-sentences it entails are true.

Extensionality problem The question of what empirical constraints, over and above extensional adequacy, interpretation theory is required to meet.

Generic semantic property Loosely speaking, such a semantic property is one whose specification can be taken to involve variables ranging over propositions, contents, meanings, or the like.

Gricean semantics Any theory according to which the meanings of linguistic expressions are inherited from the propositional attitudes (for example, the communicative intentions) of speaker/hearers.

Holistic property A property is holistic just in case if anything has it, then *lots* of things do.

Immanence A notion is immanent when it is defined for a particular language or theory, *transcendent* when defined for languages and theories in general.

258

Intentional Realism   Ontological Realism about propositional attitudes.

Interpretation   The process of assigning intentional content to the mental states of an organism (and/or meaning to its utterances).

Interpretivism   There is an "element of interpretation" in content ascription.

Isomorphism   This is, roughly, the fact that if a sentence S expresses the proposition that P, then syntactic constituents of S express the constituents of P.

Mates examples   Sentences with doubly embedded propositional attitude constructions suggest that even synonymous expressions may fail to substitute *salve veritate* in all contexts. Thus, "John wants to know whether Bill realizes that bachelors are unmarried men" may be true even though "John wants to know whether Bill realizes that bachelors are bachelors" is false.

Molecularism   A molecularist says that if there are any beliefs that we share, there must be other beliefs that we also share. But he denies that *all* our other beliefs have to be shared in order that we should share any of our beliefs. He is likely to appeal to the analytic/synthetic distinction in this regard: to share the belief that P is to accept all the analytic inferences in which P plays a role.

Normativism   Belief attributions are necessarily constrained by normative principles (for example, that most beliefs attributed must be *true*; that most desires attributed must *accord with the ascribee's interests*, and the like).

"Nothing is hidden" thesis   The metaphysical principle that if there is any fact of the matter at all about what the interpretation of a language is, then the evidence which selects a meaning theory for that language must in principle be *publicly accessible* data.

259

Peirce's thesis   The meaning of a sentence is identical with (or determined by) what would count as evidence for its truth.

Polyadicity (of a predicate)   The number of noun phrases it takes as arguments. (Thus, a transitive predicate like "hit" has polyadicity two.)

Primacy of belief   The conditions for content attribution *inherit* the conditions for belief attribution.

Principle of charity   The favored truth theory for a language L must entail T-sentences according to which most of the sentences that speakers of L hold true *are* true.

Probity principle   Necessarily, intentional systems mostly desire what it would be good for them to have.

Productivity   Every natural language can express an open-ended set of propositions.

Projectivism   A species of interpretivism; specifically, a theory of the logical form of belief attributions. In Smith's mouth "John believes P" means something like "John is in the state that would normally cause me (Smith) to say that P."

Punctate   A property is punctate just in case it is not anatomic.

Quine/Duhem thesis   The thesis that single theoretical sentences do not always or usually have a separable fund of *evidence* to call their own; their confirmation conditions are determined by their role in the theory in which they are embedded.

Radical interpretation   Interpretation that is carried out under specified epistemological constraints (for example, on the quality or quantity of the data available to the interpreter).

Robust generalization   One which subsumes a variety of otherwise heterogeneous individuals.

Semantic atomism   The meaning of an expression metaphysically depends on some punctate symbol/world relation, some relation that one thing could bear to the world even if nothing else did.

Semantic nihilism The view that there are no semantic properties.

Semi-holism The doctrine that asserts translation holism but allows punctate languages.

Strong anatomism The "long scope" or "strong" reading of anatomism: that is, there are propositions other than P such that you can't believe P unless you believe them.

Systematicity Any natural language that can express the proposition P will also be able to express many propositions that are semantically close to P; similarly, mutatis mutandis, for all nomologically possible minds.

Token-reflexive Broadly, token-reflexive features include tense and any other features of expressions that can function to relativize truth values to contexts of utterance.

Transcendental argument Any argument of the form "F-ing is impossible unless P; F-ing actually occurs; therefore P." For example, "Translation is impossible unless most of what the informant says is true; translation actually occurs; therefore most of what the informant says is true."

Translation holism The claim that properties like *meaning the same as some or other formula of L* are holistic; hence nothing can translate a formula of L unless it belongs to a language containing many (nonsynonymous) formulas that translate formulas of L.

Truth Principle Necessarily, intentional ascriptions represent a creature's beliefs as mostly true (by the interpreter's lights).

Weak anatomism The "short scope" or "weak" reading of anatomism: that is, you can't believe P unless there are propositions other than P that you believe.

261

INDEX OF NAMES

INDEX OF SUBJECTS

nomologicity (*cont.*):
  nomological relations,
    reduction to 57
  solution to the extensionality
    problem 84–92, 94–9,
    103, 238 n.
"Nothing is Hidden" thesis
    80, 81, 92, 227 n., 228 n.,
    230 n., 259

observational vocabulary 42,
    43, 101, 190, 191, 198,
    218 n., 219 n.
omniscience (*see also* God)
    159–61, 230 n.
ontology 11, 211 n.
  ontological commitments 11,
    12
optimality 147

Peirce's thesis (*see also*
    verificationism) 43, 44,
    50–2, 216 n., 218 n.,
    219 n., 220 n., 260
persons
  theory of 107, 111, 113
phenomenology 58
positivism 7, 217
possible
  worlds 85–8, 134, 158,
    230 n.
pragmatism 38, 39, 215 n.
  pragmatists 7
primacy of belief thesis 105,
    114, 115, 117–19, 122–4,
    126–8, 133, 135, 260
principle(s) of charity (POC) *see*
    charity, principle(s) of
principle(s) of rationality *see*
    rationality, principle(s) of

private language 4
probability
  subjective, conceptual role
    analyzed in terms of 180,
    181
probity 143, 260
productivity 2, 175, 176, 185,
    241 n., 242 n., 244 n., 260
propositional attitudes 108,
    115, 118, 120–2, 124, 125,
    128, 130–2, 134, 138, 139,
    146, 166, 173, 187, 193,
    240 n.
  polydicity of 141
punctate 260
  belief systems 44
  beliefs 30
  forms of life 7
  languages 5, 25, 43, 44, 70,
    92, 94, 102, 103, 133,
    209 n., 210 n.
  minds 25, 43, 116, 133,
    209 n., 224 n.
  semantic properties 32, 206,
    223 n., 239 n.
  theories 43, 44

qualia inversion 195, 196
Quine/Duhem thesis (Q/D thesis)
    37–47, 50–3, 182, 215 n.,
    216 n., 218 n., 219 n.,
    220 n., 225 n., 260

radical interpretation (RI) 59,
    61, 62–4, 70–3, 75–84, 88,
    89, 92, 93, 98–100, 102–7,
    110–12, 114, 115, 118, 121,
    132, 155–8, 160, 223 n.,
    225 n., 226 n., 228 n.,
    229 n., 230 n., 232 n.,
    237 n., 238 n., 260